WITNESS TO WAR

"Clements employs an extraordinarily restrained narrative style to recount scenes of almost unbelievable horror, scenes that burn themselves into the brain."—*Philadelphia Inquirer*

"A personal trek into and through the violence and daily life of the *campesinos*, the peasant guerrillas and their families, in the Front of El Salvador's civil war. *Witness to War* introduces the reader to the rebels, describes in detail the kinds of oppression suffered by the people, explains how the civil war developed . . . Clements has taken a major step in setting the record straight."—John DelVecchio, author of *The 13th Valley*

"Disturbing . . . Clements is a knowledgeable military and medical observer—who reports his own pain, too, to horrifying effect."—*Kirkus Reviews*

"The book charts the doctor's struggle to gain the trust of the peasants, to offer them decent medical care, to stay healthy himself and to maintain his neutrality in a bloody civil war."—*Newsday*

"A searingly personal, one-year diary."—*Detroit Free Press*

"The only current testimony from behind the lines of El Salvador's civil war . . . Sometimes gripping, sometimes thought-provoking and always interesting for anyone who wants to know what the war 'is really like.' "—*Des Moines Sunday Register*

"This is Clements's account of serving people in the jungles of El Salvador, and it offers an anguished view of the low value on life in that troubled Central American nation. . . . A testimonial reminder of how much could be done to benefit human life if political realities would allow resources to be devoted to medicine rather than munitions."—*Chicago Tribune*

WITNESS TO WAR

An American Doctor in El Salvador

CHARLES CLEMENTS, M.D.

4051

BANTAM BOOKS
TORONTO • NEW YORK • LONDON • SYDNEY • AUCKLAND

To the memories of Mohandas Gandhi,
Martin Luther King, Stephen Biko,
Oscar Arnulfo Romero, Ita Ford
and all the others whose commitment
to non-violent social change
cost them their lives.

CONTENTS

FOREWORD

AMONG THE PEASANTS IN EL SALVADOR TODAY, it is said that the vulture should be made the national bird. The creature would be an appropriate symbol, they bitterly contend, because in the past four years of savage civil war, the best and the bravest among them have ended up in a vulture's gullet.

The grim humor of the *campesinos* came back to me as I read Dr. Clements' remarkable memoir of his year in a rebel enclave twenty-five miles north of the capital, San Salvador. In my nearly four decades of close familiarity with El Salvador and its people, I know of no other visiting American who has ignored the capital in favor of the countryside, where the essential tragedy of this nation is being played out.

Dr. Clements chose to see for himself how this civil war is being fought, and by whom, and for what reasons. As a doctor he takes no side in the conflict; the ideologies of right and left are as tangential to his narrative as they are useless as a tool for understanding the enormity of what is happening in El Salvador. As he saw and now reports, there is only one reality in El Salvador—its people and the many vultures who have fed upon them.

The story of injustice in El Salvador is an old one. It doesn't take a communist to tell a peasant that he or she is

ix

hungry, or a Marxist agitator to stir protest against home-grown misery. Even I, a newcomer at our Embassy in El Salvador, could write home in April of 1948 that trouble must someday come to a society where 95 percent of the wage earners received less than a dollar a day for their labor. My Ambassador, Albert Nufer, warned the State Department at the same time that so many Salvadorans lived at or below the subsistence level that the country had become a fertile seed-bed for communism. Then, as now, the palaces and mansions of the very rich were separated by high walls from the gulleys, or *barrancas*, of San Salvador where the very poor were huddled by the thousands in cardboard shacks, surrounded by trash and junk and forced to survive with little health care and not much food.

These poor have been kept in feudal bondage by the Salvadoran oligarchy, or the Fourteen Families, as they are known. One of these land barons once invited me to his coffee plantation to show me the magnanimity with which, he felt, he treated his workers. Together, we watched a team of his laborers line up for their noon meal—one tortilla and a dab of stewed beans each—then he summoned an overseer to bring the two of us exactly what the workers were being fed.

"Don't I feed them well?" he asked grandly as we ate and sipped from our scotch glasses. Clearly he believed that he did and, once he was satisfied that his generosity had been demonstrated, we were driven to a nearby restaurant where we could dine in more appropriate surroundings.

Another *finquero*, or coffee-grower, once broke with this attitude by joining a reformist Salvadoran junta as minister of agriculture. In due course, the junta was dismantled and he fled to the U.S. While here, he spoke out against the oppression in his homeland and went, with me, to the State Department where our policy planners refused him an audience. In a few months, he risked a return to El Salvador and was there murdered and mutilated by uniformed security forces.

With few exceptions, historically the U.S. government has aligned itself with the world view and the policies of the Salvadoran rich. As a former Ambassador once told me, "After all, they have the power." When we have been wiser and more humane in our foreign policy, as we were in the early years of President Kennedy's Alliance for Progress, we have won the respect and faith of the poor. When we've abandoned programs aimed at broadening the country's economic base and fostering a gradual transfer of wealth and sharing of power, we've earned the people's enmity and distrust.

Kennedy's successors abandoned the use of economic aid as a stimulus for social change and chose to emphasize the security provisions of the Alliance. We taught security measures to Salvadoran police chiefs and counterinsurgency methods to Salvadoran military officers at our schools in the Panama Canal Zone. We sent them weapons and airplanes in the vain expectation that social stability would grow out of enforced order.

They ignored Kennedy's warning that "those who make peaceful revolution impossible will make violent revolution inevitable." This, sadly, is what has happened in El Salvador. Now we must contend with a violent, inevitable revolution in which at least 40,000 Salvadoran civilians have been killed by government security forces and the notorious death squads. President Reagan argues for more military aid to that government and has adamantly resisted all initiatives toward a negotiated settlement of the conflict. Four thousand U.S. soldiers are now stationed and battle-ready across the border in Honduras. We appear to be perilously close to direct U.S. intervention.

Such a disastrous course is inevitable if we continue to back a government making war on its own people. Dr. Clements treated and interviewed several government prisoners-of-war who obviously belonged to an army with no morale, no leadership, and seemingly no purpose other than to stay alive until the end of their usually forced conscriptions. When these prisoners saw the guerrillas and their peasant supporters for what they were, many chose to stay and fight alongside them.

There is one tradition that we still honor in this country and, before it is too late, let us begin to exercise a free people's right to choose. I share with Dr. Clements a strong devotion to the principles of Thomas Jefferson, one of which is embodied in the following passage from his writings:

> There is no safe depository of the ultimate power of society, but the people themselves . . . If we think them not enlightened enough to exercise their control with a wholesome discretion, the remedy is not to take it from them, but to inform their direction by education.

Dr. Clements is endeavoring to do just that. Far more important than the healing he did in El Salvador is his first-hand witness to the character of its people and the war they are now fighting against their government.

As I had decades before, he found the *campesinos* long-suffering, ready to sacrifice, full of love and care for their families and neighbors, and stalwart in the face of the greatest pain and hardship. Many of them have been tortured and mutilated by tormentors who have been trained in the sophisticated tactics of violence—often by our own military advisors.

I believe no thoughtful U.S. citizen can come away from this powerful document without grave misgivings as to our course in Central America. The American public was not so informed about Vietnam. They did not have the facts until too many of their sons came home in body bags. Today, we have a choice. Let us see what our tax dollars are doing in Central America. Let us decide if we want to pay the price for another intervention. Let us decide if repression is again wrapping itself in the American flag.

Murat W. Williams
Madison Mills, Virignia
February 1984

1946–47 State Dept. El Salvador Desk Officer
1947–49 Deputy Chief of Mission, U.S. Embassy El Salvador
1961–64 Ambassador, U.S. Embassy El Salvador

THE VOLCANO

WE HAD LITTLE TIME LEFT.

Copapayo and its peninsula jutting north into Lake Suchitlán were cut off. Escape was blocked by a government garrison visible to the northwest on the opposite shore. To the south, the elite Ramón Belloso Battalion was advancing steadily upon us, pushing our few defenders back toward the village.

The soldiers had been trucked thirty miles north from the capital, San Salvador, and then deployed to sweep the hills and ravines of "subversives." With little resistance, they had ground their way to a ridge overlooking the neck of the peninsula. Around five o'clock that afternoon, the battalion set up its 81s and began firing down on us.

Whump! whump! whump! We listened as the mortar rounds left their cannisters. For a moment we heard nothing as the shells sped to the top of their arc. Then they came whistling down and exploded with concussions that shook the earth and sent shattered adobe in every direction.

The young children of Copapayo—several of whom I'd

3

delivered—were my gravest concern. They were hysterical with fright. They screamed each time the mortar clusters began their descent. They clawed and tore at their mothers, desperate to escape the explosions.

There was no choice but to quiet them.

I crushed my store of tranquilizer tablets and mixed them with orange juice and brown sugar. Then, as each three-*whump!* salvo was over, I began zigzagging my way from trench to trench.

Sitting still in the trenches, the women were as impassive during the bombardment as stone figures from a Mayan relief. None of the mothers questioned what I was doing; they knew death too well. Each cooed, *"Dulce, dulce"* (candy, candy) as I dosed their terrorized infants according to my best guess of individual weight. By dark, there wasn't a conscious child under three years old in Copapayo.

Then the *guinda* (evacuation) began. A single-file column of three hundred Salvadoran *campesinos* (peasants), and a few lightly armed rebel militiamen, snaked its way up out of the trenches and wound along the peninsula toward the government lines. In the ribbons of moonlight that broke through the cloud cover, I could see the stooped *campesinos* carrying their few belongings and comatose infants up a narrow trail leading them straight through a mile-wide zone held by the government troops.

There were still the stretcher cases to see to, as well as the women who were too old, too sick, or too many months pregnant to risk an all-night march past the Belloso Battalion. In the dark, they would leave by boat. My assistant was Miguel, seventy-five, by far the oldest man in Copapayo, a *campesino* gnarled by arthritis. Miguel was no stranger to fright and flight; his memory stretched back to the great *matanza* (slaughter) of the 1930s when 30,000 Salvadoran Indians and peasants were killed by the government. He had endured at least a dozen nights such as this and had declared he would flee no more.

4

"I'm tired," he told me, "and the enemy doesn't care about toothless old men."

We took the remaining women to two small boats. Some of the grandmothers were partially deaf and couldn't hear the *whumps!* The younger, pregnant women held on to them and pulled them to the ground before the explosions came.

Miguel dropped, too, and then heaved himself up ungainly as a camel. First he made it to all fours, then using his twisted hands and strong forearms, he pushed his rump skyward. Another shove, and he was balanced again on his spindly legs.

My maternity cases, their bellies distended, could hunker down only so far. Shielding their fetuses and their own aged mothers, they formed three-generational hills in the mortar flashes. Many of them had watched their children leave with the column. They knew they might never see them again.

"Hasta mañana," I whispered to the women in my poor Spanish. "Yo voy a cuidar a sus niños." (Until tomorrow, I'll take care of your children.)

They tried to believe me.

I left Miguel at the boats with the warning that if he didn't evacuate with the women, I'd send a stretcher for him and force him to go up the peninsula with the rest of us.

"All right, amigo, I will go," he lied.

We carried the stretcher cases and the children past the enemy positions. I'm not one to pray much. If God is truly all-knowing and all-powerful, it isn't for me point out opportunities for divine intercession. But I did pray that whole long night of silent marching. I prayed for Miguel, and I asked that if any of the children were to die, that it be from an overdose at my hand—not because they awoke, whimpered, and were smothered into silence by their frightened mothers.

I knew peasant mothers who'd killed their infant children that way. Their agony never ceased. It was worse than the loss of a brother, husband, or father to the enemy, worse, even, than watching their children die of hunger and disease. It made them murderesses.

When dawn came, we were safe. Not a child made a noise that night and not a one had succumbed to the drugs. Thank you, God, for that.

We could hear the Belloso Battalion completing their siege of Copapayo, and later in the day we listened to a government radio report of the battle. The guerrillas, it said, had been vanquished to the last man.

Old Miguel.

We found him in the plaza when we returned. As a warning to the rest of us, his frail old arms had been nearly twisted from their sockets before he was shot in the stomach and left to die, slowly.

SCENES LIKE THE DESTRUCTION of Copapayo are commonplace events in El Salvador, a feature of the civil war there that has turned a mite-size, potato-shaped clump of coffee bushes and volcanos into one of the bloodiest patches of real estate on earth.

There is violence as well to the north in Guatemala. Honduras to the east is a staging area for armies attacking the Sandinista government to the south in Nicaragua. Only to the west of El Salvador is there peace and that's because for 10,000 miles there is nothing but the Pacific Ocean and a few islands. On such a due west course, the first continental landfall is southeast Asia.

In fact, you would come ashore somewhere near the middle of what used to be South Vietnam.

I have been there too.

I went to southeast Asia in 1969 as an Air Force C-130 transport pilot and remained there for nearly a year. I was a Distinguished Graduate of the U.S. Air Force Academy, an officer and a gentleman. I had hoped to become a general one day.

Instead, I became a doctor and a Quaker and, in the

early months of 1982, found myself back in the middle of another war zone. Again I saw the familiar C-130s; only this time they were not a friendly sight. As in Vietnam, they came to ferry men and materiel for a client government at war with a dedicated guerrilla insurgency. But unlike Vietnam, I was with, if not of, that insurgency. This time, the C-130s brought bombs and rockets to be launched against me and the thousands of civilians for whom I was the family physician.

At first, the civil war in El Salvador had been purely a professional concern of mine. In 1980, freshly graduated from the University of Washington medical school, I started my residency in family medicine at Natividad Medical Center, the county hospital in Salinas, California. That summer, a select committee of American health professionals went to El Salvador and returned with evidence that right-wing "death squads" were murdering surgeons in the operating room, shooting patients in their hospital beds, and "disappearing" nurses and other health care personnel from their clinics. To "disappear," in El Salvador, is to vanish permanently It means to be murdered.

The situation explained in their report, *Abuses of Medical Neutrality*, was that the country's sole medical school had been occupied and closed by the military. Not only were these gross violations of medical neutrality as outlined in the Geneva Conventions, but it appeared that a campaign of terror was being directed specifically against health professionals who served the poor or the displaced, or who had treated civilian wounds of any kind. The death squads regarded such doctors and nurses as subversives.

More troubling though was what I began to see for myself in the course of my residency in Salinas. Of the estimated 750,000 people who have fled the violence in El Salvador, two-thirds of them are in the United States. They are called "the feet people" because that's how they get here—on foot. In Salinas, many came to the local farmworker clinic where I and other resident doctors were asked to see them.

CHARLES CLEMENTS, M.D.

In medicine, you never forget a first case. Regardless of whether it is an appendectomy or a heart attack, the patient and the circumstance always stay with you. Thus, in Salinas, my first instance of a macheted breast was that of a fifty-four-year-old Salvadoran schoolteacher. It had been lopped off by government interrogators.

I also saw my first deliberate acid burns and first x-rays of badly knitted bones broken by anti-Communist truncheons. Many of the refugees were emotional basket cases: hysterics, depressives, catatonics, paranoiacs—human being after human being whose mind had been tormented by terror.

Joaquín was a typical patient at the Salinas clinic. He was middle-aged, gray, and wrinkled, with rheumy brown eyes. His servility reminded me of a broken street dog.

"Buenas noches," I greeted him. "¿Cómo te sientes?" (Good evening. How do you feel?)

Silence.

"Si tienes un problema, quizás yo puedo ayudarte," I persisted. "¿Cómo te llamas, abuelito?" (If you have a problem, maybe I can help you. What is your name, grandfather?)

Joaquín sat rigid, looking straight ahead.

"¿Tienes miedo?" (Are you afraid?)

Only when we carefully began to undress him did Joaquín stir. As if by my touch I had tapped a well of anguish and fear, he broke down completely, sobbing and blurting his story in unintelligible Spanish. An interpreter spoke for him.

Joaquín, he said, had been a tenant farmer in El Salvador, and a property title dispute with his landlord had led to an interrogation at the local police headquarters. What I thought were ringworm-like lesions with bacterial superinfection on his testicles were, in fact, the festering wounds from cigarette burns administered in the course of his questioning.

I treated the burns as he went on with his story. Arguing with his landlord, the interpreter said, had made Joaquín a "subversive." Shortly after his own interrogation, two of his teen-aged children were arrested and never seen again. In terror, he fled in the night with the rest of his family and

8

journeyed for several weeks to California. Much of the trip had been made on foot, aggravating his untreated wounds.

A physician must learn to leave patients' pain and suffering behind in the hospital. We are taught we must not assume their collective burden, or it will overwhelm us. But the tragedy of Joaquín and other refugees was not so easily put aside. The stories I'd heard of slain doctors and nurses were one thing, but treating people who still bore the marks of torture, physical and psychological, was quite another.

I began, tentatively, to share my concerns with other doctors. As past president of the American Medical Student Association, I was in touch with a broad network of medical organizations. From them, I accepted speaking engagements at which, over the coming months, my subject shifted from American health issues, such as geriatrics and pesticide poisonings, to the tragedy I saw unfolding in El Salvador.

My message of alarm met with a lot of yawns, charges of undue melodrama on my part, and the infrequent headshake over the plight of those "poor brutes" in that backward "banana republic." The audiences were polite but largely indifferent to yet another foreign carnage.

Then I gave a speech before a Hispanic medical association, La Rama. I finished with a description of a major health dilemma faced by *campesinos* in rural El Salvador. Since the closing of the medical school, they had been denied the services of senior students who previously spent an obligatory year's work in the countryside. After I passed the hat for medical aid contributions, the lights came on, and a young doctor rose from her chair.

"What," she asked quietly, "are you asking us to *do*?"

Her question troubled me. For the first time, my gentle campaign of moral and ethical suasion was open to an earnest challenge. Was talking about the problem enough? Was it sufficient, as I suggested in my answer to her, for them all to write to Congress, stressing that military aid was no solution to the strife in El Salvador? I believed that I could urge nothing more of my fellow physicians, but what of myself?

9

CHARLES CLEMENTS, M.D.

The dilemma was framed by personal history. My experience in Vietnam left me with a commitment to non-violence and later, an association with the Society of Friends, the Quakers. Having based my separate peace on moral objections to our conduct of the war, I was consequently drawn to the Quaker notion of an *inner light*, or conscience, as a person's highest authority. This tenet carries with it the duty to bear witness—to measure events with your own eyes and to attest to what you've seen. As the Friends say, "to speak truth to power."

MY FIRST TENTATIVE STEP was to approach agencies that worked in Central America: the Peace Corps, the American Friends Service Committee, and the Catholic Relief Services. What kind of work, I inquired, did they have for a physician? The response was that there was none at all. It would be too dangerous to send me.

That was discouraging, but in some ways it was a relief. It was suggested that I consider working among the many refugees in Honduras. While this was an appealing alternative, it still did not address the issues as I saw them. Then I met a journalist who told me about a French doctor who was working in one of the zones controlled by the guerrillas. Would I consider such a commitment?

I didn't know what to think. It seemed like a contradiction—a pacifist amidst armed guerrillas? Then again, would it differ from working in an area under government control? Would that be a tacit sanction of official brutality? Was there a place for a commitment to non-violence in the midst of so much violence?

I continued speaking, continued the often 100-hour weeks of a physician-in-training and continued meeting refugees. But in December of 1980, four American churchwomen who had been working with refugees and orphans in El Salvador were raped and murdered by the Salvadoran National Guard. I was both angered and saddened by the erosion of our government's integrity when, without a shred of evidence, our Ambassador to the United Nations accused the women of subversive activity. By early 1981, there were calls for more military aid to El Salvador. Someone in the State Department even announced that if we didn't stop "them" in El Salvador we'd have to fight "them" at the Rio Grande.

Secretary of State Alexander Haig affirmed the new Reagan administration's determination to "demonstrate that we can win . . . a quick and decisive victory." Aid to the Salvadoran government was increased exponentially. U.S. military advisors were dispatched with the promise of a quick return. Was this another Vietnam, another quagmire in the making?

I believed so, and I further began to believe that if I had the courage of my convictions, I was obliged to search for a way to prevent such a tragedy. The paradox of violence aside, there is always a need for healing in the midst of so much suffering, always a place to bear witness in the midst of injustice.

IN THE SUMMER OF 1981, I sent a letter to Mendes Arceo, the Bishop of Cuernavaca, Mexico. I knew him to be a conduit for humanitarian aid to El Salvador and hoped he might offer some guidance. The letter was not answered.

My discreet inquiries around the United States didn't lead anywhere, either. By autumn it seemed as though I would have to go to Mexico to approach the guerrillas' political representatives in person.

My personal affairs were in order, down to the recent and amicable dissolution of my marriage. I left enough money in the bank to cover my medical school loans for a few years and said my farewells. Only my closest friends knew that my objective was El Salvador. My parents thought I was going to work in refugee camps in Central America. Instead I went to Cuernavaca, where I enrolled in an intensive Spanish course. Aside from medical Spanish, my knowledge of the language was limited.

CHARLES CLEMENTS, M.D.

* * *

A SERENE AND MILDLY EXOTIC MOUNTAIN TOWN of terraces and narrow lanes, Cuernavaca was a pleasant contrast to the cacophony and acrid smog of Mexico City. Parts of Cuernavaca are very rich. The local tourism office boasts the highest per capita concentration of swimming pools in the world. But other parts of Cuernavaca are very poor. There are *barrios* (slums) where thousands of people live with no running water.

Before I approached the Revolutionary Democratic Front (FDR), the Salvadoran guerrillas' political wing, I decided to visit Mendes Arceo, the so-called Red Bishop, personally. The sobriquet derives from his long involvement with liberation theology, a type of Catholic ministry that preferentially concerns itself with the needs of the poor. The theology, a consequence, in part, of the reforms promulgated by the Second Vatican Council more than twenty years ago, undercut the clergy's traditional alliance with the military and monied class that had defined the historical role of the Church in Latin America.

For centuries, the Church had kept the people's eyes set squarely on the hereafter. But in the mid-1960s, Mendes Arceo, and many other Latin American priests, began to encourage a more temporal outlook among the peasants. Sickness and hunger were no longer viewed as intractable burdens of the poor but as conditions that the people themselves might overcome.

There was nothing intrinsically radical in liberation theology, but its consequence—the inspiration and organization of the poor—sent shivers through the haciendas and presidential palaces of Latin America. Even a hint of unity among the poor was seen as subversive and dangerous; it was assumed to be Communist-inspired.

My first view of the "Red Bishop" was from across the flower beds in the courtyard of Cuernavaca's centuries-old cathedral, the only place Mendes Arceo conducts audiences. His seventy-four years had stooped him a bit, but he still stood well over six feet tall. His head was shaved, and I could hear the sonorous bass of his voice.

He spoke to a little girl who skipped away with a giggle. For me, however, there was only icy politeness. The aloofness was understandable; there had been attempts on his life.

A few more words from me and the ice turned to stone. Here was a gringo claiming he was a doctor, a self-admitted former military officer with no ties to the political left and no particular experience in Latin America, talking in mangled Spanish about his interest in humanitarian work in a war zone his own government had helped create. He might be CIA or a plain fool.

Either way, the Red Bishop wasn't taking any chances. He looked sternly at me and said there were poor everywhere who needed help. That was it. The interview was over. On the way out, a priest offered me the name of a nun who he said was doing health work among the poor in Cuernavaca.

The town was filled with a mélange of political exiles and disaffected intellectuals from all over Latin America. Surely, I thought, someone there would put me in touch with the FDR. From hindsight, this entire episode was absurd.

I went to meetings and suggested I might know a doctor who would consider working with the Salvadoran guerrillas. If anyone knew anyone in the FDR, perhaps. . . ? But even if my clumsy overtures had gotten through, how would I possibly know the difference between an FDR representative, a KGB operative, a CIA agent, or anyone else? I couldn't even ask many questions for fear of provoking suspicion.

I looked up the nun. Her name was Sister Frances, and she was working with what is called a "base Christian community" in the diocese of Cuernavaca. These communities or CEBs (*Comunidades Eclesiáles de Base*) are outgrowths of liberation theology. Established by priests and nuns in many Latin American countries, the CEBs combine traditional Bible study with training of lay ministers, "Delegates of the Word," selected by the community. The teachings emphasize a God who is just and loving, who acts on behalf of the poor and oppressed. Sister Frances explained that her work was deliberately and exclusively pastoral, never political.

Sister Frances was serious but had a marvelous laugh. Unlike any nun I'd ever known, she wore street clothes rather than a habit. She was very proud of her community.

It was located in one of the poorest *barrios*, no more than a squatter settlement built of discarded plywood, sheets of tin, and cardboard. But Sister Frances saw much more there. Making agile leaps to avoid the mudholes and garbage in the rutted lanes, she led me to a community meeting one evening.

The community's Delegate of the Word, an unemployed laborer who Sister Frances said had learned to read only one year before, offered several moving passages of Bible text. I couldn't catch it all with my book Spanish, but his readings and the discussions that followed were as lively a Christian meeting as I'd ever attended.

Then the indefatigable Sister led me and the rest of the parishioners down to inspect their great triumph—a community water spigot. After months of meetings and an agreement that everyone would contribute a few centavos to the project, the spigot had been duly approved and built. I suspect that more hope than water poured from that tiny pipe, but the mere fact of its existence was a minor miracle. Sister Frances had every reason to be proud.

She certainly was accomplishing more than I was. Several weeks now into my "mission improbable," I was still going nowhere. The FDR was treating me like a bill collector. If any of my messages were getting through to them, they weren't responding. I was feeling very frustrated and just a little foolish.

There was self-doubt, too; the sort that keeps a person up at night. I tried to use that time to remind myself this was no lark I'd embarked upon. If I was going to El Salvador as a dilettante, this was the time to admit so and turn back. Sterner tests of my commitment lay ahead.

*   *   *

I CONTINUED MY ATTEMPTS to contact the guerrillas, spending my weekdays studying Spanish in Cuernavaca and my weekends at a Quaker hostel in Mexico City. The commute was always an adventure. The winding, mountainous roadway connecting the two cities is a sports car driver's fantasy, a true test of man and machine. To my dismay, the Mexican bus drivers seemed similarly inspired by the route. By day, the countryside flew past in a blur. Even more harrowing were the night rides when on each dip or hairpin curve we seemed to become airborne.

It is possible that the FDR saved me from becoming a traffic fatality.

I first received messages at the hostel to go to such and such a place and wait for so and so. No one showed up. Once, thinking my determination to meet them was being tested, I stood on a dark corner in the rain for more than two hours before giving up.

The third approach began in an equally unpromising way. A note with a telephone number on it came to me at the hostel. At the appointed time, I called the number from a public booth, but at the sound of my gringo "¡Bueno!" there was a click.

I dialed again and the same thing happened, nothing unusual for Mexico City public telephones. I tried once more and finally understood instructions for a rendezvous in a restaurant in the university district, where I was to wait for someone to approach me. I was given no name, no description.

I found the noisy, bustling cafe and sat down to wait, fully expecting another disappointment. I had spent almost two months in Mexico by then, nothing had happened and my money was running out. I was beginning to think that maybe I could find satisfying work in a Cuernavaca CEB rather than continue this silliness when a plain, middle-aged Mexican gentleman walked up and introduced himself as

15

Rogelio. There was no way of confirming who he was or whom he represented, but at least somebody had shown up.

I followed Rogelio to a city apartment where he questioned me for three hours. In Spanish, he asked about my reasons for coming and my understanding of the civil war in El Salvador. I answered as best I could in the two tenses of his language I knew.

He was searching for a deeper political affiliation. I was searching for guarantees. One, I expected medical neutrality to be observed, which meant that I could treat anyone without regard to political considerations. Two, as a Quaker, I would not bear arms. Three, I wanted to work with a civilian population.

There was no comment. He concluded by asking for references. Who could vouch for me? He asked also that I prepare some sort of resume and return to Cuernavaca to improve my Spanish. In other words, don't call us, we'll call you.

I wasn't exactly disappointed with the meeting; I hadn't been sure what to expect. But Rogelio did trouble me when he asked if I was willing to work in a government-run refugee camp. I answered yes, but told him I'd been warned against such risks. I assumed he knew as much as I about the killing of doctors, so why did he even ask? Maybe, I thought, on another hair-raising bus ride back to Cuernavaca, the guerrillas believed the murder of another gringo would be good publicity for their revolution.

Rogelio did contact me again, however, and introduced me to a second interviewer, Carmen, who questioned me several times that winter. Tough and to the point, Carmen reminded me of a district attorney. I couldn't help but feel like a felon every time we spoke.

Jaime, my third contact, was even more abrupt and intense with me. Judging from the deference shown him by Rogelio and Carmen, I guessed that Jaime was a person of some stature in the FDR, if, in fact, this was the FDR. I still didn't know for sure.

I did know that his Spanish was particularly difficult for me to decipher and that his eyes were almond-shaped, almost Asian. After many weeks, when our relationship seemed relaxed enough for me to pose a question, I finally worked up the courage to ask if he was Vietnamese.

"No!" he chuckled. "I'm Salvadoran."

It was the first time any of them had offered any information, let alone a smile.

"I do have some Asian blood," he explained. "My parents used to run a Chinese restaurant in San Salvador."

All my meetings with Rogelio, Carmen, and Jaime were held in the same small Mexico City apartment. A family I assumed was Rogelio's was usually there, too. While nothing we discussed was the least bit seditious, I still was struck by their total lack of security. It seemed to me that these people were dedicated amateurs in the ways of spycraft and clandestine operations. I was soon to be proved very wrong.

Through January of 1982, Jaime would be no more specific than to urge me to improve my Spanish. He didn't need to remind me since I have always been awful with languages. But then came the word: I was to be ready to leave for El Salvador in two weeks; I was not to communicate a word of my plans to anyone. When I asked if I would be in a referral hospital or in a clinic in the countryside, he said he couldn't tell me. I told him that I was going to need to buy medical supplies in Mexico City. He nodded, but told me to be careful. He also repeated the warning to keep silent.

I decided to prepare for the worst; that is, to assume I might be practicing in some place where there was neither personnel nor equipment. I would need a mobile army surgical hospital, a M.A.S.H. unit, that I could carry on my back. I wondered if they came complete with humor like on TV. I would probably need a lot of that where I was headed. I also needed money and advice. Ignoring Jaime, I took one last trip to Cuernavaca, where I called several private numbers in the States. I knew a small network of physicians who were ready to assist me in whatever way possible.

The next day I was summoned back to the apartment in Mexico City where Jaime, in some detail, recounted my conversations. Flabbergasted at the quality of what he knew, I was suddenly far more respectful of their capabilities. For his part, Jaime declared himself disappointed in me and said that my departure had been put on hold. He acknowledged that I had neither mentioned time nor place, but made it clear that indiscretion could cost lives and that no further willfulness would be tolerated.

I had come to the threshold and I knew it. Winning their acceptance meant my total submission. The gringo doctor was welcome as long as he did as he was ordered. What, I thought, am I getting myself into? Standing in front of this revolutionary, I wondered if my commitment to heal and to witness was strong enough to place blind trust in him.

Reminding me that I, not they, had initiated this process, Jaime said, "People's lives may depend upon your discipline or lack of it."

One of those lives, I realized as I looked at him, could very well be my own. I told him I understood.

CERTAIN NOW THAT THE SALVADORANS, and who knows who else, were watching my every move, I was up at dawn each day crisscrossing Mexico City in search of equipment. My first priorities were compactness and versatility. I couldn't count on electricity, replacement parts, or laboratory support of any kind.

An old, German-made bone saw was my first treasured discovery. It even folded! Across town, I found "cold" sterilization equipment. A third supply store provided various sizes and types of tubing. Always careful not to buy so much in one place as to arouse suspicion, I made the rounds of all Mexico City's medical supply houses.

It took forever to find reusable glass syringes, everything was disposable, and some pieces of equipment were simply not available. This I had already communicated to my physician friends at home. The proper items found their way south via couriers, mostly American tourists who had no idea what packages they brought with them.

Since I didn't dare attempt further consultations on what I should take, I tried to imagine the types of operations and emergencies I needed to prepare for. This wasn't such an easy exercise for someone barely trained as a family doctor. My minimal surgical experience had been in fully equipped and professionally staffed hospitals where all I needed to do was hold out my hand and the proper gadget was slapped into it.

Somehow I managed to pull it all together. My "Son of M.A.S.H." could handle anything and everything from obstetrics to dentistry, but it would weigh no more than seventy-five pounds and could be fitted into one backpack.

I still knew absolutely nothing about my itinerary. Jaime was only helpful enough to warn me against buying anything colored olive drab—canvas, duffles, satchels, clothing—because such a military shade is instantly provocative in Central America. When I pressed him for more specifics, he told me not to become separated from my equipment or I'd probably never see it again. He also advised me to take up smoking. I declined the suggestion, even though smoking would help combat insects, and more importantly, he said, it would be a foil against hunger.

There was no foil for my anxiety about the void that lay ahead. Although confident about the correctness of what I was doing, I began to feel the isolation, the removal from familiar things, the loneliness of living under a pseudonym—Camilo—among people who had no last names, no histories they would talk about, no identities other than as guerrillas.

I was an utterly contingent being. Unseen others now planned my every step and shared nothing of this process with me. It was the beginning of a nearly complete submersion of my individuality.

In late February, 1982, as I sat and waited with my gear in my small room at the Quaker hostel, my instructions at last arrived. I was given $200 in American money and was told to take a flight to Nicaragua the next day. That was all, except that, as usual, an unnamed someone would contact me there.

Managua, Nicaragua, population 400,000, was about what you'd expect of a Central American capital ten years after a devastating earthquake, and three years after the bloody overthrow of dictator Anastasio Somoza. Managua was only partially rebuilt; it was still in the process of becoming. Somoza's regime had barely bothered to clean up the debris after the 1972 quake. The only tall structures that remained intact were the Bank of America building and the Intercontinental Hotel. Cattle were grazing in their shadows. In the city's main plaza, the facade of the cathedral still stands, but its collapsed roof has never been replaced, and the side walls continue to crumble.

The revolutionary Sandinista government has concentrated its scant capital resources on housing for the poor, simple one-story cinderblock houses. Similarly, I noticed many newly built clinics, also of cinderblock, and many playgrounds outfitted with sculptures and futuristic equipment.

There were billboards and signs everywhere. Some denounced imperialism or hailed the revolution's martyrs. Others urged mothers to breastfeed or warned against the dangers of infant dehydration from diarrhea.

There wasn't time or opportunity to make informed judgments about the course of the revolution itself. The issues that dominate news of Nicaragua in the United States—press censorship, tensions with segments of the clergy, treatment of the Miskito Indians, Soviet-bloc influence—require more careful study than I could give them in a brief stay.

This was a society under enormous stress. There were ration lines for many food staples. American-sponsored insurgents, many of them former members of Somoza's National Guard, were active in the north and south of Nicaragua, raiding villages and attacking key economic targets. These *contras* were the recurring topic of the few conversations I overheard, as were the widespread shortages of everything from spare parts for buses to most kinds of medicine. A good deal of the latter I had intended to purchase there, but the virtual embargo thrown up around the country by the United States government had cut off most traditional sources of medical supply, along with everything else. In fact, the customs inspectors at the Managua airport nearly impounded the equipment I'd brought with me.

One surprise was the city's ethnic diversity. Not even huge, cosmopolitan Mexico City seemed to offer such an array of human types. Most common were the mestizos, a mixture of Spanish and Indian. The Irish, too, had long ago settled in Nicaragua, and part of their legacy was the occasional pair of blue eyes or shock of red hair. Black slaves once worked the east coast plantations, and their descendants were a reminder of the country's African heritage. Every now and again, however, I'd encounter an atavist, a man, woman, or child who so thoroughly resembled his or her Mayan ancestors that downtown Managua might have been pre-Columbian Tical or Chichén Itzá. The effect was eerie. In all, Managua was an ethnic microcosm of Central America. I would have liked to have spent more time there, but I was eager to move on to my goal: El Salvador.

On the radio, I listened to both the Salvadoran government and guerrilla news broadcasts about a major offensive against a region just north of the capital. According to both accounts, an area called Guazapa was being assaulted mercilessly. The clandestine rebel station reported, ". . . enemy planes dropped bombs and napalm endangering the lives of hundreds of women, children, and elderly." The government radio boasted that hundreds of subversives had been killed in an operation that would permanently eliminate this guerrilla stronghold. It sounded like a bloodbath I'd just as soon not get caught up in. Colonel García, the Minister of Defense, spoke of aerial bombardment with five-hundred-pound bombs, but reassured me somewhat when he said that the Air Force ". . . acted with complete freedom because there were no civilians in the area." I knew that I needn't worry about Guazapa being my home because I'd be working only with civilians.

MY CONTACT IN MANAGUA, also a doctor, at first suggested that I fly to San Salvador and then wait for my equipment to catch up with me once I was safely behind guerrilla lines. Mindful of Jaime's warning never to let the pack out of my sight, I told him I would prefer to enter with my equipment. He shrugged and left, saying that he would get back in touch.

When he did, he informed me I was to fly north to Tegucigalpa, the capital of Honduras, and from there I would make my way to the Salvadoran border. He gave me a very detailed list of instructions as to how to make contact in Honduras. I was to stand in a certain way on a certain corner with a newsmagazine under my left arm. When approached, I was to run through two sequences of phrases and was given an entire second set of instructions should anything go wrong at the first meeting. It was, all in all, pretty impressive and I felt as if I were in the middle of a spy novel.

The short flight to Tegucigalpa was uneventful, but my arrival there was like passing through a culture warp. While Managua had evinced a nervous élan, the Honduran capital seemed gorged, tawdry. The airport was filled with soldiers and sinister types wearing shiny suits and dark glasses.

By pre-arrangement, a Latin man in a business suit stood next to me in the baggage claim area and commented that his bag looked just like mine. Though I was reassured by his presence, I would have been much happier if he, not I, had to take seventy-five pounds of medical equipment through Honduran customs.

The inspectors looked like they came from Central Casting—scowling thugs with no necks. Around them stood armed security troops who, in my nervous state, appeared ready to pounce at the slightest nod of an inspector.

I flipped my bag onto the inspection counter with an

affected nonchalance that practically dislocated my shoulder. Eyeing me up and down, the inspector grunted for me to unzip my luggage. It was like opening Fibber McGee's closet—surgical tubing, scalpels, clamps, syringes came bursting out.

"Where is your license to import this medical equipment?" he demanded. I had had enough experience in Latin America to realize this was time for the *mordida* (the bite), a fifty-dollar bill tucked conspicuously into my passport. I handed it to him.

"*El permiso*" (the permit), I said boldly as President Grant's likeness disappeared into his ham-like paw.

"The customs duties on medical equipment are very high," he responded unambiguously.

I choked back my first impulse. "I am a guest in your country," I said instead. "At the invitation of Señora Alvarez, I am going to work in the missionary hospital of Gracias a Dios. If you require more customs duties, I suggest we get on the phone and ask her to come pay them."

The operative words were "Señora Alvarez," wife of Honduran strongman General Alvarez. I couldn't imagine any Latin American general not having a religious wife who kissed orphans and cut ribbons at important events such as the opening of a hospital.

The inspector and I stared at each other, or rather I stared at my sweaty, trembling image reflected in the silvered lenses of his glasses. After an eternity of silence, he curled his upper lip and motioned me through. With great self-discipline, I resisted leaping toward the glass doors and walked calmly outside to a taxi.

In the moonlight, I could make out rickety, lean-to slums clinging to the hillsides that encircle Tegucigalpa. The center of the city reminded me of Saigon in 1970, a neon bazaar of expensive American consumer goods. The streets swarmed with young trendies in their designer jeans and hand-made loafers. Tegucigalpa's carnival effulgence contrasted sharply with the grimness of the surrounding *barrios*. There I saw little electric light, and no one seemed to be stirring.

CHARLES CLEMENTS, M.D.

The next day my interest was focused on medicine. With what little money I had left, I went for the big As—antibiotics, anti-malarials, anti-parasiticals, analgesics, and anesthetics. When there were no more funds, I discovered my plastic was good and soon had a stainless steel pressure cooker, a tiny portable stove, and some dental pliers that could extract molars, canines, incisors, and other varieties of teeth I couldn't even identify.

MY CONTACT'S NAME WAS JOSÉ, a Latin of indeterminate nationality. He was among the most hospitable of their people I'd met. Nevertheless, the cordiality did not extend to personal small talk. In the course of a very pleasant two-hour dinner with José, I learned nothing of his past, whether he was married or not, where he'd been, what he'd seen, or if he expected the sun to come up tomorrow.

Before it did, we were driving west toward the Salvadoran border. Our transportation was José's Cherokee, a sort of stretch sedan with four-wheel drive, a cargo area in back, and sinister, smoked-glass windows. Cherokees and similar vehicles are ubiquitous in Central America, where there is a premium on a reasonably comfortable car that is also capable of traversing streams and slopes and the frequent road that is no road but only a rut in the forest.

José's choice of a Cherokee was cunning. Of all the competing makes and models of such cars, it is the preferred vehicle of the Salvadoran death squads. So frequently are Cherokees reported seen near the site of an abduction or the roadside discovery of dead and mutilated "subversives," that their appearance alone provokes dread in the country. Driving across neighboring Honduras, we were probably in the vehicle least likely to invite suspicion.

I remember the drive from Tegucigalpa principally because it was in José's Cherokee that I met Lupe. She and another Latin, who introduced himself as Francisco, were both headed to work in El Salvador, as I was, and they both said they were doctors.

To my knowledge, I have never before elicited such instant antagonism as I did in Lupe. She was short, about twenty-five years old, and sullen. While José and Francisco were patient with my halting Spanish, Lupe mocked it, or pretended not to comprehend me. Within a half hour of our first acquaintance, she had questioned my competence, impugned my motives for coming, and openly begrudged my right to sit in their company. She was so thoroughly disagreeable that I was reminded of the customs inspector at the Tegucigalpa airport.

"Lupe," I came within an eyeblink of asking, "do you have family working at the airport? In the customs branch, perhaps?"

With the tone for our journey thus set, we descended from the high hills around Tegucigalpa and drove for hours along a paved and well maintained two-lane highway. The lush countryside seemed barely inhabited. The many shades of green were only occasionally interrupted by the bright reds and purples of bougainvilleas vividly outlined against white-washed adobe houses capped with orange tiles. What settlements we encountered grew more primitive in direct ratio to their distance from the capital. We ate breakfast, for instance, just an hour or two outside Tegucigalpa and could order from a full menu in a large and well-equipped cafe. Our lunch stop's sole modern appliance was an ancient-looking refrigerator. At nightfall we bought warm sodas at an adobe hut where we were told it was the last chance for cigarettes. I reconsidered what Jaime had said about hunger and bought a couple of packs.

The road began deteriorating about midday. First we were on gravel, then dirt, and finally, nothing more than a dusty track accessible only by a four-wheel-drive vehicle. The closer we got to the Salvadoran border, the more roadblocks and Honduran army patrols we met. José's government license plates served as our visa past them.

There are several reasons for the heavy Honduran military presence along the border with El Salvador. The soldiers are there to keep Salvadoran refugees in and supplies or personnel like myself out. But there is also a historical enmity between Hondurans and Salvadorans, which last manifested itself in the so-called Soccer War of 1969. The conflict lasted only one hundred hours, but in its aftermath fully 300,000 Salvadoran *campesinos* were forcibly repatriated from their small plots in Honduras to whatever space they could find in their overcrowded homeland. Relatively underpopulated Honduras has always appeared attractive to the land-hungry peasants just across the border in El Salvador.

Today, these peasants aren't drawn to Honduras so much as they are fleeing from El Salvador. As we rode along, we saw a couple of huge tent cities, refugee camps, filled with Salvadoran peasants. They looked to me as forlorn as any POWs I'd ever seen, and I asked José about them.

He explained that they were the "lucky ones." Since the current civil war began, he said, the Salvadoran military had conducted several assaults against villages near the Honduran border. The people we saw in the camps had been fortunate enough to escape.

Many of the rest, he went on, were lost in several "hammer and anvil" operations jointly conducted by the Hondurans and the Salvadorans. These were classic military operations, at least as old as Caesar's Roman legions, designed to trap and destroy a fleeing enemy. When that enemy is a band of unarmed civilians, the strategy can be devastatingly effective.

In one well-documented massacre, *campesinos* fleeing the hammer of the Salvadoran troops made it across the Rio Sumpul at the border only to be pushed back into it by the Honduran army, the anvil. Trapped in the river, more than six hundred of them drowned or were killed by the advancing Salvadoran troops and aircraft.

By dusk, we had come to within a mile of the border. José split the group up. He went to one village, Francisco and Lupe to another, and I was dropped off in yet a third settlement. We would meet again on the other side of the border the next morning.

MY HOSTS WERE A HONDURAN PEASANT FAMILY who occupied a two-room adobe house. I have no idea how many actual family members there were. I only recall being shown to one of several hammocks in a small room. We all slept together, adults suspended from the ceiling in their hammocks and children bedded on a piece of plastic on the earthen floor. There was no more than a couple feet of free space anywhere.

One of the adults must have been tubercular. That night he introduced me to a common rural Central American habit of spitting on the floor, which wouldn't have been so unpleasant had he not been hacking so perilously close to my ear. One or more of the children cried through the night.

Dawn was a relief, even though it brought the most hazardous part of the trip—the actual crossing into El Salvador. The attempt was planned for just after seven when the Honduran guards left their nightly outposts on the border to sleep a few hours until they began the first of several sporadic daytime patrols.

I was still in possession of my large pack and had taken stern criticism from Lupe and Francisco for insisting I would take it with me across the border. They argued that I should leave it for later transport past the guards because it would attract too much attention—as if a gringo didn't already stand out in rural Honduras! But I stuck to Jaime's advice and compromised only on my duffle bag of recently purchased medicines. I didn't like it, but I left the precious pharmaceuticals and hoped they'd be brought to me later.

My Honduran host enclosed the pack in a burlap bag in an attempt, I suppose, to disguise it as a sack of corn. I watched in awe as he hoisted it, all seventy-five pounds, onto the head of his middle-aged wife, who slowly and gracefully carried it down the main path of the village.

She headed toward the unmarked border, about one-half mile away along a ridge of grass and low scrub bushes. There was very little cover until well past the border. Heart pounding, I sauntered along behind her. The men had already gone to their fields. Several women were up and beginning their day's wash. The village pigs were out oinking and rooting around for their breakfast in piles of casually deposited excrement.

No one paid me any mind. It was as if the villagers were all extras in this little drama, and it was their role to prevent any undue attention in my direction. I looked around for trees, anything I might duck behind if it came to that, but found only a few thorny mesquite bushes. It was excruciating to amble along, affecting an early morning constitutional, when I knew that at any moment I might feel the cold steel of an M-16 muzzle in my neck.

But we made it without incident. Behind a thicket of vines, the woman dropped the pack and hurried away. The Honduran guards snoozing in their bunks saw or heard nothing as I dashed the last few feet to my pack, swung it over my back, and marched with relief into rebel-held El Salvador.

FIRST TO WELCOME ME to the revolution on the morning of March 7, 1982, was Nico, a twelve-year-old *correo* (messenger). He explained that he would lead me to the others, and from there he would be our guide to the village of Quipurito, a half-day march away. Nico was an incongruous sight, a little boy with a big grin and an even bigger pistol tucked into his waistband. He was as fair skinned as I, with brown hair and a smile so full of rotted teeth that I instantly anticipated the day I'd have to pull them. He was twelve, but by North American standards his physical development was that of a slight-framed eight- or nine-year-old. Later, if there is any later for Nico, the stresses of war and hardships of life as a *campesino* will age him prematurely. If he makes it to forty-seven years of age, the life expectancy in El Salvador, he'll look more like sixty.

He silently led me to a nearby stand of cactus where the others waited. Then, for the next two hours, he communicated only with gestures and whispers as he led us deeper into El Salvador.

EVEN THOUGH I WAS IN PRETTY FAIR SHAPE, the march to Quipurito was exhausting. There was the matter of the seventy-five-pound pack I was carrying and the rugged hillsides and ravines we had to negotiate. Halfway to Quipurito, the vegetation changed from the lush lowland green to dusty scrub brush and tall, golden-dry grass that reminded me of southern California in the summer. It wasn't tropically hot, only 80° or 85°, but with the lack of shade the temperature seemed to rise with my every step. Only José and I had thought to bring canteens. Lupe polished off half my water at our first rest stop.

After a while, I noticed that we had been joined by an escort of two *campesinos* with automatic weapons. They noiselessly scouted the trail in front and guarded our rear. About two hours into the trip, they froze. In the distance, I could hear the very familiar chop of a Huey helicopter.

I had thought nothing of it. In Vietnam, every U.S. soldier knew helicopters to be their friends. Their sound meant firepower to be directed at the enemy or resupply time for food or ammunition. Sometimes they brought mail. Sometimes they came for the wounded. But to the Viet Cong—and now the rebels in El Salvador—the Hueys meant death. They could scream in over the treetops spewing machine gun fire.

In Vietnam, the enemy countered them with .50 calibre machine gun fire and were remarkably good at catching them when they took off and landed. But during my time in El Salvador, I would never see a helicopter in such a vulnerable position. They never brought soldiers anywhere near hostile fire, nor were they ever used for close air-support of ground troops. The pilots seldom brought their Hueys lower than 1000 to 1500 feet. They would hover safely out of range of small-arms fire while door gunners poured automatic rounds onto the villages. Other times the Hueys dropped huge gasoline bombs. This tactic is useful only for stationary targets such as villages.

We all flattened ourselves against the ground and waited while the Huey, which showed Honduran markings, flew past. With my burdensome pack, I wasn't very agile and rolled off the trail into some boulders. Nico pressed himself into the dusty trail and squeezed his eyes shut; he had developed a healthy respect for helicopters.

We lay there for some time, not certain if we had been seen and not certain if the Hondurans were coming back. Only after a silent signal from one of our escorts did we rise and continue on.

The closer we got to Quipurito, the more relaxed Nico became and the more eager he seemed to want to talk.

"¿Porqué un gringo se incorporó?" he inquired before asking my name. The question puzzled me. I didn't understand the verb.

"¿Qué quieres decir por incorporarse?" (What do you mean by "incorporate"?) I asked.

He explained that when you join the struggle, you "incorporate" with the guerrillas—literally, I suppose, to join their body. He went on without my prompting to explain that he had "incorporated" soon after his mother's rape and murder. He described the crime graphically, dispassionately, a recital of watching the rape itself and then seeing his mother's brains splattered against the wall. I guess being able to discuss it was a positive sign, although Nico seemed incapable of appropriate grief.

What affected me more, however, was the context in which he viewed the crime. The soldiers, he said, were no better than animals, and it was important to him, as a guerrilla, not to sink to their level. He could not dishonor himself or his mother's memory by committing similar acts. He would fight and kill and possibly be killed, but he would not degrade himself by behaving like a beast.

This was a gentleman's oath, not dissimilar from the rules of conduct drilled into me at the Air Force Academy. As startling as it was to hear from a seventy-five-pound boy, who had been quaking with fright minutes before, his words were a reassuring departure from the images of "terrorists" that were used so much in the media. His code of honor was personal, but it had the earmarks of indoctrination. He had been taught to think this way.

As we tramped on toward Quipurito, I inquired about his family and found out that on the night of the tragedy his father had fled with Nico's two sisters and infant brother to a refugee camp in Honduras. Nico went to a guerrilla camp. He was too young to be a combatant but after six months became a messenger. I asked if the gun wasn't a little too large for him. He laughed and admitted that he wasn't usually allowed to carry one. He'd been given it on this special occasion and was to fire it into the air only as a signal in case something went wrong. Though I had no doubt that he was mature well beyond his years, a twelve-year-old with a .357 magnum was still unsettling.

We had been steadily climbing into the dry foothills and began to see stubbly corn patches. Then we crossed a ridge and passed through a fortified stone fence. Nico announced we were in Quipurito.

At first I didn't see anything that resembled a village, but looking more carefully, I made out a half-dozen houses scattered among the prevalent vegetation, bamboo groves, and clusters of large oak trees. Nico had said the march would take five hours, but that was guerrilla time, not gringo-with-pack time. Though he and our escorts seemed hardly winded from the march, I was done in. Even Lupe and Francisco, who had traveled without packs, looked pretty bushed. José, his mission accomplished, rested for a short while, then said his farewells. He was heading back to Tegucigalpa. I was shown a hammock under the porch of a large adobe house and was asleep within minutes.

* * *

WHEN I WOKE UP it was late afternoon. A cluster of little boys eyed me with curiosity. Slowly, I began to hear a soft but constant slapping sound nearby. I turned to see a group of Salvadoran women patting balls of dough into tortillas and throwing them onto the top of a large clay griddle. Across a dusty courtyard of sorts were six or eight young men sitting around cleaning weapons or lounging while they listened to a radio.

A swarthy Salvadoran, handsome and thickly bearded, came up to my hammock and welcomed me. He said his name was Ramón and asked if I was hungry. When I nodded yes, he went over to the women and brought our dinner—two quarter-inch-thick corn tortillas topped with red pinto beans and a little salt. This was the Salvadoran "Big Mac," their staple meal which, for the next twelve months, would also be the mainstay of my diet.

We ate together. Ramón told me that he, too, was a physician and had been in his final year of study when the Salvadoran military occupied the country's one medical school. A number of his classmates were killed, others fled. At the time, Ramón had been serving his obligatory year in the countryside and decided then to stay with the *campesinos*. He said that other responsibilities were keeping him from practicing much medicine now. I wanted to ask about those responsibilities—he was very patient with my Spanish—and a million other things, but I held my tongue.

I was less restrained with my food. As I gobbled it down, Ramón ate slowly and deliberately, as if no meal should be taken for granted. Some several minutes after I was done, he finished his last morsel and then asked if I would mind seeing a patient. I was pleased by the request for a consultation, and told him so.

We walked across the village to a two-room adobe house where I found a young woman, possibly twenty, lying on a low pallet, breastfeeding her newborn infant. There was very little light inside, barely enough to make out the patient and the worn features of an older woman, presumably her mother, who sat by her side quietly brushing flies from the baby's eyes.

A dog chased a chicken through the room as Ramón introduced me and explained that he reluctantly had performed a Caesarean section. That was seven days ago. The baby seemed to be doing well, he went on, but the mother was now feverish with lower abdominal pain and a vaginal discharge.

There was no soap in the house, so we scrubbed with the bars I'd appropriated from my hotel room in Tegucigalpa. Then I began my examination. Her incision, done with razor blades, was ragged but healing nicely. I saw no sign of infection around it.

Her uterus, however, was flaccid. I noted the discharge was the color and consistency of melted chocolate. These symptoms, together with her history as provided by Ramón, pointed to a diagnosis of post-partum endometritis, a simple womb infection that is quite common, especially following Caesarean section.

Endometritis was Ramón's diagnosis as well; he seemed pleased and relieved that I shared his opinion. Better still, I had with me a supply of ampicillin capsules that would be far more effective in combating the infection than penicillin, the only antibiotic at Ramón's disposal.

After examining the baby as well, I asked Ramón about his decision to operate. There had been no alternative, he said. The mother had endured seventy-two hours of obstructed labor because her pelvis was too small. She would have died had he not surgically removed the baby.

"Where did you operate?" I asked, expecting him to indicate the direction of his clinic. Instead, he gestured toward the adjoining room and a small table that stood at its center.

"Our clinic was filled with stretcher cases," Ramón explained. "We had to operate here."

He was so matter of fact about it!

The Caesarean had been done at night by candlelight using only local anesthesia. While he cut into her with his razor blade scalpels, the patient had been awake and alert.

To me, it was a miracle that Ramón had saved both mother and child. I couldn't imagine then attempting such a procedure myself. But this case was my introduction. Within months, I would be performing amputations with a Swiss Army knife and suturing wounds with dental floss.

This was to be battlefield medicine in El Salvador.

I ARRIVED THERE in the middle of the local dry season. It hadn't rained anything but bullets and mortar rounds for many weeks, and it wouldn't rain again until May. The sun seemed to have sucked the countryside dry. Dust coated everything, and the region's few stream beds were sinews of baked clay.

Quipurito had been largely destroyed during a government offensive of the preceding November. Once the soldiers left, its three hundred or so citizens returned to patch up their old houses or build new ones.

What I encountered was thirty to forty adobe huts, some brand new, others partially rebuilt, a few abandoned entirely to the weeds. Wherever possible, the houses were sited under oak or broad-canopied *ceiba* trees for protection against the sun as well as from the government helicopters.

The huts were connected by narrow, winding lanes and rocky footpaths along which grew a smattering of tropical flowers, mostly brilliant red hibiscus and bougainvillea, that lent some color to the otherwise drab landscape. Insects of every imaginable sort kept up a background din of chirps and buzzes. The air smelled of desiccated vegetation and sweat, tortillas and garbage.

The courtyard, where I had slept the day before, was the community center. Ramón, after our first consultation, revealed that his "other responsibilities" included being the local guerrilla comandante. He held his meetings in the court-yard and maintained his headquarters there.

The clinic, where Lupe, Francisco, and I slept that first night along with the patients and staff, was located some distance away. It was no more than a converted adobe hut, indistinguishable from any of the peasants' houses except for the amount and type of trash strewn around it. Quipuritans, like most *campesinos*, were casual about sanitation.

The building was alive with fleas. As soon as we had strung our hammocks and had settled in for the night, they swarmed and skittered all over us. Luckily, I received few bites. Francisco and Lupe, however, awoke the next morning covered with them, especially in places where a band or strap of their clothing had been tight against their skin. I assumed I was spared because I slept naked. They angrily assumed I was spared because I used a private hoard of insect repellent.

At daybreak, we learned that a Honduran border patrol had captured and killed the two *correos* sent to retrieve Francisco's and Lupe's packs. A third messenger entrusted with my duffle of medicines had managed to elude the soldiers.

Lupe, Francisco, and I were stunned. We had taken our own safe arrival for granted.

While I made it my first task to find a shovel to start cleaning up around the clinic, she led its staff of young *sanitarios* (peasant health workers) to the courtyard where she undertook to explain a battlefield tracheotomy. Never mind that Lupe had never performed one herself, her clear intent was to upstage me.

Ramón, I remember, regarded us both with amusement. There we were, two-thirds of his medical-relief column, and the first thing one of us did was teach tracheotomies while the other attacked the trash. He was too much of a gentleman to tell either of us what fools we were making of ourselves.

At midday, the *sanitarios* returned with bewildered looks; one appeared worried and kept rubbing her throat. They, and Lupe, found me in a circle of *campesinos*, who were equally confused by my primitive Spanish and pantomime of someone shoveling garbage.

I would later wonder at their patience with me. I came into their midst thinking I was well-prepared to help civilians living under primitive conditions. Part of my medical training included a year of work with villagers in India, and I had taken a master's degree in public health. The theory and practice of preventive medicine, the importance of sanitation, the organizational approach to community health were all very familiar to me. It seemed only logical to apply these lessons to their situation.

What I didn't then understand is that in El Salvador medical treatment is viewed as a semi-mystical affair in which every ache or pain is treated with a pill or an injection, if possible. The practice is not fostered by doctors; most rural Salvadorans have never seen a doctor. It is a result of medicines of every type being urged on the people by over-the-counter diagnosticians. Product safety regulation is unknown in that country.

Typical of the abuses is the widespread use of steroids among the peasants. Most steroids are powerful and quite dangerous to use without supervision. Yet Salvadoran pharmacists routinely suggest one such drug as an appetite stimulant for children. A mother whose child might be malarial or full of parasites will be advised to give the youngster this product to make him eat better, which is a little like prescribing chemotherapy for a common cold.

A real doctor with a bagful of medicines, then, is practically a shaman to the peasants. The residents of Quipurito were understandably perplexed when I tried to hand out shovels instead of shots.

There was also the question of priorities. After repairing and rebuilding their shelters, the villagers had begun to dig bomb shelters and to fortify their earthen battlements. Another government offensive was imminent. It made no sense to tidy up the clinic just so the government Hueys could bomb it again.

The *sanitarios* saved the situation by telling me that the assembled *campesinos* had come great distances to be treated. Unless I started seeing patients soon, many would have to return to their villages without having received any care.

THE AFTERNOON INTRODUCED ME to a fair sampling of the range of medicine I'd practice over the next year. In varying order of importance, the *campesinos'* health problems were a function of inadequate diet, chronic disease, woeful sanitation, lack of education, and warfare.

Obstetrics and pediatrics were important because of the high birth rate. Having many children is typical of Third World nations where children are a poor family's insurance against old age. As I had seen in India, the peasants of El Salvador routinely expected half their children to die before reaching their teens. As long as this continues to be the case, the women will continue to bear as many children as they can lest they and their husbands attain old age with no family, especially sons, to care for them.

Many of my patients were pregnant women suffering from obvious anemia. Beans and tortillas are poor sources of iron. The little iron they get, they lose to pregnancy, malaria, and parasites. The children, too, were anemic from malnutrition and parasitic infections. Many of them suffered from chronic diarrhea and, consequently, dehydration.

There were several wounds to attend to, including that of a woman who had recently delivered a baby after walking six days with a grenade fragment in her leg. Her baby was fine by local standards; it was underweight for its age, anemic, and covered with lesions caused by scabies, a kind of mite. The mother's leg wound, which had abscessed, was even more serious. I had to make a channel for it to drain.

Like Joaquín, the *campesino* whose torture wounds I had treated in Salinas, there were several depressives at the clinic. Years of fleeing government offensives, watching each other die, and struggling in the interim to find enough to eat had left these people mentally disorganized. One moment they would stand listlessly before me. The next, they would fall into spontaneous sobs.

The clinic exhausted me. I was overwhelmed by my sense of inadequacy before the challenge of easing their tragic burden of disease and trauma. After treating fifty or more of them, I ate my beans and tortillas and retired to my hammock where not even the fleas could distract me from the sadness I felt.

I conducted another clinic the next day, then toured the village. Everyone seemed occupied with some task. Most of the men were working on bomb shelters or digging trenches. Many of the women were busy grinding corn for that night's dinner. Some of the adults attended a prayer meeting, while others were gathered in literacy classes.

When the children's school let out, I found Nico drilling his squad of *correos*. They listened in sober silence as he delivered a little speech, no doubt in emulation of the ones he had heard Ramón deliver to the guerrillas. At his command, they all saluted and then broke for a soccer game. For the next two hours, they could be heard laughing and shouting a half mile away.

AFTER SUPPER, everyone joined in the courtyard for a sort of village sing-along. The songs were all revolutionary numbers that sounded, to my ear, like a cross between Mexican and U.S. country-and-western music. The words to one of them went something like, "We're not Russians, and we're not Cubans, too. We are the Farabundo Martí Liberation Front." In Spanish, it all rhymed.

Several guerrillas, or *compañeros* as they are called (a term that combines our sense of partner and friend), were standing near me. I asked one of them why they would sing such a song that seemed to repudiate their leftist allies.

He was puzzled that I would ask such a question. According to him, the guerrillas resented that every newspaper they saw or broadcast they heard seemed to credit the Cubans or the Nicaraguans with supplying them arms. Their victories were being wrongly credited to foreigners. They were irritated by the inference that they couldn't fight for themselves, and they even suspected the Cubans or Soviets didn't mind this propaganda.

In one of my several long conversations with Ramón, he explained that the sensitivity over foreign involvement in their civil war was partly a matter of pride and partly a question of practicality. Accepting Soviet-bloc weapons or allowing a Cuban or Nicaraguan to fight alongside the *compañeros* would be inviting even more direct intervention by the United States. The guerrillas were not about to give the Reagan administration a pretext for sending U.S. troops against them.

Ramón was a study in contrasts. His rhetoric in front of the guerrillas was heated and full of obligatory slogans and epithets. He referred to the president as "the Fascist Reagan" as mechanically as you might say, "my brother-in-law Bob." In private, he was reflective and compassionate.

He clearly detested bloodshed. Several *campesinos* had told me of his daring in the last government offensive, how Ramón and his *compañeros* had fought very bravely to hold off the enemy soldiers long enough for several hundred civilians to evacuate into the hills. But he declined to discuss these battlefield exploits.

We talked one night about my conversion to non-violence and on another about Ché Guevara, the Argentinian of Cuban revolutionary fame who, like us, was a doctor. On a third occasion, he outlined his ideals of a future Salvadoran health care system not dissimilar from the socialized medicine of Britain or Canada. When he spoke at all of his military duties, it was only to explain his efforts at erasing illiteracy among the volunteers and to overcome their machismo. A guerrilla had to be more than a fighter, he believed. The *compañeros* had also to be examples to the rest of society.

I dwell on Ramón because he, like Nico, was my introduction to the revolutionary ethos, the character of this insurgency. They did not just oppose the old order, they were fighting for a new one.

It would be easy to romanticize the two of them, the traumatized orphan and the heroic comandante, especially when their principles and dignity are contrasted with the terrorism wrought by the Salvadoran right. But a truer portrait would be of a man and a boy caught in the vortex of revolutionary violence.

In a rational world, Nico would have a kite and a pet dog and his mother's lap for comfort. Ramón, then thirty-two and married, would have been a contented country doctor. Instead, Nico will probably catch a bullet and die with a revolutionary slogan on his lips. Ramón is already gone.

Months later, a *sanitario* told me Ramón was resting in his hammock when the pin from a grenade on his hip fell to the floor with a tinkle. There was no time to heave the device out the door. As three of his men looked on, Ramón threw himself into a corner and absorbed the full impact of the exploding grenade with his body.

They rolled him over to find him barely breathing, clutching his lacerated liver and intestines. A call went out for a medic, but the comandante refused any treatment. He said that to operate was a waste of equipment and anesthesia. Then, for the last minutes of his life, Ramón spoke of the future. For his death to mean anything, he told them, they were not to mourn him but to carry on.

I WAS SEVERAL DAYS IN QUIPURITO before being told of my ultimate destination—Guazapa. To my great dismay, it was not free of civilians as I'd been led to believe by the radio reports I'd heard in Managua. There were 9,000 *campesinos* there and they had sustained extensive casualties in the recent offensive. Ramón told me the government body counts were comprised almost exclusively of slain civilians.

Guazapa, like the region around Quipurito, was referred

to by the guerrillas as a "control zone." Nowhere in the country were they yet strong enough to actually hold territory or to engage the enemy in set battles. Control zones were rebel-occupied in the sense that death squads did not operate in them, and the soldiers entered only during invasions.

The bulk of controlled territories lay in the north and eastern sectors of El Salvador. Guazapa was more isolated, an area of about two hundred square miles surrounding a dormant volcano twenty miles north of the capital, San Salvador. It would be a three-day march south from Quipurito, across government-held territory.

Ramón's last words to me were a request. An American film crew had come to Quipurito, and they wished to interview me for a freelance documentary they were producing. At first I refused them, but Ramón urged me to reconsider, suggesting I might accomplish much if Americans heard me explain why I was there.

I did so with great reluctance; my commitment did not include propagandizing for the revolution or for myself. I was not in El Salvador to endorse killing under any banner, or to imply any individual courage. I'd seen enough of heroes in Vietnam to eschew the notion of becoming one myself.

The film team, headed by a Californian named Frank Christopher, agreed to focus on medical issues. When it was over, Christopher and his cameraman, the late John Chapman, surprised me with the announcement that they were coming along to Guazapa. We left the next morning.

Thirty of us made the trip. Along with myself and Lupe (Francisco remained behind in Quipurito), there were the four U.S. filmmakers, a *campesino* family traveling to Guazapa for a reunion with their sons, and our guerrilla escort.

The trail was steep and serpentine as we marched down from the highlands of Quipurito and across the dry hills of Chalatenango Province. Our column leader, a martinet, kept up a murderous pace that soon had myself and most of the older *campesinos* gasping for breath.

Endlessly, it seemed, we'd plod down one side of a hill

only to grope our way up the other. Because it was the dry season, fresh water was as scarce as the sun was merciless. What little water we did find came from foul mudholes.

The vegetation was mostly tufts of grass poking through the rocky soil and a few isolated scrub trees. On a couple of occasions, we came across a native fruit tree that the guerrillas would expertly strip of its plum-like fruit. Otherwise, I saw only a few patches of corn stubble and parched bean fields.

We saw more vultures than people until we neared Guazapa. Since El Salvador is the most densely populated country in the western hemisphere, I wondered where all the people had gone.

The answer lay with the government Hueys we saw from time to time that day. For months, they had ferried invasion forces in and out of Chalatenango, bringing scorched-earth devastation to the entire region. We passed gutted village after gutted village, uninhabitable ruins whose owners had long since fled to Honduras or guerrilla-controlled zones to the north and east. Not only were the houses ruined and the livestock butchered, but objects as benign as fruit trees were often, apparently purposefully, destroyed. What I didn't see first-hand were the ruined granaries. The government soldiers had seen to it that starvation would set in before the May rains brought another planting season.

The column leader allowed us but three brief stops during the first day's ten-hour march. Juanita, a middle-aged (that is to say, old) peasant, complained from the first hour of chest pains and shortness of breath. It might have been angina or asthma, exhaustion, dehydration, or all four; there was little time to diagnose and treat her on the trail. John Chapman, the American cameraman, collapsed about eight hours into the march with vertigo, nausea, vomiting, and teeth-rattling chills: heat exhaustion. By the time we stopped that night, fully a third of the column, guerrillas included, were stumbling and straggling.

For me, it was the beginning of many months of foot

agony. The pack of equipment shifted my center of balance and with its added weight put tremendous pressure on the balls of both feet. As a result, I later developed plantar fasciitis, an inflammation of the connective tissue. In time, all ten toenails turned black and fell off.

WE BIVOUACKED THAT FIRST NIGHT in a ravaged and deserted village. John Chapman's symptoms had worsened throughout the day to the point where he had to be carried in a makeshift stretcher. After seeing to Juanita, and the less severely disabled members of the column, I stayed up with John all night. He could not take liquids because of intractable vomiting. The only available remedy for nausea was in suppository form and long since gone liquid. In desperation—and hope—I injected him with an anti-psychotic drug because I vaguely remembered it had a strong anti-emetic side effect. It worked and its use marked the beginning of much seat-of-the-pants medical care.

From midnight on, I rehydrated him with spoonfuls of a Tang mixture. The column leader told me to "make" him well by morning because we had a rendezvous with a ferry in forty-eight hours and there could be no more delays! Several other members of the column collapsed before we made it.

The next two days of marching differed little from the first except for the random gunfire we began to hear. Most of it was far off and indistinct. Save for the unmistakable staccato of the machine guns, it sounded like deer-hunting season in the mountains of Colorado.

The last and most difficult part of the journey had to be accomplished at night. We made it to a point overlooking the north shore of Lake Suchitlán, a distance of about forty miles north of San Salvador and about twenty miles from the Guazapa volcano. To our left, I could make out the lights of the giant Fifth of November dam. Ahead, across the lake and to our right, I could see nothing. There was no moon yet and all of the Guazapa "control zone" was blacked out.

As we began the long descent down to a gravel, east-west highway and then to the boats that would take us across the lake to the village of Copapayo, my only sensation besides fear was the electric shocks of pain running up my legs from my abused feet. Silence, I thought, seemed paramount; it was from the shore below us that we'd heard the machine gun fire earlier that day, and there was no way of knowing if enemy troops were still in the vicinity. But I didn't know then that the army troops try to avoid fighting at night. We came crashing down the slope like a herd of buffalo. A couple of the *compañeros* even stopped to light cigarettes! The author of the "Night-fighters' Manual" would have blanched at their recklessness.

Across the deserted highway, we passed several adobe houses that had burst like egg shells from the impact of five-hundred-pound bombs. A phosphoric ash, presumably from rockets used to spot the targets, glistened in the dark like snow on the ground.

We made Copapayo by midnight and at dawn pushed immediately on to the village of Tenango directly east of the volcano. We rested there and ate before leaving at nightfall on the last leg of the trip. In the dark, we traversed an enormous chasm I would come to call the "Grand Canyon."

The moon came out that night, casting a soft blue light on us in the canyon. There was a short briefing held, in which we were given instructions for crossing our final obstacle, the heavily patrolled, paved road that connects San Salvador to the south with the town of Suchitoto and its garrison five miles to our north, near Copapayo. For the first time, I sensed battle tension among the guerrillas; unlike our pell-mell charge down to the lake, this crossing would be dangerous.

After we climbed up the western slope of the abyss, we walked single-file toward the road, keeping a distance of five yards between us. Once there, the *compañeros* fanned out on both sides and then with hand signals sent us running, one by one, across the road.

Once reassembled on the far side, we resumed our march

up the volcano itself, a black, forbidding mass in the moonlight. Since I knew we were nearing the heart of the control zone, I expected to see fortifications. If this were Viet Cong territory, there would be trenches and tunnels and bunkers honeycombing the mountainside. Nothing of the sort was in place on Guazapa. Along the winding trail, the only structures we saw were three- and four-house settlements called *caseríos* smouldering in ruins. The air was thick with the stench of death—livestock, I hoped—from a government attack just a few days ago. I had to hold a handkerchief over my nose as we skirted the bombed-out settlements and moved north along the side of the mountain to our destination, the village of Llano Rancho. As the sun rose behind us, I saw the first tiled roof. A collective sigh went out of the column. We had made it.

Someone handed me a cold tortilla that I sat chewing while staring up through the mists toward the volcano's summit. I was suffering acute fatigue, a boneweariness lightened only by the satisfaction that after nearly half a year of trying I had made it to this village on the eastern slope of an extinct volcano in El Salvador. Ironically, after all that trouble, I was within an easy hour's drive of San Salvador and, had I wished, might have made it to the airport and back to California for a late lunch that day.

The view from Llano Rancho was magnificent. Far below the coffee bushes that surrounded us, I beheld sugarcane fields together with low brush that gave way to a panorama stretching north to Lake Suchitlán and east into the heart of El Salvador. As I swallowed the last doughy morsel of my tortilla, I reflected on the somber, primitive beauty of the country.

Later that morning, I was introduced to Jasmine, the medical *responsable* (director) for the Guazapa Front. Jasmine was a stout and stolid Salvadoran who did not invite familiarity. She wore her hair in two utilitarian braids and kept her smile, which was lovely, mostly to herself. I imagine she was somewhere in her late twenties.

Her expression did become considerably brighter when we went through the pack of medical equipment and the duffle of medicines I brought. In total, the supplies and medicine were about what a rural general practitioner in the United States would need for a week of routine doctoring. But they were twice the total Jasmine had on hand to minister to 9,000 civilians and 1,000 combatants in Guazapa. She fingered several of the instruments as if they were rare and precious objects; to her, they were.

After a day's rest, she had me brought to Palo Grande, a village a short distance from Llano Rancho where their central "hospital" was located. It was a small adobe structure divided into three rooms and outfitted with a porch. The hospital was a pathetic, dusty affair with no electricity or indoor plumbing. I counted six beds.

There was also the same inattention to basic sanitation that I had seen in Quipurito. Used syringes, moldering wound dressings, discarded ampuls—the septic refuse of medical work—lay strewn around the ground. This time, I ignored the mess and followed Jasmine into the building to meet her patients.

One was a silent *compañero* with a palate injury and a great jagged hole in his skull. He lay motionless while a young girl, one of Jasmine's nurses, spoon-fed him some liquids. Another patient had been blinded. His left hand was amputated, and his right hand was a burnt and mangled stump. The other two patients were a little girl and an old man, both with several leg wounds from mortar fragments.

Only the absolutely immobile, Jasmine explained, were kept in the hospital. All the rest of her cases were seen on an outpatient basis. If they couldn't walk, their families or friends brought them to the hospital on stretchers, often over very tortuous terrain.

Elsewhere on the Front, her network of *sanitarios* ran small clinics where the care was even more haphazard than it was here. This was make-do medicine. With her limited formal education, Jasmine said, and with limited supplies and limited time, she couldn't begin to address the basic health needs of the people, let alone see to the sick and dying left after each enemy offensive. She was plainly very grateful I'd come to help.

THE GUAZAPA FRONT, at that time, was filling with guerrilla columns as the rebel command prepared an offensive to disrupt the March 28, 1982, national elections. On about the sixteenth, or a couple days after I'd arrived in Llano Rancho, I heard U.S. Ambassador Deane Hinton on my pocket radio. "The forthcoming elections," he told an interviewer, "will be the most revolutionary event in Salvadoran history." He went on to encourage the guerrillas to lay down their arms and to participate in the elections.

Hinton was being either naive or disingenuous. Any election in El Salvador was a sham as long as the death squads remained unbridled. Only eighteen months earlier, six FDR leaders tried to hold a press conference in San Salvador. They were kidnapped by a truckload of uniformed soldiers and several men in street clothes. The next day the mutilated bodies of the six were discovered strewn outside the city. Thousands more trade unionists, teachers, doctors, and peasants had been murdered since. Under those circumstances, campaigning for office under the FDR banner was tantamount to suicide.

The guerrillas quite naturally took Hinton's call as evidence of U.S. treachery. It is difficult to trust a man who invites you to walk into a bullet. Unfortunately for me, their suspicion wasn't confined to the Ambassador. Any *norteamericano* was apt to be viewed with hostility.

A note about *norteamericanos*. Many Latins see it as a sign of cultural arrogance for us to assume the term "American" applies only to ourselves. To underscore that point, they call Mexicans *Mejicanos*, and Canadians *Canadienses*. Americans are *norteamericanos* or, sometimes, *Yanquis*.

I felt shades and varieties of their aversion the moment I

stepped into José's Cherokee. Few of the others were as overt as Lupe, but many of the *compañeros* were distinctly cool or avoided my company altogether.

My decision to keep a diary did nothing to allay this distrust. But I felt it important to maintain a record of my time there for several reasons. For one, I have forgotten much of what happened around me in Vietnam. If I was to bear witness to what I saw in El Salvador, I wanted to retain details, not just impressions. I also did not know if I'd leave Guazapa alive. The revolution could swallow me the way it had so many others. If it did, I wanted some tangible artifact by which my family and friends might understand what I'd done.

It turned out to serve another function, as well. There were so many obstacles to open communication in Guazapa, my poor Spanish, the culture gap, the need for secrecy, etc., that I needed some outlet for my thoughts, especially complaints. Had I not deemed the diary a necessary exercise as well as a therapeutic one, I would have dumped it after the first few baleful stares. The best I could do was to try not to seem too secretive about it and to hold my peace the many times I knew it had been taken and read.

Jasmine wasn't nearly so paranoid as the others, or so spontaneous, either. Hers was an extremely sober nature. She wasn't an automaton; Jasmine was as compassionate as she was earnest. She simply had no time for distractions.

She also knew nothing of the terms of my service. Either Jaime and Carmen in Mexico City hadn't troubled themselves to pass along this information or, as was likely, the rebels' tenuous system of radio relays and codes, which changed daily, was overburdened by the several sentences it would take to explain Quakerism.

It didn't occur to me to repeat my conditions when I met her; it was difficult enough with her poor English and my worse Spanish to discuss the simplest issues. Had I thought to bring it up, I might have saved myself a tremendous amount of distress.

But I didn't.

When Jasmine suggested I go southwest around the volcano to El Salitre, I assumed it was because the civilians there needed me. She said that since we were the only two doctors for 10,000 people spread over two hundred square miles, it made no sense for us both to be stationed in Palo Grande. Unaware of my moral preference for working among civilians, Jasmine didn't add that Salitre was one of the staging areas for the guerrillas' election day attack on San Salvador. She didn't tell me that I'd be expected to accompany them.

SALITRE WAS NEAR THE SOUTHERNMOST BORDER of the control zone, an irregular area that would have appeared on a map as a great runny egg. Its yoke, the volcano peak, was held by government troops and resupplied by helicopter. They launched periodic raids from this base, as well as random mortar attacks and sniper fire. ·

From Llano Rancho, located a mile or so down the eastern slope from the base, the Front's farthest reach was twelve miles northeast to Copapayo on the southern shore of Lake Suchitlán. Due north from Llano Rancho was the farm belt, several square miles of flat, arable land where *campesino* collectives grew corn, beans, and sugarcane that once belonged to the local *dueño* (landlord). Northern Guazapa's principal villages, Delicias and Chaparral, were the most prosperous of all the Front's communities. The countryside just west of the volcano was rugged, largely uninhabited, and of little consequence to either the guerrillas or the government.

The southern sector was nearly as forbidding as the west. Much of it was on a thirty to forty percent grade and is covered with dense underbrush. The trails were no more than footpaths laid out not for convenience but for the best cover from surveillance. To the soldiers in the volcano-top bunker, we'd appear as ants dodging among pebbles and leaves below them.

El Salitre itself was well hidden from the garrison, the

only positive thing I noted upon arrival. After four and a half hours of steady pounding down and around from Llano Rancho, plantar inflammation had made balloons of my toes. The few children who greeted us in Salitre found my limp highly entertaining.

None of the Front's villages differed significantly from the rest. Each, like Quipurito, consisted of a handful of widely spaced adobe houses connected by dirt paths. In some, the people cooked and washed communally. The cultivation of the local corn or bean patch or the gathering of firewood was also communal. An individual's responsibilities in these various tasks reflected his or her interest in collective life. Not everyone chose to join the collectives or, if they did, devoted themselves full time to them.

This was pre-Columbian collectivism, a loose form of social organization that has a far longer history in Central America than do the coffee bushes or even the Spanish language. The native tendency to dwell together in this way has always been an obstacle to the imposed system of huge plantations. To overcome it, the *dueños* had to destroy it. They legally expropriated or stole the communal lands and then turned the population into landless workers.

A hundred years ago, the landowners planted the country with the indigo bushes for making dye. When that market collapsed, they ripped up the indigo and replaced it with coffee. For a time, the plantations produced handsome foreign revenues for El Salvador. Per capita income was high by Latin standards. But the cash crops didn't require nearly the labor that thousands of *milpas* (corn patches) did, and, since the indigo and then the coffee bushes had replaced the *milpas*, there was less food to go around. Later in this century cotton and grazing cattle displaced more *campesinos*. Where once the peasants ate regularly, if not well, and enjoyed a measure of tranquillity, vast numbers of them began to crowd San Salvador looking for work. The rest fled to Honduras or stayed hungry in the countryside. The goal of both twentieth-century *campesino* rebellions has been to win back what the *dueños* have taken from them.

* * *

I GAVE THE SALITRE CLINIC a brief inspection and found it in appalling condition. It was really only a mud hut, about half the size of Jasmine's hospital. It contained a single rickety operating table upon which I found a haphazard collection of medical equipment. The few odds and ends were not put away, the local *responsable* informed me, because there was rarely time to gather them and flee from surprise attacks. Within five weeks, the village would be assaulted and the clinic razed.

The *responsable's* code name was Camilo, like mine, but unlike me he enjoyed instant warmth from Lupe. It turned out they had trained together in Mexico, and she had come to Guazapa to work next to him. Having accomplished her goal, I hoped, would make her a bit more tractable around me. It didn't.

As we began to see patients, Lupe would literally grab them from their place in line and then conduct her own private examination. She would not, as a matter of policy, consult with me at all.

One of these cases was a woman who complained of severe headaches. Lupe took a brief history from her and learned that the headaches had bothered the woman every day for six years. No aspirin or any other medicine relieved the pain.

There are several possible diagnoses for such severe headaches, including cranial lesions, a blood clot, a tumor, or, most likely in my view, the headaches were psychosomatic, the result of stress.

Lupe at least should have taken a thorough medical history and then checked the woman's retinas and pupils for signs of intracranial pressure. Instead, she broke open an ampul of Demerol, a powerful synthetic morphine, and administered an injection.

Of course, the patient felt very good, very soon, and was deeply appreciative for the relief. Lupe smiled. When I later offered her a look at a medical text in the hopes she might pick up a little something about headache diagnosis, she rejected it and haughtily offered me a piece of fruit brought to her by the grateful patient.

Lupe had violated two canons of medicine: Do not do harm to the patient and always be sure you know what you do not know. The Demerol had masked all headache symptoms and had thus prevented any accurate diagnosis. Moreover, we had only ten ampuls of Demerol at the clinic, and we couldn't waste the drug on headaches. After the woman came back a third time for her Demerol shot, Camilo and the other *sanitarios* firmly told Lupe to stop the treatment.

But Lupe wasn't the only source of strain. Since my first day in Llano Rancho, the only reason it seemed anyone approached me was because they wanted medicine, money, clothes, or, most often, my small radio. Batteries were scarce, and I tried to conserve mine. I used the radio only to monitor newscasts.

The young medics, however, would tune in music stations and listen until the batteries went dead. No one was the least bit apologetic about this, nor did they ever offer to replace the batteries. They all assumed I was rich and could easily afford to replace the batteries myself. On more than one occasion when I had not replaced them a *sanitario* would filch the batteries from my diagnostic kit and use them in a radio.

It took me a long while to overcome my irritation with their total disrespect for my meager private belongings. Having my precious radio treated like a toy was infuriating. The same was true for what I took to be their puerile selfishness whenever I asked for something.

Each night a guerrilla or two would sneak down from the slopes of the volcano near Salitre into government-held towns to buy little luxuries such as condensed milk, candy, or cookies. When I asked one of them if he would pick up some medical supplies he wanted to know if I was going to pay for them.

I directed his attention to a pile of recently purchased socks and women's underwear. "If the *compañeros* can afford those things, can't they afford to buy some medicine?" I asked him somewhat self-righteously.

"Those things are different," he replied without a flicker of concern. "They're war supplies."

Another irritation was weapons training. I was expected to take instruction with everyone else, even though I thought I had made it clear in Mexico I would not be a combatant. To that point, the only weapon I'd handled was an old revolver given me one night when I was awakened and told to go stand watch at the clinic. I remember shivering in the cool breeze that blew down from the volcano and praying I wouldn't have to stop anyone. My dread fantasy was that a *compañero* would open up with his M-16 after I mangled the Spanish passwords. As it was, the only sound I heard that night was the thunderous flatulence of a nearby horse.

In weapons training I discovered what, I will wager, is a universal military truism: All arms instructors are asses. At the Air Force Academy, my training had extended to bedding down each night with my M-1. We were expected to take our rifles apart and then reassemble them in the dark several times through the night and then report on our success each morning.

Like most of my arms instructors at the Academy, the guerrilla who explained the M-16, the G-3, and the ᶠAL rifles in Salitre was a self-important and windy bore. He stretched a five-minute talk into two stuporous hours. I finally wandered off to bathe in a nearby spring and returned only to find him still at it. The *sanitarios* stood by politely, their eyes glazed over.

I know that part of my crankiness during those first days in Guazapa came from the constant torment of my feet. They itched and burned and ached and smelled bad. The insects were annoying, too, from the interminable drone of the cicadas to all the winged and crawling little monsters that feasted on my imported gringo blood.

Food, or rather hunger, was becoming another pre-occupation. I really didn't mind the beans and tortilla routine. There just was not enough of it, nor could I vary my diet much. Once in a while, I was offered a piece of candy or a cup of sugary black coffee. The odd avocado turned up now and again.

I began having food reveries, such as the time a kindly old man gave me a small bunch of thumbsize bananas. Coveting them, I sat down with my back against a tree and proceeded, in a very disciplined fashion, to consume them, thirty-two chews per bite.

That was Academy training. An underclassman at the Air Force Academy dined erect and rigid on the edge of his chair with his eyes fixed on the rim of his plate. If I was ever caught looking at the food itself, if I spilled any, or if I neglected to chew each bite thirty-two times, a senior would bark, "Mr. Clements, ground your fork!"

Then he would order me to sing three verses of "The Star Spangled Banner."

"Do you think you are sufficiently capable of self-discipline to continue chewing thirty-two times per bite?" he would ask.

"Yessir!" Mr. Clements answered.

Under a tree on a hot Guazapa afternoon, the gringo Camilo fell into Academy procedure as readily as Cadet Clements had. Thirty-two chews per bite. Yessir.

THE FIRST FRESH GUNSHOT WOUND I treated was self-inflicted, not deliberately but because the guerrillas were extremely casual about handling loaded weapons. It always made me very nervous to walk among them because they never put down their rifles (not even at dinner or on the way to the latrine), and the barrels were pointed every which way.

The patient—code "green" for a minor casualty—was brought to the clinic with a clean hole through the fourth metatarsal of his left hand. He had shot himself while on the trail returning from an ambush near San Salvador. The guerrillas' objective there was the buses to be used to transport voters on election day. Eighteen empty buses, or so he claimed, had been blown up that day. I could not repair his damaged tendon nor did I have any wire or plate to hold the bone together, much less plaster for a cast. All I could do was dress and splint it.

As he spoke, we received word by radio that a second casualty, a "black" or critical injury, was being brought to Salitre. Camilo seemed to panic at this news; it was clear from his instant confusion that he was as new to guerrilla medicine as I.

He was in charge, however, and I had no choice but to accept his decision to grab a hammock and head out looking for the injured man. We had no idea which trail he was being brought in on, and I was too lame to make much of a stretcher-bearer. Nevertheless we headed out.

We skidded along down the first likely trail until we met a party of returning fighters. They said the casualty was being brought up by another route. We turned around and scrambled back up the hill to Salitre. Exhausted and with my feet on fire with pain, I hobbled back to the clinic at just the moment that our patient, who had sustained a head injury from a fall, was being brought in. Quickly, I ordered the unconscious man laid on our operating table, which just as quickly collapsed.

We moved him to a pallet in a corner of the clinic and I called for my diagnostic kit. Naturally, the batteries were missing so I had no way of examining his eyes for symptoms of neurological damage. My external examination revealed no obvious fractures or other signs of gross injury. If I could have determined that he was hemorrhaging, and where, I was prepared to drill burr holes through his skull to help relieve the pressure.

Since I couldn't, I asked that a *correo* be sent to the central hospital for batteries and several doses of intravenous steroids with which I might prevent inflammation of his brain tissue. Until the *correo* returned, all I could do was put the man on saline solution and wait.

He did regain consciousness for a time, and I was relieved we could give him fluids orally. In two days, we would have gone through our entire stock of intravenous saline solution on his case alone. As it was, he died the next day, and we buried him without my ever diagnosing or correctly treating his injury.

It is hard to say if even the most advanced medical care would have saved this man; severe head injuries such as those that often kill prizefighters are very difficult to treat under the best of circumstances. I did, however, rage inwardly at my total inability to help him. Like the night of my first clinic in Quipurito, I again felt despair.

Life in Salitre was not unrelievedly grim, nor was I ever bored. One night, for instance, I returned from clinic guard duty to find a stranger slumbering in my pile of blankets under a tree. Tired and cross at what I took to be yet another example of arrogant presumption, I brusquely rousted the intruder. He left mumbling something to himself. The next day, I learned that I'd ordered Raul Hercules, the guerrilla comandante of all Guazapa, from his sleep. I went looking for him to offer an explanation, but it was too late. He'd already gone.

Then there was "El Cubano." I kept looking for evidence of Cuban or Nicaraguan or even Soviet advisors among the insurgents, certain that there must be at least a few.

One day I was sure I'd discovered one when I saw a circle of *compañeros* joking and teasing a very dark-complected and frizzy-haired young man they called "El Cubano." They ran their fingers through his hair and laughed, "When they kill you, they'll know they have a Cuban."

When he came to the clinic with a minor problem, I accosted him.

"¿Cubano," I asked. "Cómo se llama usted?" (Cuban, what is your name?)

"¡No soy Cubano!" he protested.

I didn't believe him. "¿De qué parte de Cuba viene?" (What part of Cuba are you from?) I pressed.

He laughed and then everyone in the clinic laughed. "El Cubano" was a native of Guazapa and was called that only because the guerrillas imagined he was what Cubans looked like. My interrogation had amused everyone greatly.

Later, in another part of Guazapa, a *campesino* asked *me* if I was Cuban. Later still, villagers from just outside the Front listened to a bit of my suspicious Spanish and wanted to know if I was a Russian.

They had heard the phrase "Soviet-backed" insurgency on Voice of America so many times they assumed it was true.

In general the Salvadoran insurgents showed little sensitivity to outside involvement with their revolution. I met a Mexican, an Argentine, and a Colombian there. But with me or Nicaraguans and Cubans, they were skittish.

That sentiment subsequently hardened into official FMLN policy when the United States State Department produced a Nicaraguan prisoner who swore he had fought with the FMLN under orders from his own government. When he was brought to Washington, he recanted the whole business at a press conference. Even with such "evidence" of Nicaraguan participation in the civil war discredited, the guerrilla command didn't want to give the United States any possible justification for intervening more directly in the civil war. At the time I left El Salvador in early 1983, no Cuban or Nicaraguan was allowed to serve in any capacity with the guerrillas, nor had I ever seen or heard of one among the rebels I was with.

It was many months before I was given the merest hint of guerrilla policy on this level; indeed, even the location of Front headquarters was a mystery until well into the summer of 1982. For the longest time, I had trouble even making out who was a column leader (their equivalent of a company commander) and who wasn't.

After all the years I spent living on military bases, attending a military academy, being educated in everything from hand-to-hand combat to paratrooping to pilot training to months of a combat tour in Vietnam, it was extremely frustrating to be in the middle of a military camp where I knew or understood next to nothing. From what I saw there seemed few more highly trained military men than myself among the guerrillas. Yet, at that time, even the most airily disengaged tortilla maker generally knew more than I knew, and much sooner.

IT DIDN'T TAKE ME NEARLY AS LONG to figure out that I was the only fully educated doctor in the region, even though Jasmine was perhaps the better qualified of the two of us. She had far more practical experience in battlefield medicine. Ranging in experience down from her, the likes of Lupe or Francisco or Camilo were equivalent to civilian paramedics in the United States. There were about a dozen similarly experienced *sanitarios* in Guazapa. The rest of the health workers had learned what they knew from Jasmine and the *sanitarios*. Most knew how to administer an intravenous injection, perform wound debridements, give a few basic medicines, and carry out similar emergency services.

Given the practical medical concerns of the Front, Jasmine's and her staff's training were well-adapted to their tasks. While in general the care they could provide was severely deficient, this was not for want of enthusiasm or dedication. They did very well with what little they had.

I saw my role as a complement to this system. Although I was bound by oath to treat anyone who required my aid, I wished to be primarily responsible for obstetrics, pediatrics, and preventive medicine.

Typical of the cases Jasmine referred to me was a *compañero* who had somehow driven a needle into his soft palate while mending a canvas pack. She had tried to remove the needle at the central hospital, but had succeeded only in driving it farther into his throat. I, in turn, had no better success.

The patient arrived in the middle of the night by

"Salvadoran ambulance," a hammock slung between two bamboo poles and hefted down the dark trail by some sturdy *compañeros*. I wanted to operate immediately, but someone had taken the operating lamp batteries. Candles would not provide enough light for me to see into his throat.

As soon as the sun was high enough, I had him brought outside on a bed. One of the *sanitarios* held up a shiny tin can, the bottom of which reflected sunlight into the man's mouth. I could see that the area around the perforation was very swollen. He couldn't swallow or move his neck, and I knew I couldn't touch the wound without provoking a gag reflex.

My single ampul of anesthetic was a type usually used for setting acute fractures and would be effective for only five minutes. Worse, it wouldn't suppress his gag reflex. Luckily, local application of lidocaine did. Unluckily, the delay in operating had allowed the needle fragment to work its way even farther into his palate. In the brief time I could keep him under, I couldn't find the needle and had to give up after accomplishing no more than an even bigger surgical hole in the back of his throat.

I had to wait for the wound to abscess before I could go in again and finally remove the needle. That was several days later and only after a tremendous amount of agony for the patient. He eventually healed and continued to serve as one of the leaders of the agricultural cooperatives.

FIVE DAYS BEFORE THE FIGHTING was to begin, Jasmine made one of her periodic trips down to Salitre. I was glad to see her and asked if we might talk. I wanted to clarify my responsibilities vis-à-vis civilian and military medicine. She said that it was a very busy time for her, but we would talk in a few days. She seemed preoccupied; I would soon see why. She brought with her a few supplies for the *sanitarios* who'd accompany the guerrilla columns into San Salvador as well as a few words of advice for them.

I could understand a lot more Spanish than I could speak, so I was pretty well able to follow her talk, even though her voice was soft as usual and was nearly drowned by the roar of the cicadas.

First, Jasmine reminded them of how important their role was, and she emphasized the importance of maintaining discipline. I could feel her struggling when she turned to the subject of wounded *compañeros*. They must not be deserted, she said, but sometimes it would be impossible to evacuate them. In these circumstances, well . . .

Jasmine didn't say to kill the wounded or leave them alive. But she did point out that no injured prisoner was known to survive capture and that everyone realized what might be in store for them in such a case. The government troops are especially cruel to the wounded. She reminded them of the *sanitario* who had recently been skinned alive, piece by piece.

As a doctor, I was stunned by what she was telling them. Yet, Jasmine could not have been more humane or more professional at that nightmarish moment.

At this time, as many as five columns of guerrillas had amassed in Salitre, about four hundred combatants in all. One of their commanders approached me and asked if I'd give his men a physical exam. It nettled me that Jasmine hadn't made my mission clear to everyone. I contemplated refusing the request. But I wasn't at all certain what would happen if I said no; my position among them was fragile enough.

So I examined the guerrilla column. I found the young men surprisingly fit. Most of them had gunshot scars. One, named Rubén, proudly showed me twelve places on his arms and legs where he'd been hit. Many had pale tongues and lips, and through my stethoscope, I detected a surprising number of heart murmurs. This was a reflection of the nutritional conditions. There was next to no red meat in Guazapa; most of the *campesinos'* livestock had long since been slaughtered in enemy offensives. Malaria, which destroys red blood cells, is also very common. Furthermore, almost every one of the fighters suffered from periodic parasitic intestinal infections that cause blood loss through hemorrhaging. As a result, their hearts have to pump oxygen-poor blood that much faster. The inevitable result: murmurs of chronic anemia.

Such widespread anemia should have caused more apparent lethargy among them. You'd expect them all to tire easily. Yet from the marching I'd already done with the columns, I could personally attest to their remarkable durability. This was very surprising, but no more so than the camp meeting that followed my physical exams.

A POLITICAL OFFICER from the FDR, who identified himself as Saul Villalta, opened the meeting with a very precise and comprehensive review of the past ten years of Salvadoran history. The speech was tedious at times, but relatively free of rhetoric.

He explained to the guerrillas how a center-left coalition headed by José Napoleón Duarte, a Christian Democrat and former mayor of San Salvador, and Guillermo Manel Ungo, a Social Democrat and attorney, had won an apparent election victory in 1972 until the army rigged the returns and declared its candidate, a colonel, the winner.

Villalta, who was thirty years old, was stout, neatly dressed, and obviously educated. He looked like a bureaucrat. In a well-modulated voice, he went on to relate how there was similar fraud in the 1977 elections. Now yet another farce was about to unfold. Thus the aim of this offensive was to disrupt a false process, to show the world that the people of El Salvador did not endorse this American-sponsored exercise.

Unlike past guerrilla operations, he said, this one had political, not military objectives, even though the targets were to be government military installations. On no account were civilians to be harmed and any looting or other breaches of discipline would be dealt with severely.

The FDR man's analysis included an overview of the Salvadoran economy: where the money was, who controlled it, and why it was now necessary for them all to risk their lives to overthrow this U.S.-backed tyranny. Peaceful means of accomplishing their goal had been exhausted. There was nothing left but to fight.

He asked for comments or questions and received several. Once again, I was surprised. No soldier I ever knew had been invited to question an order or a strategy. But there in that guerrilla camp one *compañero* rose to ask why they were bothering to disrupt an election when elections had always been frauds and never changed anything anyway? This one, he added, was only a U.S.-sponsored charade to legitimize a client government.

Villalta congratulated him on a very good question and replied at length. He said it would be very important to expose the election as a sham, to demonstrate that the issue in El Salvador was freedom for the people. Now there was no freedom: not of speech, not of the press, not of assembly, not even to feed their families. Since the election was rigged to ratify this oppression, their only recourse was to disrupt it.

As it turned out, this rebel strategy was based on a good deal of wishful thinking and woeful miscalculation. It didn't reckon with a voting registration system that would allow each vote to be traced to the person who cast it. Not only that, but failure to vote was declared an act of treason. Any citizen could be stopped at any time and commanded to present his or her identification card. The lack of an election stamp on it could mean immediate arrest or worse.

At the time, I had no sense of this guaranteed propaganda disaster for the insurgents. The *compañeros* in Salitre spoke of it being their "final offensive." There was talk of a triumphal entry into San Salvador, a casting off of their hated oppressors, an end to the death squads. Peace.

*   *   *

ASTUTELY, THE GOVERNMENT MADE PEACE the focus of its propaganda campaign, the carrot, if you will, that went with the stick of the election laws. The advertising appeals in the Salvadoran news media did not encourage voters to stand up and be counted for this party or that. Without ever explaining why an election would mean peace, the message that it would was drummed into the electorate, as if saying something loud enough and long enough made it so.

Along with a core of Salvadorans, who still believed in the electoral system, plus the well-to-do and the military whose interests would be served by a staged event that both consolidated their position and appeased the U.S., the threats and cajolery brought a huge turnout. On election day, 1982, the image the world saw was of a Salvadoran military fighting to protect the integrity of a democratic election, while the left mounted what appeared to be a national terror campaign that utterly failed.

No matter that government employees had to prove they voted in order to collect paychecks. No matter that the final ballot tally exceeded the estimated number of eligible voters. No matter that the death squads promptly began murdering centrist or moderate electees—especially if they were known to support land reform. Details like these were lost in the more powerful impression that the left couldn't win a fair election, so they'd tried to shoot their way into power.

The guerrillas' misplaced confidence in a popular uprising was based on faith in the broad sympathy of El Salvador's urban poor. The vast majority of their supplies flowed to the rebels not across the border but out from San Vicente, San Miguel, San Salvador, and other cities. They relied on an impressive underground network of supporters who risked their very lives for the cause.

Over Radio Venceremos, the guerrillas' clandestine station, these people were urged to prepare for the offensive, to hoard gasoline, dig trenches, do anything to aid the *compañeros*. But it was asking the impossible. The urban cadres had answered a similar call in January of 1981 and had suffered a bloody defeat. Two years later, they still hadn't recovered. Now, as then, it was the army, not the rebels, that controlled cities where revolutionary organizations were still weak. In that circumstance, it was better to wait, vote, and fight another day.

AS THE ELECTION APPROACHED, I assumed that Jasmine would leave the civilians to me while she and the *sanitarios* treated the *compañeros*. I was astonished, then, when Rosa, one of the local *sanitarios*, came up to me on the afternoon of the twenty-fifth and announced I'd be leaving with a column in an hour.

"Leaving for where?" I asked.

"I can't tell you. Ask Jasmine."

"Whose order is this?"

"I can't tell you. Ask Jasmine."

"Where's Jasmine, then?"

"I don't know."

"Don't you know that with my feet I can hardly walk at all?"

Rosa shrugged.

"Plus I'm here to work with civilians, not to go into combat."

"Oh," Rosa replied. "You'll be setting up a field hospital with *many* civilian casualties to see. It might even become permanent if the offensive goes well. Don't worry, just pack a few things and be ready in an hour."

I was perplexed. Someone had decided to send me into the conflict. It seemed a clear violation of my carefully negotiated agreement to work with civilians. Not only that, but I was now being told to prepare to march maybe thirty miles to San Salvador on a pair of badly infected feet.

Jasmine was nowhere to be found, and there was no time to go looking for her. I had to trust that she knew of this order and endorsed it. Just before nightfall, I was hobbling off with a column of seventy-five *compañeros* and three *sanitarios*, including Lupe.

Once underway, I was told that the destination was San Antonio Abad, a lower middle class suburb of San Salvador. The objective might as well have been Brazil for all the chance I gave my feet of holding up.

With darkness, the trail grew doubly treacherous. Yet the column leader hardly slackened the pace at all. I began chanting obscenities to myself; they weren't directed at any one thing, just general singsong imprecations against the idiot cosmos.

Suddenly, a sheet of small-arms tracers exploded in the forest before us. Dozens of weapons opened fire simultaneously and just as simultaneously the whole column dove off the trail for cover. The pain in my feet wondrously disappeared for a moment as I hugged the ground while bullets zinged overhead.

We all waited for several minutes until word was passed down the column that a guerrilla squad had accidentally encountered a government patrol just ahead. Under no circumstances was there to be further engagement, so all there was to do was to stay silent and hope the government troops did not retreat back on top of us.

After a time, the fighting died down, although it was impossible for us to tell if the insurgents or the government had won the skirmish. We waited for at least an hour after we heard the last gunshot and then pushed on. To make up for lost time, the column leader doubled the pace to a near trot. I barely kept up by use of a sort of sonar. That is, I listened closely to the footfalls just ahead of me and tried to aim my steps accordingly.

When the trail steepened or narrowed, we'd give up walking altogether and make our way through the dark on all fours. Groping along, I reconnoitered each boulder or tree root by touch and then gingerly clambered over or around it. Every obstacle left scratches and bruises. Rivulets of dusty sweat ran down my forehead and stung my eyes.

After several hours of this, I had no emotion left in me. My arms and legs seemed to work autonomously; I didn't feel anything except thirst. Whole stretches of that night are a blank to me.

With dawn we crawled off the trail into the bushes and rested. Someone handed me a piece of candy and a couple cookies and my last memory was of savoring sugar as I fell into a coma-like sleep.

By mid-afternoon I was awake again, if not entirely sentient. Sensation returned to my mind and limbs slowly, the way it does when you awake from a general anesthetic.

Looking back to the north, I had my first, long-distance view of the Guazapa volcano, 5,000 feet high and maybe ten miles away as the crow flies. In the near distance there was a smaller, steeper peak, also apparently an old volcano. By my addled recollections of the previous night's march, I believe we went straight up and straight down that mountain. In all, we must have covered at least twenty miles.

The view south was equally forbidding. Part of San Salvador was visible from my vantage; the rest was obscured by the massive San Salvador volcano to its west. In between, the terrain seemed to even out in places, but I knew we'd avoid these open, farmed areas and stick to the densely overgrown hillsides and canyons. At least another night of hellishness remained.

That thought precluded any appreciation for the beauty of it all. As I pulled out my diary to record the moment, my focus turned inward. In retrospect, the mood was a spiritual analog to my physical condition: alone, exhausted, and suddenly very vulnerable.

I realized as I read back through my diary that all the wonder and randomness of my first days on the Front had overpowered my contemplative processes. The entries seemed to gallop everywhere, moving lickety-split from impressions of Nico and Ramón to the many notes on my foot problems to complaints and questions, questions, questions.

I had very thoroughly thought out my decision to come to El Salvador and believed my conditions for being there had been accepted by others. Now exigency was challenging principle. Partly because of a failure in communication (of which I was ignorant), but also because my private concerns counted for nothing to these people, I had been stripped of choice. All the things I'd fretted over and then put aside in Salinas—Could a true pacifist function in a war zone? Was morality a luxury?—returned as concrete dilemmas.

Another person might not have been so unsettled by such a realization. "Be sure you are right and then go ahead," Davy Crockett is supposed to have said. But I had thought I was right once before—that time I went willy-nilly to the edge and found there something that would forever alter my life.

Vietnam.

I WAS RAISED IN A MILITARY FAMILY, and what I remember of my early boyhood comes back to me as a kind of endless Fourth of July. My father, an Air Force colonel, took us to bases in the United States, the Pacific, Britain, and Europe. Everywhere we lived there were military ceremonies, marching bands, flags, American eagles, uniforms, and salutes.

The tone of our household was similarly patriotic. My father exercised great moral authority over my brother and me. He was our dad and leader who, along with my mother, taught us respect for traditional Americanism. Duty, discipline, and principle were emphasized. Laxity, untidiness, and raucous displays of any sort were discouraged. I don't think it is entirely coincidental that both my parents later developed ulcers.

My older brother, Manen, who is named for my father, was very popular, a gifted athlete, and a good student. I was the kid brother. I suppose that I resented the favoritism he seemed to receive from our parents, and I vividly recall several knock-down battles (always out of Dad's presence) that Manen inevitably won.

In fact, he was always better at everything. Yet I never quit trying, was disinclined by nature to sulk, and eventually turned myself into a compulsive competitor. Young Charlie Clements tried to be better at everything.

Such a boyhood is notable for the things that don't happen to you. Moving from military base to military base, I never developed much of a sense of place, of home and hearth, of Christmas at Grandma's, or summers at the lake. I was born in Myrtle Beach, South Carolina, in 1945 and have a number of relatives who live near Tuscaloosa, Alabama, but I regard neither locale as home.

When I was twelve, we returned from Germany to a base near Austin, Texas. I was well-traveled, but that did not convey much social advantage in the rural public school I attended. American football or baseball didn't excite me. I had no heroes on the Packers or the Yankees. I'd grown up playing soccer. The World Cup meant much more to me than the World Series.

American television was a novelty, too. Not nurtured on it, I knew nothing about the *Mickey Mouse Club* or *Leave It to Beaver*. Moreover, television-watching was limited in our household.

I was a very good student, especially in science and mathematics. When my public junior high school appeared no longer equipped to challenge me, my parents sent me to an excellent Catholic school near Austin, where I completed my secondary education with various honors and awards.

One other note about my younger days. My parents, moderate Republicans, didn't discuss contemporary affairs, national politics, or world events at the dinner table. Racial discrimination, I remember, troubled them, but in no sense could they be called civil rights activists. I remember respecting Martin Luther King, Jr., because he was a good man and a man of principle. But I had yet to feel what he was saying, understand his analysis of racism, or realize the symbol of hope he was to people of whom I was barely aware.

The same went for the youth culture. I knew more about cars than music or dancing. In the spring of 1964, my freshman year at the Air Force Academy, an upperclassman, seeing to my social development, one day approached me with a list of questions about contemporary events. It was like one of those *Time* magazine quizzes, and I sailed right through it until he got to the Beatles. I'd never heard of them.

For all the martial influence of my boyhood and my compulsive, almost ascetic, will to succeed, I really wasn't much of a militarist. While I uncritically accepted the honorable role of the military, I was drawn more to scholarship than soldiering. As a result, my parents were truly surprised and delighted the day I announced that I wished to follow Manen to the Air Force Academy.

Were my psyche to be plumbed, no doubt someone would find lingering sibling rivalry at the base of my decision to go to the Academy, or maybe I was driven by the need to please my father. I can offer a simpler reason, however. I wanted to study astronautics, and schools such as Cal Tech or MIT weren't within our means. From my perspective, an Academy education seemed equally prestigious, and it wouldn't cost a cent. If I did well, I knew the Air Force would pay for graduate school, too.

I saw the chance to become an astronaut, a general, or perhaps I'd someday hold high appointive office in the Defense Department. The Academy seemed a perfect match for my aptitudes, my aspirations, and my attitudes. As I defined myself then, it was.

I DID VERY WELL AT THE ACADEMY. Throughout the four long winters I spent in Colorado Springs, there were few distractions and plenty of pressure to work harder, always work harder.

Academy standards in the sciences and engineering were quite high. The rest of my courses, however, were more or less a matter of swallowing and regurgitating. This left plenty of time for the varsity track squad. At one point I was a quarter of the Academy's nationally ranked mile relay team.

There was no time or inclination, of course, for thoughts

on the growing anti-war movement except to note that the demonstrators looked hairy and dirty and were probably just lazy. Never mind. We Junior Birdmen would protect them from themselves.

To be fair about this self-characterization, however, I was very queasy watching the combat films and listening to all the tales of derring-do that were part of our training. I found the swagger of the returning fighter jocks a bit much, and the scenes of napalm attacks and bombing runs left me decidedly cool on the glories of fighter-piloting. Furthermore, I suffer from motion sickness.

I never dreamt of soaring aloft. My hero at this time, if I had any, was Robert McNamara, who seemed to be converting the entire government into systems thinking. I was coming to the view that everything was reducible to computer analysis. All decisions could be qualified and quantified, maximized, minimized, and optimized. Brave New World.

By the Academy's criteria of military acumen, classroom excellence, and athletic accomplishment, there was only a single more perfect cadet than I in the 550-man graduating class of 1967. Dan Twomey graduated first in the class and also won the Rhodes scholarship that I coveted. As number two, my consolation prize was to be sent to UCLA to study for a Master of Science in operations management.

The Air Force curries and pets its prized few. I would get my graduate degree in eight months and then have another chance to compete for the Rhodes. A vision of myself as the modern scholar-soldier was beginning to take shape; I would be a new breed of Renaissance man in uniform.

Not even troubling reports from the Academy perturbed me at UCLA. I learned that several of my instructors had been sent off to Vietnam and that many pilots were now being extended for second tours. Clearly, the demand for bodies was rising, and my turn would be next.

The Air Force never directly pressured me into leaving my studies and heading for flight school. The impetus honestly came from within. Call it a sense of duty or obligation or maybe the realization that I really should get my wings if I wanted to go far. But I didn't have to think too long or hard before making up my mind to suspend my studies and get ready to go to war. Before I completed my master's course work that spring, I applied for flight school.

Just how I would serve in Vietnam remained to be decided. I had many choices, from piloting F-4 fighters to B-52s to any number of other aircraft. Before I went to flight school, I wanted to have a clearer notion of what I might someday be doing. The best way for me to do that was to head for southeast Asia for a first-hand look at what was going on.

In the early spring of 1968, I used my vacation time to fly by military transport first to Anchorage, then to Taiwan, and then down to the Philippines and across to Thailand. Without military orders, it was impossible to go to Vietnam.

I spent a week or so at Air Force bases in all these countries, talking to pilots and other officers about their experiences and soliciting advice. Somewhere in this period, and I cannot tell you exactly when, I decided to avoid killing people if I could. It may have been after talking to helicopter pilots whose involvement with air rescue seemed like a positive way to be of service. I certainly wasn't impressed with the professionalism of the fighter pilots. All the talk I heard in Thailand was of drinking and screwing and "offing gooks." Whatever the moment, I left southeast Asia for India with an emerging sense that I would do my duty without dropping bombs or pulling a trigger.

I also can't explain why I went to India except that I'd never been there, and it was on the way to Europe where I hoped to catch up with several old friends. You could say I went to India because it was there.

What I found appalled me. India was my first direct exposure to what I'd learn was the general condition of Third World countries. There were beggars everywhere. One morning, I awoke in my hotel room in a suburb of Calcutta to see an old man in an even older wooden cart slowly making his way among the street people, checking them for life signs and hoisting the dead ones onto his cart. The scene sickened me. I left on the next plane.

Third World poverty and illness was until that moment only a television reality to me, something I'd seen at a safe distance. But being among these people filled me with guilt, not guilt at having caused their misery, but guilt at having money or eating in a restaurant when I knew that right outside there were people begging for food. I could not cope with what I saw and fled India after only three days.

MILITARY FLIGHT SCHOOL is as Tom Wolfe has described it, a celebration of macho "right stuff" as epitomized by the "rightest" of them all, the jet fighter pilots. Only the top few in a class of fifty become fighter jockeys and are sent forth screaming along at the speed of sound, cannons and missiles blazing. Below this elite, the rest of the class sorts itself into the "mid-stuff," transport and helicopter pilots; and finally the "low stuff," bomber pilots. This is not to disparage those who wind up flying B-52s, but by the "stuff scale" of flight school, a B-52 is a battered station wagon while an F-4 is a Corvette.

My training began at Reese Air Force Base in Texas in April 1968. It was important from the beginning, as it was until the end of my Air Force career, to affect the "right stuff" pose. Though I had no interest in fighter planes, I did have a Corvette. All the way through school, beginning with the T-41 propeller craft and on to the end when everyone flew supersonic T-38s, we drank and flew and flew and drank and generally carried on like the boys that we were.

It was a new feeling for me not to want to finish first or even near the top in pilot school. I knew if I did the pressure to ask for an F-4 assignment would be difficult to resist. On the other hand, I soon found that that would be no problem, since qualifying for advance helicopter or transport pilot training was going to be struggle enough.

My first serious obstacle was my T-41 instructor, a taciturn sort who smoked incessantly in the cockpit. What with the extreme heat of the Texas summer and the smoke fumes in the sealed cockpit, my natural motion sickness was intensified, and I felt on the verge of vomiting most of the time. Like many of the instructors, he took a dislike to me as an Academy graduate and thought I was a sissy about his smoking.

PILOT TRAINING TOOK A YEAR. After making it past the T-41, I settled into the middle of my class and went on to earn my wings. I wouldn't be forced to choose a fighter jet, nor would I be stuck flying B-52s for the Strategic Air Command. My first choice was the CH-53 (Jolly Green Giant) rescue helicopter, but none were offered to my class. As a result, in the late spring of 1969 I headed for Sewart Air Force Base near Nashville where I'd receive advance instruction on the C-130 Hercules transport.

The C-130, a Lockheed-built, four-engine turboprop, is a versatile craft, capable of taking off and landing on short runways under adverse conditions. It was the Air Force's principal transport in Vietnam—the "workhorse of Asia"—and was popular with many trainees because experience with it qualified them for a future career as airline pilots.

The three months at Sewart were intense. Although I continued to drink and fly and fly and drink in the "right stuff" way, I began to get a more practical feel for what lay ahead. We drilled continually for so-called LAPES (Low Altitude Parachute Extraction System) missions. We'd come down at 120 knots to no more than twelve feet above the ground, open the cargo doors, and disgorge huge amounts of equipment that were pulled from the cargo bay by monstrous parachutes. More often than not, the gear got tangled or fell apart or broke when it hit the ground.

We also ferried paratroopers all over the hills of Tennessee and practiced repeated takeoffs and landings from unprepared, unlit airfields. In every phase of the training, the emphasis was on staying low, getting in and out fast, and avoiding hostile fire. We all took that part of the course very much to heart.

Next came survival training. We were taught mountaineering in the Cascade Range near Spokane, where they also took us to a mock prison camp. There we learned to resist interrogation; we were deprived of sleep and fed fish heads and rice. Heavies with Russian accents grilled us. Next, off Okinawa, we were bounced into the water for our course in survival at sea. Then they dried us and dropped us into the Philippines for jungle survival.

Finally, in the autumn of 1969, I was assigned to the 50th Tactical Airlift Squadron, based in Taiwan. By then, Richard Nixon had been in office for several months and the American people were being told that the South Vietnamese had begun shouldering an ever-greater responsibility for prosecuting their own war. It was Vietnamization, the light at the end of the tunnel. Americans would soon stop dying.

One of my very first hints that all was not as it seemed came with the realization that our official combat strength was a sham. Many hundreds of thousands of Americans fought in Vietnam without ever having officially been stationed there. While in-country troop strength may have remained below the 500,000 or so official maximum, pilots such as myself weren't counted. Even though I flew over fifty combat missions out of Saigon or Camranh Bay, my "official" base was Taiwan, and therefore, I didn't count.

Another way the numbers were rigged was to shorten a tour. Some of my classmates, for instance, did three 179-day stretches as B-52 crews based in Thailand. Yet because the Air Force only counted 180 days as a full tour, they never were officially based in southeast Asia.

Our squadron flew from Ching Chuan Kang Air Force Base in Taiwan on eighteen-day rotations to Vietnam itself. Once there, we'd fly fourteen hours, have twelve hours off, and then fly fourteen hours again. It required setting your personal clock ahead two hours every day. Soon, your body clock was as out of sync with real time as everything else around you.

As a result, the days passed in a blur and whole periods of Vietnam are a blur. One moment in the cockpit of a C-130 is much like any other; it is a dimly lit cocoon from which life is observed as if on a screen. Without a compass, I couldn't tell a sunrise from a sunset. Much of the time, I felt as passive as a TV addict.

When I wasn't flying, especially in the first few weeks there, I was either asleep, drinking in the officers club, or lying on the beach at Camranh Bay, watching air strikes against the distant green hills, listening to others fight the war. After each eighteen-day rotation, I returned to Taiwan for seventy-two hours of even further insulation from reality.

I couldn't feel what I didn't experience, and I didn't care. While the duty was perilous enough (flying whale-size bladders of gasoline into fire bases under siege or ferrying frightened paratroopers into enemy country involves certain risks) my thoughts were more fixed on the upcoming Rhodes scholarship competition and my second chance of going to Oxford. Vietnam didn't really concern me.

The Rhodes competition very much did. I was only marking time in Vietnam, though doing my duty, of course, until I could get on with my education. At Christmastime, 1969, I was scheduled to return to the States for the finalist interviews.

But then the ground began to shift.

SEVERAL OF MY ACADEMY CLASSMATES were also flying in Vietnam. I saw one of them, an F-100 fighter pilot, one afternoon in November. He had just won his squadron's "Top Gun" award for the month and was showing it off.

"How'd you get it?" I asked idly as we sat drinking in an officers club.

"I was coming back from a mission," he answered, "and I

saw a bunch of slopes standing around in a rice paddy. I radioed to the base, and they radioed back that this was a free-fire zone and so I strafed 'em."

He went on to say a body count confirmed thirty-one kills.

"How'd you know they weren't farmers or something?" I asked.

"Who the hell cares?" he replied. "They were gooks in a free-fire zone, so I offed 'em."

This flyer was no stranger to me; we'd been friends at the Academy. I just couldn't reconcile a fellow officer and gentleman committing such indiscriminate slaughter, much less being proud of it and even winning an award for it. Though it was happening all around me, the episode troubled me greatly.

Looking back, it is obvious that I went to Vietnam with a set of very naive preconceptions about the war. I was amazed, for instance, by my first personal contacts with our ground troops—"the grunts." I guess my model of the infantryman was of a determined defender of liberty, the average WW II Joe fighting for his country as a matter of conscience and patriotism.

What I found were scared kids, many only seventeen, who wanted no more than to stay stoned and stay alive. For some reason, my model infantry units were largely white like the officer corps around me. My conception was very different from the units of conscripts I picked up and delivered dead and alive in Vietnam. I'd never met a ghetto kid before, a poor Black or Hispanic, yet I came to understand that they were fighting in gross disproportion to their numbers at home. They were cannon fodder. At various times in the Vietnam War, fully a quarter of all American casualties were sustained by non-whites.

Had I been less rigid in my beliefs, the ugliness and injustice of what I saw might have elicited a shrug or a sad shake of the head. What happened, however, was that I began to sense a betrayal. I learned, for instance, about body counts. Not only did we inflate the number of enemy dead, but our own casualty figures were manipulated.

After one week of particularly heavy losses, I was sent with my crew to a small base to pick up the dead. When I got there, a bluff sergeant offered me a hearty welcome and announced that he couldn't release the bodies right away. It wouldn't look right—too many American dead in one week.

"We're gonna hafta leave 'em on ice a bit longer," he explained with a laugh.

Deceit and self-delusion were the order of the day. On another occasion, I flew several tons of materiel to one jungle base, only to return later that day to pick up the same equipment and fly it back to its original location. Since I wasn't doing this for fun, I made an angry inquiry of the shipping sergeant.

"Look, Lieutenant," he responded. "We're just trying to justify your keep here."

"What do you mean?"

"Well," he said as if talking to a child, "if we don't fly so many cargo-ton miles and prove to Congress that we need these C-130s here, you might get sent back to the States and we wouldn't have the capacity when we need it."

Then there was Terry Savery, a fellow C-130 pilot, who had flown several hundred combat missions. Though he loved flying with a passion, he had come to have his doubts and was, at the time I met him, filing for conscientious objector status.

Terry was lean and mustachioed, with a big smile. His style was aw-shucks, belying his brilliance as a debater. I learned this when I picked an argument with him, intending a little intellectual sparring to tune-up for the upcoming Rhodes competition.

I confidently began by asserting we had to defend the South Vietnamese from an unprovoked Communist attack, just as I'd learned at the Academy. Terry rejoined with a cogent summary of our several violations of the 1954 Geneva accords. Essentially, he pointed out, we had created the war and sustained a slaughter ever since by massive infusions of money to a corrupt government that brutalized and exploited its own people.

I responded with a recap of the domino theory and finished strongly, I thought, by arguing that we were fighting for the right of these people to have democratic elections.

Terry caught me off guard when he brought up Dwight Eisenhower, one of my parents' heroes, and told me that Ike had said we couldn't allow free elections in Vietnam, because Ho Chi Minh would sweep them. Since that amazing concession by our former President, Terry maintained, we had slogged on in the path of the French, killing hundreds of thousands of nationalists who rather than being a strategic threat to us were merely trying to rid their country of hated foreign influence.

I wobbled away from these sessions a bit disturbed, but essentially still believing my side of the argument. This was the first time I'd been forced to articulate something I'd always taken for granted.

For all our contention, however, Terry and I were also becoming friends. I was amazed at the ease with which I took to someone who held such patently dangerous notions. I respected the quality of his mind, as well, and that disarmed me.

JUST BEFORE THE END OF THE YEAR, I flew back to the States for the Rhodes competition. I was not, as yet, consciously disaffected from the war. For all I'd seen and heard, I still clung to the argument that our objectives, if not all our actions in Vietnam, were right and honorable.

Yet a process had begun. Flying first to Anchorage, then on to Colorado Springs, and finally to Pasadena where the Rhodes committee had gathered, I worked hard to reshape my presentation. Its thrust was that the military needs a well-rounded breed of officer, a man who knows the classics of literature as well as the mechanics of modern warfare, a man with a sense of history and a knowledge of society and culture. I proposed to be such an officer. Tacitly, the argument suggested such leaders did not then abound in the American military and that might help explain Vietnam.

In Pasadena, the other Rhodes finalists were overtly hostile to me. Once again, I encountered obviously intelligent and non-radical minds set against everything I stood for in my uniform. I was out-numbered and out-gunned and I retreated.

To this day, I cannot say if it was my uniform or myself that lost me the Rhodes scholarship. Whatever the case, something in the package was found wanting in comparison to the other candidates. My candidacy was refused.

This was a bitter disappointment. All across the Pacific on my way back to Taiwan I replayed my appearance before the committee and wondered what had tipped the scales against me. My case must have struck them as artificial, as though I really did not know why I stood for what I said I stood for.

If so, they were right.

Soon after I returned to Asia, our squadron was reassigned to Saigon. This was my first extended stay in the capital and my first close contact with the Vietnamese themselves.

When I wasn't flying, I walked the streets and saw all the hookers, beggars, and little boys with shoe-shine kits mixing with the American servicemen. It was also my first close view of the pervasive corruption in South Vietnam, the plainly marked PX boxes of cigarettes, stereos, and scotch being sold by local vendors, the inordinate luxury in which the wealthy lived as compared to the slum hovels that surrounded the city.

In bars, I met several military and CIA intelligence officers and listened intently to their tales of the Phoenix Program, a rural "pacification" program in which thousands of suspected Viet Cong sympathizers and anybody else who got in the way were eliminated.

One CIA officer claimed to have recently planned the "elimination" of a member of the South Vietnamese Assembly. He explained how the politician had raised certain embarrassing questions about the incomes of several Vietnamese generals and had otherwise discomfited the government. Besides, the politician was thought to be "pink."

Radio Hanoi announced nearly every day that "American air pirates" had once again bombed the north. I dismissed the charges as so much propaganda until a classmate explained the Armed Reactive Reconnaissance program to me. In its essence, the program called for American reconnaissance planes to provoke anti-aircraft fire which then justified "reactive" bombing strikes. President Nixon, meanwhile, could say with a straight face that American planes in the north fired only when fired upon.

By this time I knew the President to be either a liar or a dupe; neither possibility spoke well of his leadership. But his routine deceptions seemed inconsequential when compared to his flat denial that we had no combat forces in Laos. I watched a rebroadcast of this speech in Saigon and was infuriated by Nixon's patent betrayal of his public trust. Watergate had not yet happened, and it was then very difficult to accept that the President of the United States would knowingly deceive the public.

I knew we were maintaining secret air strips in Laos; CIA pilots flew Air America C-130s on daily supply missions to these bases. I had Academy classmates flying unmarked aircraft out of some of those fields. At that time, we'd already lost more than three hundred aircraft in Laos.

Whether this was just macho bar talk, and there was a lot of that in Saigon, I'll never know. However, once I mentioned a special mission on which I'd flown State Department representatives into neutral Cambodia for negotiations with Prince Sihanouk, the premier. A "spook," an agent I'd known for some time, scoffed and said I was a naive fool if I didn't know what that mission was about. Sure the diplomats were flapping with Sihanouk but while they were doing that "his" boys were negotiating a coup with Lon Nol. General Lon Nol, he said, wasn't so queasy about his country's neutrality, and would allow us to invade the sanctuary. I didn't think too much about it at the time.

The bombing of Cambodia was another official secret. I had personally seen vast regions of the country that looked like moonscapes from our saturation bombing. Yet there was the President, denying it all. It was disturbing. The American government was dangerously widening the conflict at the very time the public was being told a far different story. I understood for the first time what the domino theory really meant. In the name of liberty and freedom, we were sinking the entire region into conflagration. We would destroy it in order to "save" it.

Then in March, the coup occurred; Lon Nol came to power. A month later, my squadron took part in a massive airlift of men and supplies to the so-called Parrot's Beak region, an area on the Vietnam-Cambodia border from which we intended to invade Cambodia directly. The build-up was enormous, essentially a train of C-130s flying continually back and forth. On some days, I flew as many as twelve round trips.

In the midst of this, as I grew angrier and angrier at what I was certain would be an all-out escalation of the war, I declared myself unfit for duty and took the first transport available back to the States. Any Air Force pilot could do this under almost any pretext. I pleaded a head cold, but in fact was fleeing the grotesqueries of southeast Asia in order to think things out.

I ARRIVED IN THE STATES as news of the invasion broke. Opposition to the war clearly was no longer a fringe attitude, nor, as Kent State demonstrated, was the price of protest limited to a lump on the head or a night in jail. Fresh from the war zone, I found the country in an ugly and scary mood.

I flew to Kansas to attend my brother's wedding. Although he and I have always had a good relationship, I wasn't able to clearly communicate the stress I was feeling to him, nor to the other pilots or classmates at the wedding, nor to my parents. The nature of Vietnam duty was, they all said, that you had to do it only for a year. What was so tough about staying a few more months?

After the wedding, I went to Los Angeles where I renewed my acquaintance with Terry Savery. He had been granted conscientious objector status and was now a civilian.

Terry recollects our conversations then better than I do. He found me deeply agitated, angry at what I'd seen in Vietnam, unhappy about my own role in the war but still unwilling to say no to it. Despite his many arguments, the core of which I now embrace, duty remained stronger than doubt.

We drove north to San Francisco where I attended my first anti-war rally. At some point in the evening, the microphone was passed to me and I found myself talking to a crowd of approximately 1000 people about how many other servicemen also opposed the war, were refusing to fight any longer, were being court-martialed, and all the rest. This was my first, and for many years, only, public denunciation of the war. I remember the short speech more for the depth of my emotion than for any cogency in what I had to say. It was a turning point.

I knew as I returned to Taiwan that I wasn't going to fly anymore, and I further realized that my military career was over. It only remained for me to disengage myself in an honorable fashion so as not to disgrace myself, my family, or my uniform.

Before I could be ordered back into Vietnam, I made an appointment to see my squadron commander. I went to him in the unreasonable hope that I could explain my position and possibly be transferred to some Stateside duty where my management training at UCLA could be put to quiet use. I was determined not to defy, or even unduly antagonize, my superiors. But, I believe, a guilty plea to rape would have dismayed the Colonel less than my explanation for wanting a change of duty. He fidgeted in his chair and could barely bring himself to look at me.

When I finished, he said, "Lieutenant, there are a lot of things that we don't like about the service, and we don't all like our jobs all the time. I'm not always happy with what I have to do. However, I recommend that you keep doing the fine work you've done. You only have six months left and then you can leave and forget about it. You have responsibilities here, and it's easier to carry them out than to jeopardize a brilliant career."

It was pragmatic advice, much like what my father had given when I complained at the wedding in Kansas. Military men aren't supposed to question too much, but I wouldn't be deterred.

"Sir," I went on, "my decision is based upon moral judgments that have nothing to do with my respect for the service or my country. I honestly believe it would be safer for my crew and better for the Air Force if I were reassigned."

"Lieutenant, you are making a grave mistake," he countered. "Why don't you take a week off from flying to think it over?"

"I already have, sir. I have given this choice very careful thought."

The Colonel rose and signaled the end of the conversation. "In that case," he said, "I recommend that you go see the base psychiatrist."

It might have gone worse for me. In the Air Force, a visit to the shrink is the kiss of death for an officer's career. By suggesting I go, the Colonel had obviously already written me off. From my perspective, my Air Force career was over anyway. The Colonel could have forced the issue by commanding me to fly. If I refused, a court-martial was inevitable.

Thus I took his handling of the matter as a hint that my case would be dealt with quickly and quietly and that was fine by me. However, the First Sergeant quietly informed me that a special version of our conversation had been prepared, typed, and placed at the ready in the Colonel's desk drawer. In it, he ascribed to me several shrill anti-war remarks, attacks on the military, and treasonable opinions. Had I been court-martialed, I assume this document would have surfaced as evidence.

I regarded my trip to the psychiatrist as routine; in order to be taken off flight duty, I'd have to have a psychiatric exam anyway. The doctor was young, slightly portly, and wore glasses. He also seemed sympathetic.

We talked awhile, and he agreed to ground me temporarily. Meanwhile, he suggested, I should explore filing as a conscientious objector and even recommended an Air Force attorney to me.

Captain Bob Patrick was an acquaintance of mine. We spent several days discussing a possible case for conscientious objection (CO), but he finally had to advise me against filing. To be granted a CO exemption, you must demonstrate aversion to all wars. Since I believed that I would have fought in World War II, I was only a selective objector. Under the law, you cannot pick when and where you'll fight.

So I went back to the psychiatrist, who still seemed sympathetic. He said that the only thing to do was to try to build a case for sending me back to the States for a full psychiatric appraisal. Out of it might come a decision that I was unfit to fly and the recommendation that I be given a desk job.

The doctor and I met many times and most of the interviews were genial. Over the course of a couple of weeks he probed my feelings on a variety of issues I raised and showed particular interest in one incident that I felt was only tangentially involved with my decision to stop flying.

This was the death of a cheerful and friendly Academy graduate, an acquaintance of mine, whom I'd visited in Pleiku on a couple of occasions. He was a C-47 pilot and was listed as missing in action.

His loss weighed upon me somewhat, but no more so than that of the many other officers I'd known before they were killed. What made this one different was that about a week after he was reported missing, I flew into a base to pick up some bodies and quite by accident saw his name on a body bag. All that remained of him were four large lumps of disconnected flesh. His and the other corpses had been lying in a swamp for many days, and their stench filled the aircraft. Though saddened and sickened by the experience, I had not been overly traumatized.

The psychiatrist suspected otherwise, and questioned me very closely about the impact of the incident on my thinking. Was I preoccupied with death? Was I disturbed in ways I couldn't even realize?

We concluded our talks in late May of 1970, then I heard nothing for three months. It was three years since I had graduated from the Academy and had been commissioned. My automatic promotion to captain came through in June.

I reported each day to my squadron desk job and tried not to dwell on all the difficult possibilities that awaited me if I wasn't sent home for evaluation. It didn't help that many of my former pilot buddies now shunned me; few knew exactly why I wasn't flying, but nearly everyone knew I'd been to the psychiatrist and that was reason enough to avoid taint by association.

THE GOOD NEWS FINALLY CAME IN SEPTEMBER: I was to depart immediately for the Brook School of Aerospace Medicine near San Antonio. With high hopes and a light step I went to my apartment, packed a few things, and said so long to the psychiatrist.

Less than thirty-six hours later, I was seated across from a crewcut Major at Brook, a West Point man with pilot wings, parachute insignia, and a small chest full of medals.

"Don't worry, Clements," he announced immediately. "I understand you perfectly. I've reviewed your whole case. You're in the old three-year slump, but I'll have you back in Saigon in a week!"

My instant thought was "The hell with you!" but I decided not to share it.

Instead, I launched into a reasonably well-controlled tirade about all the things that had been bothering me, why I had come to Brook and why, under no circumstances, was I interested in going back to Vietnam. As far as I was concerned, the war was over.

The crewcut seemed to stiffen a bit. He ordered up a battery of psychiatric and psychological tests and that was the last I saw of him. After a couple days of testing, I was called back to his office, handed a sealed envelope, and told to report to Wilford Hall hospital across town at Lackland Air Force Base.

I picked up the envelope with no little trepidation. I knew it contained the crewcut's recommendation, and I suspected very strongly that, despite what I'd said to him, he had not abandoned his three-year-slump theory of my case. If he ordered me back to Saigon, I'd have to refuse and a court-martial, as well as a prison term, would be unavoidable.

On the other hand, I thought as I was driven over to Lackland, I'm just as likely to be carrying my orders for re-assignment. Everything I'd sensed since my first chat with my squadron commander told me that the Air Force wanted this handled with discretion. They wanted me out of the way. I wasn't creating a stir, why should they?

Why, indeed. My driver left me by a side door at Wilford Hall and then quickly pulled away. I walked into a small reception area where an orderly took my envelope, placed it in a file, and then directed me to follow him.

We walked down a corridor and then up several flights of steps to another corridor where a security officer buzzed us through the locked door. I smelled medicines and disinfectant.

All of a sudden, in a flash of this-can't-be-happening-to-me recognition, I knew it had. I wasn't going to Saigon or anywhere else. This was a psychiatric ward and I, Captain Charles Clements, was an inmate!

TWELVE YEARS LATER, my stay at the military hospital in San Antonio was a distant and no longer painful memory. I was now on my way to San Antonio Abad, El Salvador, with a column of guerrillas fighting a war very much like the one I'd left. The major difference, of course, was that now I was on the other side—or at least I was as far as my own government and that of El Salvador were concerned. If this election day assault ended in a government body count, my corpse would be toted up as that of just another dead rebel.

I put away my diary and sat on that hillside willing the sun to never go down. Once it did, there would be another night of tramping through the dark. The anticipation of all that pain was depressing.

As I looked around, I caught sight of Arlena, one of several female guerrillas who had joined the assault columns in Salitre. As with everyone else, I didn't know Arlena's real name, just Arlena and her nickname, *La Chinita* (the Chinese).

She did look a little Asian, as had Jaime in Mexico City. I learned from someone that Arlena was indeed part Chinese, and I wondered if her family knew Jaime's. Since I didn't know his true name, there was no way of finding out.

Actually, I was curious about her on several scores and resolved to strike up a conversation. She was pretty in a plain way, with dark, expressive eyes and a shy manner that was unusual for a combatant. I guessed her background was relatively privileged and protected in the way of Latin families who raise their daughters according to very strict notions of femininity.

La Chinita was hungry. She reached for a small plastic bottle of honey and somewhat furtively opened the container and took a long swallow. It was meant to help sustain the wounded over the two days it would take to return from San Salvador. Yet she'd finished almost a third of it in one drink.

She looked around to see if she'd been noticed, and blushed furiously when she saw me staring at her. I smiled to reassure her that I didn't care about the honey, and took her expression of relief as my chance to start a conversation.

She told me about her parochial school and the nuns there who raised issues that she was forbidden to talk about at home, things like why *campesinos* worked all day in the

CHARLES CLEMENTS, M.D.

fields for only one-and-a-half *colones* ($0.45). When one of her classmates, who was distributing leaflets, was "disappeared," Arlena joined others in a peaceful protest on the steps of the cathedral. The National Guardsmen and National Police appeared and began firing into the crowd "with one of these," she said as she motioned toward her automatic weapon. They killed twenty-three demonstrators.

That was May 1979. Her parents knew she had been at the demonstration because of the blood on her dress. They locked her in her room. A friend helped her escape, and together they ran away to join the urban militants.

Arlena was then fourteen. She stayed in the city two more years until the failed offensive of January, 1981, when heartsick at the slaughter, she resolved to take up arms herself. Arlena was the single member of the column to show the least fear of what lay ahead.

Lupe, by contrast, was her accustomed self: stubborn, hostile, and grittily determined. Yet for all her gratuitous unpleasantness, she was beginning to insinuate herself into my field of respect

I learned during our day's rest that her knees were acutely arthritic and the stress they endured surely was as painful as my feet were to me. Before we trudged off again, I made the mistake of suggesting ways that she might cushion her stride a bit to ease the strain on her knees. She denied that they bothered her at all and told me to mind my own business. Halfway through the first night's march, I heard her sobbing from time to time as we struggled along the trail. But she never lagged and never complained.

The second night's march took nine hours and brought us, at dawn, to the western slope of the San Salvador volcano. We were about 750 feet above the city and about six miles from the *barrio* of San Antonio Abad.

Unlike the previous day when my thoughts ranged everywhere but El Salvador, I spent the twenty-seventh in keen anxiety over the imminent attack on the capital. I was also grumpy over the condition of my feet, and the two emotions combined to keep me alert and concentrated through the day.

Around me, the guerrillas looked to their sorry store of weapons, cleaning and recleaning them, and checking their ammunition. When they went to battle the next day they would be armed with U.S. M-16s, Belgian FALs, German G-3s, plus a few old M-1s and .30 calibre carbines. With the exception of a rusty Chinese RPG II grenade launcher—the only non-western weapon I would see all year—there were no heavier weapons among them.

Since everyone in El Salvador knew the attack was coming the next day, their enemy, who vastly outnumbered them, had plenty of time for defensive deployment. Against the lightly armed guerrillas, the soldiers had not only their M-16s, but also M-60 machine guns, M-79 grenade launchers, 90mm recoilless cannons, armored personnel carriers, light tanks, and their Hueys. The battle had a single possible outcome.

I was sufficiently ignorant of the true state of affairs to be hopeful for the rebels. After having endured the two-day march, I was proud to still be standing and ready to set up the field hospital as near the fighting as possible. My first duty as a doctor was to save lives, and I was determined to do so.

It began to rain on the afternoon of the twenty-seventh. At dusk, the column began moving down toward San Antonio Abad. I stood up to go with them when Raymundo, one of the column leaders, approached me and very firmly announced that because of my feet I was being left behind! My safety was one question, but he explained that they were more concerned that a lame doctor might slow down the column and jeopardize everyone's life.

The news angered me. After all that strain, they had discovered what I'd warned them about in the first place! Now that I'd made it, I was eager to press on, to complete my assignment. Instead, the guerrillas were going to leave me sitting under a coffee bush in the rain.

I made no effort to hide my confusion as they headed past me down the volcano toward the city. Arlena, *La Chinita*, flashed me a silent and nervous smile as she slung her M-16 over her shoulder and walked off. A *compañero* asked if I wanted a weapon and I curtly declined. Someone left me a chunk of French bread and a small container of custard pudding. Then they were all gone.

After a sleepless night I sat there forlornly in the damp, watching first the arcs of light over San Salvador and listening to the growing crescendo of small-arms fire. As it grew lighter, I could see the Hueys converging on their targets, and I heard the delayed reports of explosions far across the capital.

It was going to be a long and anxious day for me alone with my radio and my resentment and my injured feet. I worried about the column, wondered how they were faring in San Antonio Abad, and hoped that their casualties were light. I wouldn't allow myself to dwell on what might be happening to Arlena and the rest. Nor could I imagine the truth, that the column had been marked since it left Salitre and that it was now marching straight into an ambush.

SKY OF THE LONG DAY

THE RADIO BROADCASTS I MONITORED THAT DAY left little doubt that the guerrilla assaults had failed. The voter turnout was huge and only in isolated instances had the elections been disrupted at all.

I began to worry more and more about my own safety. What if the column didn't return or had to retreat by a different route? There was no chance I could find my own way back to Salitre. For all I knew, the entire Guazapa Front had fallen in a government counteroffensive. I had visions of hobbling down into San Salvador, mud-caked and bearded, covered with sores, in search of refuge.

About dusk, the first few of the fighters returned. Among them was Comandante Paco.

"What happened to the others?" I asked. He shrugged and mumbled. "We became separated."

Comandante Raymundo, I learned, was dead; a burst of machine gun fire from a Huey had cut him in half. But there was no word of Lupe and the other *sanitarios*, of Arlena, or of most of the sixty or so guerrillas who hadn't yet returned.

They had left me next to no medical supplies, just the few items I carried in my personal kit. As the wind and rain picked up with the coming of dark, the only thing I could do was boil a T-shirt for sterile bandages.

One of the wounded was Jorge, a teen-ager who had been among the very few people kind enough to personally welcome me to Guazapa. Jorge had four bullet holes in him—one in his neck and three in his calves—and all from a downward trajectory.

"What happened?" I wanted to know as I began to clean the wounds.

"A helicopter strafed us," he said, "soon after we entered the *barrio*."

"How'd it go?"

"Not well."

"How many losses?"

Jorge hesitated.

"Some. We don't know how many."

It was nearly midnight before all the survivors were back. Twelve of them were wounded, three seriously. Thirteen other *compañeros* lay dead in San Antonio Abad. Arlena, I was told, had taken a mortal wound to her abdomen and couldn't be evacuated. She shot herself in the head rather than face capture. According to my later information, the soldiers' vengeance against her corpse was to cut off her breasts.

Lupe and I and the two *sanitarios* worked through the night and into the next morning to debride and bandage the casualties. Those that would talk spoke of their surprise at the enemy's preparedness. Most would say very little except that two government M-16s had been captured. They didn't mention that six of their weapons had been lost, that fully a third of their number were dead or wounded.

Several of the *compañeros* foraged for bananas as we attended to their comrades. Lupe, especially, showed her mettle with the injured, performing extremely well under the conditions. She and the two *sanitarios* moved from patient to patient, injecting local anesthesia, removing huge chunks of traumatized, burnt, or otherwise damaged tissue. Once a wound was clean, it was daubed with honey, a practice I'd read of but had never seen done. For reasons unknown to me, the substance *does* seem to enhance healing.

What few details I could gather about the mission made me wonder at their strategic planning. San Antonio Abad, it turned out, was prepared for an assault. Why had they attacked a well-armed and numerically-superior foe at his strongest point?

Paco was acting peculiarly, as well. Late on the twenty-ninth, as we prepared to move out with our wounded, the other surviving comandante, Luís, suggested we try stealing a truck and then driving at least part way back rather than take the larger risk of moving slowly, on foot, with all the injured *compañeros*. It seemed a reasonable idea. We knew government forces were searching for us.

Paco, though, would hear nothing of it. He delivered a long speech to the camp, full of rhetoric, about the struggle being more important than our lives, *patria o muerte* (the motherland or death) and all the rest. It was a calculated appeal to macho instincts, a call to manly sacrifice that most of them found difficult to resist. Luís bowed to Paco's rhetoric, and we pushed off at dark on March 29. Ten formed a vanguard, twelve *compañeros* shouldered the six hammocks bearing the injured, then came the walking wounded and our rear guard.

When we started out from Salitre, we'd been fresh. There had been great hope and expectation. But now we were all dog-tired, hungry, and understandably deflated by the failed attack. Discipline broke down, as people shouted back and forth to one another, lit cigarettes, and cursed. At times, the column stretched over as much as a mile and a half of terrain.

Moving back up into the hills, we passed several huts where the guerrillas would break off and go in to beg a tortilla. I remember Luís pulling one young fighter from a kitchen table.

"But I'm hungry!" the youngster moaned.

"We all are," Luís replied and pushed him back into line.

The pain in both my feet exploded again. Since my days at the Academy, I have often used self-hypnosis to overcome physical obstacles. I used it, for instance, to smooth and lengthen my stride in the last turn of the 440 when I was on the mile relay team. But self-hypnosis didn't do much good while we were marching. The pain was a maddening presence. After having played no significant role as a physician and, worse still, feeling that I'd been duped, the physical discomfort seemed far harder to bear. Only the groans of the wounded reminded me of my relative comfort.

In the middle of these pained reflections, someone handed me an M-16 in the dark and motioned for me to relieve a *compañero* in the vanguard. It wasn't a moment for quibbling. I accepted the rifle, but decided not to chamber a round. I don't know if I would have used it to defend the wounded if we had been attacked.

As we shuffled on, the sight of me with a weapon seemed to alter the *compañeros'* attitude toward me. Whereas before they'd ignored me or muttered irritably about my slow-footedness, they now made me feel like one of them. If I stumbled in the dark, someone would grab my arm and curse for me.

"¿Puta! Eh, Camilo?"

Or I was passed a piece of fruit. It never ceased to amaze me how, in those pitch-black canyons, their sense of smell alone guided them to fruit trees that they stripped while hardly breaking stride. My state of mind being what it was, their acceptance of me was heartening. If nothing else, it eased my isolation and discomfort.

After our first night's return march, we were still well outside the Guazapa Front in government-controlled territory. The stretcher cases doubled the time it would take to get back. Just before dawn we passed within a few hundred feet of an army outpost that, luckily for us, was then under attack. Otherwise, we surely would have been detected.

In this zone, it was extremely dangerous to abet the guerrillas. Nevertheless, as we rested under some trees that day, the local *campesinos* made two excursions to our camp bringing tortillas and beans and some fruit and water to the *compañeros*. I imagine anyone would be responsive to the needs of sixty armed guerrillas, but this aid was offered, not solicited.

What impressed me was that the guerrillas insisted upon paying for the provisions. Such a scene, I knew, would have been unthinkable in Vietnam for either a troop of GIs or the South Vietnamese Army. These villagers, at least, saw the *compañeros* as their friends and partners.

I cannot convey the physical torment of our next two nights of marching back to Salitre; I won't try. Suffice it to say we made Guazapa—*territorio libre*—at about daybreak and were met by a relief column bringing food and fresh help to carry the wounded.

I was light-headed from exhaustion. In the last hour and a half of daylight hiking to Salitre, the column began to stretch out two, maybe three miles. All was quiet and peaceful in the early morning sunlight.

Maybe it was the daylight that allowed me to walk more carefully and therefore with less pain. Maybe it was because I'd made it back whole and alive while a third of us hadn't. It could simply have been my utter fatigue. But all the walls around my emotions were suddenly breached. My eyes began to fill. Tears, real tears such as I had not been able to shed for ten years after Vietnam, poured down into my matted beard. It was a wonderful, cathartic release of emotion.

IN SALITRE, WE'D BEEN CALLED "THE LOST COLUMN"; until we neared the control zone, it had been feared that the entire detachment was wiped out. Radio stations in San Salvador announced three times the actual guerrilla casualties; we surmised they counted every civilian victim of the "clean-up" operation as "subversive." As it was, the number of casualties (thirteen dead, twelve wounded) was the highest ever sustained by one of their columns. Of the eleven other detachments sent from Guazapa against San Salvador on election day, none lost more than a single *compañero*.

The radio reports continued to affirm the early news of the offensive; it was a propaganda victory for the government. Only later as the actual results of the showcase voting became known could I see how they added up to a potential embarrassment for the United States.

The American hope had been to excise both the left and the extreme right from El Salvador's political spectrum and to install a tractable centrist government. The clone of any state legislature would have suited United States strategists fine. Once in place, the United States would be duty-bound to defend such a client, paving the way for more military aid to crush the guerrillas for good.

However, the Salvadoran radical right and its leader, Roberto d'Aubuisson, emerged from the balloting stronger than ever. D'Aubuisson, a founder of the ultra-right National Republican Alliance (ARENA) party, was widely known as a death squad organizer and probable participant. Most people assumed he helped plan the 1980 assassination of Salvadoran Archbishop Oscar Romero. Whoever he accused of being "subversive" was apt to die or disappear soon thereafter. In the months following the election, d'Aubuisson would lengthen his announced list of leftists and their sympathizers to include Ambassador Deane Hinton and the whole of the United States Congress.

President Carter's Ambassador Robert White had called d'Aubuisson a "pathological killer." Now the Reagan administration had to bring enormous pressure behind the scenes to keep him out of the president's chair. In the end, a moderate banker named Alvaro Magaña, labeled a "Jewish Communist" by d'Aubuisson, was given the figurehead title of provisional president. D'Aubuisson took the less-visible post of Constituent Assembly president, and another election was planned.

My own post-election resolution was to clarify my position on the Front. The mission to San Antonio Abad had convinced me I had been too hesitant in asserting myself and too cautious where issues of great importance to me were concerned.

The long march back gave me an opportunity to reassess; it was the first time since my arrival in Guazapa that I had a chance to reflect. I knew I had to accept the possibility of being killed there, but I was not going to die with a weapon in my hands. As soon as I found Jasmine, I told her I wanted to meet with someone with authority, possibly even Raul Hercules, to whom I could explain a few things.

In the meantime, the guerrillas themselves conducted a post-mortem of their failed election day offensive. In an open review called a *balance*, they gathered in their camps all over Guazapa and posed some very tough questions to their leadership.

The survivors of the San Antonio Abad assault column met under a eucalyptus stand near Salitre. Before them, comandantes Luís and Paco at first tried to paint the day as a triumph. But the *compañeros* were having none of that. Fighter after fighter rose to criticize the choice of target, the lack of maps, the poor advance scouting, and the bickering between Luís and Paco.

Several column members were upset that two prisoners, National Guardsmen, had been executed that day. Usually, POWs were given the chance to join the guerrillas or were relieved of their uniforms and other useful equipment before being released in their underwear. At the *balance*, the failure to follow this standard practice was attacked as a case of unnecessary barbarity, even if the executed prisoners were members of the hated Guard.

The meeting lasted for three hours. The *compañeros* discussed each other's actions that day as well as my and the *sanitarios'* performance. Lupe got in her licks; she accused me of not helping enough with the wound dressing. Others criticized her for being too bossy and uncooperative.

The next day, Jasmine summoned me by radio to Palo Grande. When I arrived, she took me to an adobe house close by the hospital, a house I had noticed before to be filled with children and assorted adults and presided over by a gentle, gaunt giant called Salvador.

Actually, he stood only a little over six feet, but that was at least four inches higher than the next tallest man in Palo Grande—me. I found him cordial and diffident in a way similar to Ramón; he was respectful of my skills and grateful I had come to help. Only after talking for some time did I learn that he was a former secretary of the National Union of Day Laborers, now acting as head of all civilian authority in Guazapa.

Salvador listened with surprise to my story. He said that no one had informed him of any conditions of service and for that he was apologetic. Had he known, I would not have been sent out with a column.

Our meeting went well. Salvador later came by the hospital to inform me that I was thenceforth to concern myself exclusively with civilian medicine. Jasmine would see to the combatants. While a teen-aged *sanitario* named Dorita would be official *responsable* for public health, I was free to plan its organization and implementation. I would consult with him and Jasmine, and she would present our proposals and initiatives before the many committees established to pass on Front policy. From what I'd seen already of their structures, I could guess how many hours of wrangling and debate this arrangement would save me. I was pleased.

I BEGAN BY RECONNOITERING THE FRONT. In its full, irregular extent, Guazapa was about the area of Denver, Colorado. Traveling north from Palo Grande to the farm villages of Delicias, Chaparral, and the rest was relatively easy; all could be reached in a few hours' walk over level ground.

Access to the eastern part of the zone was another matter. The Suchitoto highway cut Guazapa nearly in two. It was heavily patrolled and could be crossed only in the dark. Yet unless a person was willing to try the even riskier boat ride across Lake Suchitlán, there was no other way to reach Copapayo, Tenango, Guadalupe, and the rest of the eastern settlements. Even then, there remained the "Grand Canyon" to negotiate. In the dry season, it was arduous. When the rains came, the stream running along its bottom would swell into a torrent, wide and deep enough to uproot trees and roll one-hundred-pound boulders along its course.

There was very little local military action initiated by either side during April of 1982. As I toured the zone, getting to know both the villages and clinics, I noticed the fields were filled with farmers preparing the soil for the May rains and planting time. Among them were *compañeros* from the San Antonio Abad column, fighters happy to take advantage of the shooting lull to put down their rifles and pick up a machete or planting stick.

Many hailed me as I passed. I didn't know their names yet, but I found they'd given me one. Because of my limp, my gray hairs, and the fact that I was the only member of the column over thirty, they had nicknamed me *abuelito* (little grandfather) and cheerfully called out, "Hola, Camilo, abuelito," when they saw me. I guess I looked as used up to them as poor Joaquín in Salinas had to me, and sometimes I felt that way.

On the first of May, the skies opened. Slanting torrents turned Guazapa into a mire. In no time, the dusty trails became tricky mud-slicks; in places the goo was knee-deep. Along them, the bare earth exploded with weeds first a foot high, then a yard. By the end of the rains in July, the foliage had grown to eight feet and more.

My boots, for which I'd paid one hundred dollars in Tegucigalpa, would sink into the mud, then come sucking up with an obscene glop! sound at each step. They were the most expensive item of apparel I'd ever purchased; my previous record was seventy-five dollars for a suit from Sears. They were sold to me as the ultimate in rugged footwear, the sort of thing men wore to build skyscrapers, run Arctic oil rigs, chop timber in Oregon. These all-world boots didn't withstand two weeks of the Salvadoran rainy season. One sole and then the other tore from the uppers. I mended them with thread and wire or plastic filament, but still they came apart. *Glop glop glop* through the mud and then *flap flap flap* as I trudged into a village. My blackened, nailless, and mildewed toes stuck out through shreds of sock and the gaping fronts of the boots.

May's first droplets were the farmers' cue to hit the fields with their planting sticks and bags of seed. Everyone was out planting, from the individual *campesinos* to the elementary school classes and health collectives who each tended their own *hortiliza* (garden), as they called it.

It wasn't yet apparent to me how close to starvation the Front was, or how deeply the *campesinos'* spirits were tied to the earth's cycles of fertility. One morning in May, I came squishing and grunting up the eastern side of the "Grand Canyon" near Tenango to encounter an old man stooped in the rain with his planting stick, concentrating fully on the small holes he made and then sowed with three or four kernels of corn.

I introduced myself, breaking his reverie. When he looked up and offered his name, Chepe, I could tell he was mostly Indian. After we exchanged pleasantries, I asked why he had seemed so absorbed in poking holes in the wet soil. Chepe answered that like his Pipil Indian ancestors he must stop and apologize to the earth each time he wounded it with his stick.

Once the crops, mostly corn and beans, but also radishes and cabbages and squash, were planted, the farmers fought the weeds and prayed for a bountiful July harvest to end their increasing hunger. The previous year's crops, usually enough to sustain them through the winter dry season, the rainy season, and planting time, had been largely destroyed in the spring offensives against them. Not only Chalatenango to the north, but Guazapa too, was quickly running out of food.

Rationing became necessary and then increasingly severe. First, we were cut to twice-a-day meals of two tortillas and a half-cup of beans. Then there were no beans. The tortillas, now made of yucca root, kept shrinking and growing coarser, too. By June, these virtually indigestible disks and cups of a clear, thin soup were all that sustained us.

As always, the children suffered the most. Nearly half the population of Guazapa was under twelve, yet less than one hundred scrawny old cows provided fresh milk for them. As the rest of the food disappeared, I saw more and more of the youngsters with the distended bellies of serious malnutrition and the flag of blondish hair, a sign of protein deficiency.

I had with me, as a special reserve, one hundred dollars donated by Los Niños, a California-based child welfare agency. The money was earmarked for pediatric crisis. We decided to buy milk with it. One of Salvador's most reliable aides was sent to Suchitoto, where an army officer agreed, for an outrageous price, to sell him a sack of powdered milk that was clearly labeled as a United States government donation and not to be sold.

I was hungry all the time, a condition made less tolerable by the restaurant advertisements I heard over my radio. Just twenty miles away in San Salvador, I was told, "American-style" hamburgers were available, along with chicken and barbecue. I had come into the Front a vegetarian, but it was torture to listen to the announcer linger seductively over the word B–A–R–B–E–C–U–E.

Even the wildlife in Guazapa, what there was of it, seemed to be going hungry. One night, the Salitre village skunk sneaked away with my hat for the salt in its sweat band.

Several weeks later and hungrier than I ever believed possible, I was crossing the "Grand Canyon" with my escort when we encountered another skunk and dispatched it with a machete. He sprayed us all before expiring, a minor nuisance to starving men. We skinned, spitted, and roasted him on the spot. As I savored my share, two spoonfuls, I briefly contemplated replacing my hat with his hide.

Along with the hunger and discomfort came misfortune. One night, a flapping boot sole caught on a root or a stone and I took a header down into the canyon. Slaloming through the muck on my butt, I stopped my slide after a hundred feet and counted myself lucky that the only damage was a few cuts and bruises and a shredded workshirt—my last shirt.

When my watch crystal was shattered, I learned how to live by local time.

"How long is it to the next village?"

"Abuelito, the sun will be hot before you get there."

In May, it became, "You'll never make it before the next rain."

Then I lost my flashlight. I didn't mind this so much until I contracted amoebic dysentery. At night in the rain, there was little time to grope my way to the bushes.

My Air Force survival training was of no help. It did not contemplate situations of institutionalized deprivation and hardship. I was unlikely to lose my way on the Front or have the leisure to set snares for game animals long since eaten by the *campesinos*. Besides our hunger was collective, not individual. Knowing how to root for edible insects was useless because for all their great numbers, the bugs of Guazapa were too small to efficiently exploit as a food source for even one, let alone thousands of people.

The year I spent in India was more useful to me. I had gone back there on leave from medical school and the experience had taught me patience and sensitivity to the poor's perceptions of their would-be benefactors. High-yield strains of wheat and other grains are fine, if you can afford the fertilizers to make them grow and the pesticides to save them from insects. Gasoline motors to power irrigation systems are an improvement over ox power only if you can afford the fuel. Birth control pills make sense as an appropriate, low-tech method, but until a woman's fear of abandonment in old age is conquered, she will continue to have children. As that first day in Quipurito had demonstrated, to neglect such lessons was to imperil my credibility.

Before urging measures like latrine-building, garbage disposal, water sterilization, and personal hygiene, I strove to foster trust by providing acute-care doctoring, pills, and injections, to the extent that my meager supplies would allow. It wasn't always necessary to have the requested drug; bright red vitamin pills had a powerful placebo effect for a wide range of psychosomatic complaints ranging from headache to otherwise inexplicable toe trauma.

There could be problems, however, even when I had the drug of choice. American medicine may be rightly faulted for concentrating too much authority in the hands of physicians. Many useful medicines would be much more widely accessible, and probably cheaper, if prescriptions weren't necessary to obtain them.

Still, the system does restrict the possibility of abuses such as are common where people are free to purchase nearly any medicine they like. I saw it in Salinas where farmworkers and refugees would arrive at the clinic with their ampuls of injectable vitamins or cold remedies they'd acquired over-the-counter in Mexico.

A Salvadoran example was Miguel, whom I met one afternoon while holding a clinic in Copapayo. His arthritis was advanced and quite painful. When I offered him the indicated four aspirin to ease the condition, he demanded *butazolidina*, an extremely potent anti-inflammatory agent. It probably was effective in his experience. The difficulty is that it can dangerously interfere with red-blood-cell production in the marrow. In the United States, its use is confined to very specific cases and then only with concurrent laboratory monitoring.

Yet Miguel was insisting on it! He wouldn't consider taking aspirin or drinking willow bark tea, which contains the same active ingredient. His wife, he told me, used to regularly buy butazolidine ampuls from a pharmacist in Suchitoto and to administer them by injection every two weeks.

I imagined what her shopping trips were like.

"I'll take this bolt of cloth, a sack of salt, and a few candles," she might tell the store owner. "And, oh yes, give me a six-ampul pack of butazolidine, 10cc size please. Don't forget the syringes!"

In time, Miguel came to accept that aspirin was the proper medicine for his arthritis, and he even begrudgingly agreed to try the willow bark tea recipe. Once converted to this "new" medicine, he became an effective advocate for its use.

Miguel was one of several people in Copapayo to whom I became closely attached and whose memories I'll always carry. Copapayo was the first village I encountered on the Front and, as it turned out, it would be my point of departure a year later. In between and since, I associate it with my finest—and saddest—hours.

FROM THE LATE 1960s through the mid-1970s, Copapayo came under the influence of Father José Alas, a Catholic priest who introduced liberation theology to parishes in much of north and northeast Guazapa. Along with Father Rutilio Grande, since murdered by uniformed assassins, Alas awakened the *campesinos* to the power of unity and the possibility of this-world relief from their suffering.

His ministry provoked retaliation: Alas was repeatedly threatened by the death squads and was once beaten nearly to death. In 1977, he was finally driven from the region, but his teachings and the example of his courage left their mark on the people. Copapayo remained a spiritual legacy of the Christian base communities he founded.

When I later met Alas in the States, where he was working as a loan consultant to the World Bank, I told him how the first question I was asked in Copapayo was if I knew him and had I seen him lately. They were surprised when I answered no. The *campesinos* assumed that the Father would be well-known wherever he went.

Alas was eager for news of Copapayo, particularly word of a remarkable family, the extended clan of Frederico, the village's most prominent citizen.

There were fourteen of them in all, ranging from ten-year-old Noe, a Down's syndrome child, up to the venerable Frederico and his wife, Isabel, who ran the house as well as led the local Association of Salvadoran Women. In the immediate family there was Janet, twenty-six, the *responsable* for health care in the eastern sector. One brother, Selvin, who was a little older, acted as head of agricultural production in the same area. His wife, Lia, was a seamstress, in charge of the village shop where hats, packs, and uniforms were sewn. Another brother, Aurelio, was a guerrilla. Sister Lola, about twenty, was a schoolteacher in Copapayo. Two younger brothers were members of the local militia.

At one time or another, I treated them all. Frederico, for instance, was nearly crippled by arthritis. Selvin carried in his neck two .22 slugs from a death squad pistol. Janet and I removed them using local anesthetic.

It was very unusual in Guazapa for an entire family to be intact and living under one roof. It was also rare for every single member to be incorporated. This family's commitment to the revolution was total.

Frederico was the son of a pioneer; his father had settled their land. The several acres they owned, plus some livestock and a rather large, by local standards, three-room house in Copapayo, was property he held in trust for the fourth generation, Selvin's son. The family had suffered relatively little before the revolution. They were not as dependent upon the local *dueño*, and there were enough colones in the family bank account to provide a few amenities.

Unlike the vast majority of their friends and neighbors, this family couldn't expect much material gain once the revolution was won. If his family's safety and well-being were

Frederico's only concern, he might have evacuated them long ago to the States.

But Frederico had a dirt farmer's obstinacy about staying on the land. With his family, he also believed that the Christian and patriotic thing to do was to stay and contribute to the struggle. They didn't see this commitment so much as a responsibility as an opportunity to help build a better, more just society in El Salvador. From Uncle Gabriel, a leader in one of Copapayo's base Christian communities, or CEBs, to Isabel, who gave pet names to all her pigs, it was unimaginable to desert their homeland.

There was no revolutionary rhetoric heard at Frederico's table. Rather, there were stories. He told me how proud he was the time Father Alas had asked his opinion on some question; no one except another *campesino* had ever asked Frederico's view on anything. He recalled how in 1969 the National Guard had surrounded the church in Suchitoto, demanding that Alas leave town. Peasants from all the surrounding base communities converged on Suchitoto, shouting for the soldiers, not the priest, to go away.

To Father Alas, my most welcome recollection was of Frederico saying the priest armed the people of Copapayo with courage, not weapons. The guns came after Alas was driven away. His legacy was the *campesinos'* dignity and self-esteem.

Of Frederico's family, I got to know Janet best. She was the ablest and most helpful of all the village medics, a tribute to someone with only a third-grade education. She took her responsibility for health care in the eastern sector very seriously, working long days and somehow also finding time to attend adult literacy classes. Her limited ability to read and write were an embarrassment, a handicap Janet meant to overcome.

Because of this diligence, the eastern sector of the zone was a model of organization and achievement for the rest of Guazapa. Without her, the public health campaign would have floundered.

She showed me how leadership was exercised by example on the Front. To get a *campesino* to dig a latrine, you first had to persuade the village *sanitarios* to dig one for the clinic. Likewise for the treatment of infant diarrhea. We taught the health workers that diarrhea kills because of dehydration, and showed them how to mix a rehydrating fluid of boiled water, sugar, and salt. They took the remedy into the *campesinos'* homes where mothers, at first skeptical, soon found that the liquid worked. There was just as much diarrhea to contend with, but suddenly it wasn't so deadly.

LIKE THE CAMPESINOS THEY SERVED, the *sanitarios* required demonstrable, preferably instant, proof of an idea's utility. In the rainy season, for example, it might take two hours to search around for the wood for a fire to boil the contaminated water. In the dry season, by contrast, some households would have to travel up to a half-mile to the nearest source of water. In either case, it was difficult for them to appreciate why the children should be given some to wash their hands.

Record keeping was another alien concept. We established sixteen clinics in villages around the Front. Unless my schedule was seriously disrupted, I could visit each of them once every two weeks. Between fifty and one hundred peasants would line up for treatment. Afterward, we held classes for the medics. I explained to them that with 9,000 people in our care, we could not remember each one's case history. We had to take careful notes and keep them for reference when the patient came in again. The *sanitarios* seemed to understand the concept, but they didn't practice it. With paper scarce on the Front, pages of the notebooks were used to light fires or for trips to their newly dug latrines.

They did put the paper, including our records, to one ingenious use. To sterilize gauze or one of its substitutes for debriding wounds (diapers, mosquito netting, old clothes) the material was cut into two-inch squares, then rolled and folded into a piece of paper. These and anything else that was to be sterilized were sealed in a large tin. It was placed inside an even larger can, packed with sand, and then baked for several hours over a low flame. A temperature high enough to achieve sterilization, but below the flashpoint of paper, was attained in this way. When the cans cooled, the sterile pads were removed and stored for later use inside their protective paper envelopes. By this method, we were able to sterilize and recycle disposable surgical gloves up to twenty times.

The peasants were skeptical at the introduction of natural remedies. Their forebears, like Miguel's mother, had been conversant with the pharmacopoeia growing wild around them. Almost any of their grandparents had ten times the knowledge of natural medicine that I possessed, but that lore had been lost with the advent of easily available drugstore remedies.

The willow bark tea was slow to catch on, as was the sedative we showed them how to brew from the leaves of the mock orange tree. Despite the fact that stomach gas, acidity, and ulcer-like pain were common complaints, they showed little interest in learning how to prepare an antacid from the fine ash of their cooking fires.

They resisted expanding their diets, as well. As hungry as they were, the *campesinos* dismissed as "rabbit food" the papaya, yucca, and other fresh leaves I urged on them for their vitamin content.

My "nail cocktails" received the greatest initial contempt. Anemia was a very serious problem. There was anemia of chronic childbirth—most women by age forty had experienced a dozen pregnancies. There was anemia due to intestinal parasites as well as malaria, which destroys red blood cells. There was anemia due to blood loss from wounds. The most common anemia, though, was the simple anemia resulting from the iron-poor diet of beans and tortillas. Soaking several nails for twenty-four hours, cleaning them with a piece of lemon, and then drinking the rusty water provides a small quantity of absorbable iron. You'd have thought they were being asked to drink turpentine from the initial reactions.

Some of the mothers suspected I was trying to induce abortions with the drink.

I tried to address these fears at the pre-natal sessions. The first few hours of every visit were set aside for the needs of pregnant women who didn't have the strength to stand all day or who were too shy to be examined with men around.

An important requirement for preventive medical care during pregnancy is a thorough history. Among other things, I needed to know how many pregnancies they'd had, how many miscarriages or abortions, and how many stillborns. To alert me to the possibility of perinatal deaths or fatal birth defects, the last piece of information I needed to know was how many children were still living and how the others had died.

I soon learned that asking these questions, especially the last one, often stirred the women to paroxysms of grief. Camila, thirty-eight, was not atypical. She said she had had nine pregnancies including her current one. There had been one miscarriage. Her composure gave way when I inquired about the others.

Three children survived. Two others, a boy and a girl, had died of a fever and diarrhea, respectively. Both had been lost in the years when Camila and her husband had chosen to pay their mortgage, a sum equal to half the value of their crop, rather than keep the money to feed their children. Each year, the choice was always the same. If they paid, the children's lives were endangered. If they didn't, their land could be repossessed.

Another two children were killed in a massacre during the early months of the civil war. Their memory haunted her.

"Why didn't you flee?" I asked.

"Because we didn't know then," she answered through her tears. "We had never been to a demonstration or belonged to an organization. We didn't know we were the enemy."

My diary became a receptacle for this pain as well as for my personal frustrations. My handwriting became a furious scribble as I complained that I'd be happy to dispense all the analgesics and iron pills in the world if we only had them. In a few brief weeks, I'd seen a dozen deaths that could have been prevented with an adequate store of medicines. Hunger gnawed at my spirit, too, as did the daily deluge of the rainy season and the dysentery that was slowly robbing me of my strength. I didn't have the proper antibiotic for it; neither tetracycline nor sulfa tablets had any appreciable effect in controlling it.

THE *DE FACTO* TRUCE WAS LIFTED IN MAY. We began to see government Hueys appear between the cloudbursts.

One afternoon, a crowd of fifty patients was standing outside the clinic in Guadalupe when the dread chop of an approaching Huey came from over the valley rim. I ran to the door to see the helicopter bearing straight down on us at a tremendous speed.

This was a flight profile, or angle and speed of attack, that I had been familiar with in Vietnam; a full-tilt, treetop boogie with the "gookmobile's" M-60 machine guns blazing. Until that moment, I'd never seen a Salvadoran Huey flown that way.

We all froze, transfixed by the thunder of his huge rotor, and expected at any instant to see the fire and lead of his port guns.

"So this is what it's like," I thought. "We're caught in a free-fire zone, and here comes a Top Gun."

The episode was over in an instant. The Huey screamed right over us and continued south. Some of the *campesinos* fainted. Many of the children began to wail. Thankful for their safety and mine, I could only surmise that the Huey had been returning from Chalatenango, his ammunition spent.

For a long while, the violence—or the threat of it—was like that: random, unexpected. Sometimes, the government soldiers would infiltrate the Front from their command posts along the Suchitoto highway. They would lie in wait along the well-traveled paths between Palo Grande and the farming villages to the north. When a target appeared, they would fire a few rounds and then run before the guerrillas or militia could engage them.

We were always alert to the possibility of a sniper attack on these trails, but not always alert enough. One afternoon in May, I was trudging through the sector when a woman not twenty-five yards in front of me dropped dead to the ground with a single bullet through her heart.

Her toddler stood screaming on the trail. I ran to him, cupped a hand over his mouth and pulled him down into the mud beside his dead mother. For fifteen seconds I cradled him there as he put up a ferocious struggle. The bearded foreigner scared children all the time, and perhaps he thought I was the one who had shot his mother.

I picked him up under my arm and ran bent at the waist through the sodden underbrush until I had him safely out of the way. I waited a few moments and then returned to the trail to confirm his mother's death. I then hid her body lest the soldiers come and mutilate her.

Her orphan and I then cautiously picked our way around the scene of the ambush and made our way to Llano Rancho. The little boy's father had already been killed some months earlier. With his mother now gone too, his care and that of his brothers and sisters fell to an aunt, herself a widow.

The *campesino* families of Guazapa were continually shuffled and mended in this way. The house where I would later live, for instance, was headed by a widow with five children. Besides myself, residing in its one room were her aunt and a female cousin, an elder uncle, a niece from yet another arm of the family, an old man who had been the mother's father's longtime friend, and two more children whose relationship to the rest was never clear to me.

With the notable exception of Frederico's clan in Copapayo, intact nuclear families were almost unknown in Guazapa. Western sociologists, concerned about the effects of divorce, the trials of single-parenting, or the plight of latch-key children, might learn a lot about broken homes if they visited El Salvador.

Not long after I had witnessed the murder on the trail, a sniper round whizzed past my ear in a similar ambush. In the same period, Janet and I were set at by a rabid mongrel dog that we killed with a club.

The three incidents prompted concern among my patients and the health workers that their doctor might get killed. Until this time, I'd only accepted an armed escort when crossing the Suchitoto highway. Now, they wanted me to be guarded at all times.

At first, I yielded to their wishes and permitted an escort to accompany me on my rounds. But I felt like a hypocrite. If my Quaker principles kept me from defending my own life, how could I ask someone else to? If my body ended up on some Salvadoran roadside, so be it. Martyr, fool, or anonymous statistic, at least I would have remained true to my conscience. After one-and-a-half circuits, I persuaded my protectors that I could manage on my own with a pistol. I carried an old Smith and Wesson .22, like my grandfather's, for two weeks and then passed it on to a *sanitario*. Nobody seemed to notice, or else they figured I was hopelessly beyond reason.

The subtler challenge was to my neutrality, part of my commitment to non-violence. On one level, it was impossible not to be sympathetic to these people who, for decades, had been used as the Salvadoran national doormat. Peaceable protest had brought them nothing but more repression. They at least had a rationale for fighting; they wanted their land back and they wanted their freedom.

I saw no counter-justification behind marauders like the Ramón Belloso Battalion, the death squads, or the intensifying air war against the villages of Guazapa. A system that must make war against its own people, that defends itself by murdering its priests, its professors, and its physicians can hardly claim to be civilized, much less to have staked out the moral high ground.

In a practical way, my neutrality was undermined by

circumstance. Leaflets dropped on the Front announced a reward of five thousand *colones* (about $1,500) for anyone who brought in a foreign subversive, dead or alive. I might not be willing to defend myself, but I certainly wasn't about to endorse efforts to eliminate me. Try as I might to avoid taking sides, I found myself writing "we" in my diary for the *campesinos*, and "they" for the government. In time, "they" yielded to "the enemy."

The brutality of the Salvadoran government forces provoked implacable hatred among the guerrillas and their supporters, but something else was needed to account for the people's disdain. From my first day in El Salvador when young Nico explained the importance of fighting more bravely and more honorably than a government soldier, I heard nothing but contempt for the military among the *campesinos* and *compañeros*. They regarded the soldiers as cowards and called them *chuchos*, slang for "little dogs." I was told that the troops rarely searched for the insurgents and that every one of the many invasions of the Front had been conducted against the villages where the soldiers knew no guerrillas were to be found.

They also rarely fought at night. On the last day of April 1982, a group of us climbed up from the "Grand Canyon" and prepared to make our usual night crossing of the Suchitoto highway. This was the most hazardous zone around the Front. Not only was there a substantial government garrison in Suchitoto, but several permanent outposts, as well as constant patrols, were maintained along the whole length of the road.

Yet unless there had been an alert or recent skirmishing nearby, we always took the same trail and crossed at about the same time of night. It was so routine that a person could almost set his watch by us. "What an invitation for an ambush," I thought. In Vietnam, the trail would have long since been mined and monitored.

We passed close enough to several government camps to hear their radios playing music in the night. I wondered if the soldiers were trying to lure us into a fight, and asked the *compañero* behind me if he thought we might be walking into a trap.

He just laughed at me. "Camilo," he said, "the chuchos play their radios so we'll know where they are. If they didn't, we might catch each other by surprise, and they'd have to fight. This way, we can cross the highway, and they don't get hurt. They are cowards."

The next day was May Day, and we all celebrated at the hospital in Palo Grande. As galas go, it was a pretty tame affair. Everyone received an extra tortilla, a piece of candy, and a couple slices of mango.

I remember it, though, for the discussion I joined that afternoon. Gathered around the small porch in Jasmine's hospital, several *campesinos* and *compañeros* offered their understanding of the day's significance. The more political of the *compañeros* thought of it as a sort of worldwide proletariat day celebrated with military parades and speeches in communist countries. One *campesino* was sure it was a celebration of the spring rains and planting season in El Salvador.

Few of them were at first ready to accept that the May Day was celebrated not only in socialist countries, but elsewhere to mark an event that occurred in the United States more than thirty years before the Russian Revolution. It is, I explained, a commemoration of the Haymarket Square Riot in Chicago. There on May 4, 1886, eleven people were killed and one hundred others injured when workers demonstrating for the eight-hour workday clashed with police. When I further explained that American labor's traditional day of celebration is not May Day but in early September, the group was even more lost. *Yanqui* ways puzzled them greatly.

PERHAPS MY MAJOR SURPRISE in El Salvador was the low number of civilian war wounds I encountered. While the guerrilla columns were filled with those carrying shrapnel and old bullet wounds, the civilians seemed remarkably free from such traumas.

Since civilians were the most common targets of government invasions, I didn't understand their relative freedom from injuries. When warfare returned to Guazapa, I would learn the horrible answer to this mystery.

For the time being, it was chronic ill health that concerned me most. Take, for instance, the widespread incidence of malaria.

I could have practically eliminated malaria on the Guazapa Front for ten cents per week per person; that's the retail cost of a prophylactic course of chloroquine tablets. Unfortunately, the only person regularly supplied with chloroquine was myself. I carried this personal supply under the assumption that I was worth more to the civilians on my feet than supine and riddled with fever.

I lived by this rule until a May afternoon in Tenango where I was taken to see a pregnant woman shaking so violently with malarial chills that even strong boys couldn't keep her on a cot. I gave the woman a full dose of ten chloroquine tablets, a five-weeks' preventive supply. In a short time other emergencies consumed my entire stock.

The only recourse was to exploit the local source of quinine, the *quina* (cinchona) tree. I walked up to Copapayo and found Miguel, who remembered using *quina* bark to dose malaria and knew how to find the trees.

According to him, his mother used "three fingers" of bark per cup of *quina* tea; three fingers being a single plane equal to that of three closed fingers.

I planned to take an epidemiological approach with the *quina* medicine. Peasants in separate villages would be given one of three strengths—two fingers, three fingers, or four fingers—and we would then adopt the most effective as the standard for the Front.

As usual there were problems. We had no microscope, so each case had to be diagnosed clinically. Not only did I have to train each of the *sanitarios* to differentiate between the chills and fever of malaria and the similar symptoms of so many other common tropical diseases, but the peasants themselves had to be taught not to assume every headache or fever meant the onset of malaria.

Since our paper always disappeared, record keeping was impossible. Nor were follow-up examinations complete because the people came to the clinics only if they were sick, or if they knew we had medicine.

On top of that, a summertime outbreak of dengue fever, similar to malaria and also mosquito-borne, skewed the project even more. Hundreds of *campesinos* with dengue were initially diagnosed as malarial and given *quina* tea or chloroquine, neither of which has any effect on dengue.

So much for science around the volcano. Without case controls I had no way of being certain if the *quina* helped or, if it did, what the most effective dose was. My guess is that we achieved some amelioration, but only a slight one. By autumn, *quina* bark tea-lover Camilo came down with malaria, too.

In some regards, my advent on the Guazapa Front was like introducing a food processor to a *campesino* kitchen; I could whir and spin and effect wondrous things in their eyes. Yet I often questioned my overall value to them.

One afternoon, a government air attack on the farm village of Chaparral left several people dead and a thirteen-year-old boy critically wounded with a piece of shrapnel in the side of his chest.

Jasmine and I examined the boy at the Palo Grande hospital. His lung exam was negative and pulmonary function seemed normal. His abdomen was tense, but that was probably because of the pain he complained of.

We debated performing a laparotomy, or exploratory surgery, to search for internal damage. Had I seen him in an American emergency room, x-rays of his abdomen and thorax would have been routine, as might have been a peritoneal lavage, a procedure in which fluids are pumped in and out of the peritoneal cavity. If they return red with blood, then internal damage has occurred and you operate.

No such procedures were possible in Guazapa. My only choice was to risk the laparotomy or to trust that clinical diagnosis of a superficial wound was correct. With our stock of general anesthesia about gone and his condition apparently stable, I decided not to operate.

Jasmine monitored the boy through the evening, then I stayed with him from midnight on. By dawn, he was able to sit up with no pain and was talking about how he wanted to go home.

I was immensely relieved. His mother, six months pregnant, had lost another son just two days before. Her older boy had been caught by government troops in a town south of Salitre and his mutilated body found on a trail hours later. They had been burying him when news of the younger boy's injury came over the village radio.

This son, I was pleased to tell her in the morning, was doing fine. Every vital sign was stable except for a slight tachycardia, or fast heartbeat. I left him to go prepare an IV solution. When I returned he was dead. The *sanitario* reported the boy suddenly sat straight upright in bed, complained that he was hot, and expired. There had been no warning, no hint at all that his life was endangered.

Here was a stark instance of my impotence as a physician. For all my education and training, all the slick, high-tech doctoring I could do, I'd been helpless to save this boy. In the United States, the loss of such a patient would be totally unacceptable; in Guazapa, we encountered God's will more frequently.

I guessed that the young boy died of a ruptured spleen, or perhaps an embolism. I'll never know because his mother, still traumatized by the mutilation of her other son, refused to allow an autopsy. She wouldn't talk to me. She just sat there in the hospital, holding her dead child and praying.

Over time, I learned to adjust my expectations. I was the product of a medical system that puts extreme emphasis upon absolutely correct diagnosis. In the United States, a doctor will order every conceivable test to arrive at a diagnosis rather than risk peer criticism, a malpractice suit, or a patient's life. The patient price is inflated by this caution, but cost is no object when your career is at stake. In Guazapa, there was no such thing as a second opinion, no CBCs, EKGs, CAT scans, or anything else. While no one was about to sue me if I made a mistake, the patient would be just as dead.

One case in point was an old man I examined in El Zapote, a village about two hours' walking distance northwest around the volcano from Palo Grande. David stood on his crutches outside the clinic for an entire day, waiting until all the other patients had been seen. Then he came hobbling in and asked that the female *responsable* leave the room along with the young girls who assisted her.

His embarrassment had been more acute to him than the pain of a right testicle swollen to the size of a tennis ball, so inflamed and tender that David winced even in anticipation of my touch. With the women gone, I tried to elicit a medical history from him. An old hernia scar suggested one diagnostic possibility, while the swelling and inflammation suggested another. The old man might be herniating again, or he could be suffering from a torsioned testicle in which the organ twists on its pedicle, threatening strangulation of vessels and tissue. The third possibility was epididymitis, an inflammation of an excretory duct.

To differentiate among these diagnoses, I needed old David's help.

"Do you have regular bowel movements?" I asked in Spanish.

"Sí."

"Does it hurt to urinate?"

"Sí."

"Is the swelling recent?"

"Sí."

David's answer to everything was "Sí," no help at all in arriving at a very serious decision as to his probable condition. I did the best I could with him and decided after an hour's interview and physical exam that he most likely had a treatable case of epididymitis. A five-day course of tetracycline was indicated.

The most difficult part was next. David's condition *could* require emergency surgery. He had to be monitored in my absence. Someone had to be shown what symptoms to look for if it was a hernia or a torsioned testicle. Someone had to watch him and notify me instantly by radio if there was a change. That someone would be Sara, the sixteen-year-old *responsable* or one of her equally young assistants.

I don't know if the old man or the women were more embarrassed as I explained how his testicles should hang and how to watch them for a change in angle, etc. He stared up at the ceiling in mortification, and they stared down at my demonstration in dread obedience to their duty. Never was a medical lecture delivered under more trying circumstances.

For six days afterward, I heard nothing. The afternoon of our May Day discussion, I hiked back to El Zapote to learn that no one had seen David since the examination. The news angered me. Sara knew as well as anyone that David might not be able to make it back to the clinic, that he could be dead or dying. Despite all my precautions, he had been left to his fate.

Following her directions, I set out for his house, a strenuous four-mile trek that exhausted me and must have been torture for him to negotiate on crutches. All the while, I was certain old David was dead.

His house was deserted.

"They're probably out burying him," I thought.

But off in the distance, I could make out a figure with a hoe in a cornfield. As I drew nearer, I saw David vigorously working his *milpa*. He looked up at me with a huge grin, gave a satisfied pat to his scrotum, and offered profuse gratitude for the tetracycline cure.

After resting overnight, I walked back to Palo Grande to find Jasmine busy with several wound cases. An overnight guerrilla sortie had not gone well.

She directed me to the village radio room where I was handed a stack of garbled messages from Delicias. From what I could make out from them, a young mother apparently had fallen into a coma or convulsions or both. They needed a doctor immediately.

My first fear was eclampsia, a condition observed among young mothers in which high blood pressure leads to convulsions. Eclampsia is a mystery; no one knows what causes it. If untreated, it begins as a hyper-reflexive state and quickly moves into convulsions and then complete, constant muscle spasms and occasionally death.

The medicine of choice for eclampsia is magnesium sulfate, which acts to relax the muscles. I, of course, had none and so prepared to treat the woman as best I could with intravenous fluids and tranquilizers.

Time was critical; eclampsia attacks swiftly. A *campesino* saddled a bony old nag that I mounted and spurred north toward Delicias at a wobbly gallop. Three hours later, I reined into town like Don Quixote atop Rocinante and was directed to the patient's house. Another mile and a half over some corn stubble and through a canebrake and I had arrived.

I walked into the adobe hut and was delighted to see the mother alert, if stark raving mad. She was spitting and screaming, throwing food at her frightened husband and parents, crying.

The scene was disturbing, but it wasn't eclampsia. I quickly diagnosed her condition as postpartum psychosis, a self-limiting affliction that would pass in a short time. Provided she could be made to eat and was kept from harming herself or her child, she would recover.

Her family did not share my relief. They were half-convinced she was possessed by demons and thought me very brave indeed to approach the woman, put my arm around her shoulder, and try to comfort and calm her.

She fixed me with intensely curious eyes, a frequent symptom of psychotic states. The woman spit on herself and me, rubbed the saliva over both of us, and continued to rave. But gradually, she calmed down, the first sign of control she'd shown in two days.

Her family's terror was understandable; madness frightens everyone. Even I, a doctor, might have been more wary of her, less likely to risk having an eye poked out, had not the Air Force schooled me in the ways of the insane. After all, I was once diagnosed a head case myself.

*   *   *

"DEPRESSIVE: ACUTE, SEVERE" was my official mental state in September 1970 when the Air Force committed me to Wilford Hall Hospital. After a lifetime of obedience and smug conformity, I'll own that I was acutely and severely depressed to be handed a robe and slippers and told to report to the dayroom to meet the rest of the inmate patients.

This was on the fourth floor of Wilford Hall and I was designated a class 4–B patient; that is, I was grouped with the most severe cases. The ward was locked and guarded—by other patients. The windows were barred. We were regarded as too sick, even, to use the telephone.

My first mistake was to protest. That first day, I told anyone who'd listen that I most certainly was not crazy and I wanted out—now. I also didn't care to associate with mental cases and tried retreating to my room to think and to avoid their company.

This behavior was immediately reported to the staff and I was called before a beefy lieutenant known as "Big Nurse" among the patients. Only later, when I became a physician, would I realize that, although very professional, she too was a victim of institutional ways.

"Captain Clements," she said firmly, "the patients say you are rude and sullen and uncooperative. You didn't attend your group therapy session."

"You're damn right!" I shouted at her. "I don't belong here!"

She sighed and rubbed her chin.

"There's no use getting angry, Captain. You're here because of a decision by two Air Force psychiatrists. My job is to help you resolve your problems."

"My biggest problem is the Air Force," I answered.

She was impassive.

"How long are you going to keep me here?" I asked.

"That depends on you," she answered.

"What do you mean?"

"We have a system here. The patients help to evaluate

one another. If you don't go to group therapy and don't try to get along, you won't be able to make any progress."

In short, she was telling me that my "peers" would decide how well I was doing and what privileges, such as the telephone, I would be allowed. Periodically, they would vote to determine if I was fit to become a 4–A, then a 3–B and so on until I was 1–A and ready for release. Each promotion carried with it a new level of freedom. At 4–A, for instance, I could use the telephone and walk downstairs for my meals. At the 3 level, I could take escorted walks outside the building. At 2, I would be allowed passes to leave on my own and so on.

"One flew into the cuckoo's nest," I muttered.

"Captain?"

"Nothing. But tell me, why can't I at least have a razor and why won't you let me eat with a knife?"

"Well," she replied, "there's some thought that you might be suicidal. We don't want you to harm yourself."

"Suicide!" I yelled again. "If you think I'm going to kill myself over the Air Force, you're sadly mistaken. I wouldn't give you the satisfaction!"

The rest of the conversation only distressed me further. She told me that I would see a psychiatrist regularly and that "it was felt" I should begin anti-depressant drug therapy. I felt hopeless.

That night, I met my roommates. One was catatonic. The other, a sergeant, told me how each night he flew through the window for assignations with his girlfriend in town. Good Lord!

I soon realized the futility of my anger and the absolute need to use a telephone. Beginning the next day, I tried to make friends with the other inmates, spoke of my hopes of getting well at our group sessions, started my drug therapy, and prayed for deliverance.

This went on for several desperate days until one afternoon when an old friend, Captain Ray Brill, burst onto the ward, brushed aside a protesting orderly, and found me in the dayroom.

I had seen Ray the night before I was committed and,

though he didn't share my views about the war, he was supportive. Now he was deeply concerned.

"What the hell happened to you? You disappeared!" he said.

I have never been more grateful to see anyone in my life.

"Ray," I answered, "I think I need a lawyer."

We talked for several minutes and Brill agreed to find me an attorney and do anything else he could. Short of shooting our way out, I told him, there wasn't much anyone could do.

Two days later, the patient council voted me into 4-A and access to the pay phone. Brill had contacted Maury Maverick, a local attorney familiar with military law and willing to help me if he could. I called Maverick, and we agreed to meet.

My first week of confinement had passed before we could meet. During that time, the bleakness of my situation became ever more apparent. As well, the anti-depressants were blurring my vision and making me groggy. They left my mouth constantly dry.

"Perhaps I am crazy," I thought.

Maverick didn't do much to lighten my mood. We quickly disposed of filing for a conscientious objection or for a writ of habeas corpus, because I had no basis for my decision other than my sense of right and wrong.

It was clear that the Air Force held all the cards. If I attempted any legal challenge to my incarceration, they could instantly declare me fit for duty and assign me back to Vietnam. When I refused, as I would, it would be a clear case of disobeying orders. I might fight it all the way to the Supreme Court, but the end, without a doubt, would be a stretch in Leavenworth. He said they would throw the book at me. I was, after all, the "right stuff" gone wrong.

My alternative, we both knew, was hardly more attractive. But if I went along with the Air Force, I had the chance of finally being declared unfit for flying and reassigned. The unhappy truth was I should stay put at Wilford Hall, do as I was told, and hope for the best.

This I did for nearly four months. Slowly, I was promoted up through the various levels until I was allowed out of the hospital entirely. I even became president of the patient council before leaving.

It was a difficult time for me. Adjusting to the ward and the shrinks and the other inmates was nothing compared to the trauma of feeling your whole life collapse around you. I remember going to see the movie *Catch-22* at the base theater and wondering why everyone was laughing; I walked out in the middle.

I went home at Christmas to find my parents a little ill at ease with me. Both assumed I was in the hospital for good reason, probably something to do with combat stress. I tried to talk to them about the war, but to life-long Republicans my accusing President Nixon of being a liar was tantamount to, if not imbalance, treason. We couldn't talk about the war.

At last, my case came up for review. On March 3, 1971, an Air Force Evaluation Board met at Randolph Air Force Base. Veterans Administration Diagnostic Code Number 9405, Captain Charles L. Clements, was determined to have a "disabling depressive reaction, mild to moderate social and industrial impairment." The board agreed my condition was permanent and recommended a psychiatric discharge. In some ways I was fortunate—a less sympathetic psychiatrist would have sent me back to duty for a court-martial.

I was, in their estimate, ten percent disabled. Had I been thirty percent or more depressive, I would have qualified for a pension. As it was, they issued me a severance check, and I was gone. Several friends in San Antonio held a ceremony to properly muster me out of the service. I was called before their picnic-board and in my best khaki uniform, I was mustard-ed in the finest Dijon tradition—from head to foot. Good-bye to the Air Force. Good-bye to everything I had striven toward for twenty-five years

IF I HAD COME TO DELICIAS feeling like a latter-day Don Quixote astride his half-starved Rocinante, the trip back to Palo

Grande was more evocative of Ichabod Crane on Halloween. After sedating the young mother and wiping most of her spittle from my face and hands, I left instructions for her care and then headed back for Palo Grande.

It was late afternoon by now. Massive cumulus clouds were piling up on the horizon and a breeze was coming from the north. A diffuse luminescence seemed to emanate from the trees and ground, an eerie glow such as that from mercury-vapor lamps in the fog.

My old horse plodded along while I scanned the landscape for signs of life. No one was out. For an hour we just clopped along, Rocinante the oblivious nag and I her careworn master.

Then the rain started. At first the drops were gentle, almost soothing as they plopped down on us. Soon, however, the wind freshened, the rain grew heavier, and I could see thunderheads marching toward us from the volcano.

We were going to get soaked.

The first few nearby thunderclaps didn't seem to bother the horse. But a white ball of electricity just to our left did, and we were off at a shambling gallop. Up ahead, I saw the tree and the limb into which Rocinante was about to hurtle me. Just as I leapt to safety, the whole tree exploded from a direct lightning strike. I looked up from the ground to see a smouldering remnant of shattered trunk and branches.

Now the rains came down in earnest. I found the horse, calmed her down, and remounted. But she would not walk straight into the stinging pellets. Instead, I had to steer her at 45-degree angles, like a sailor tacking into a heavy headwind. Even that worked only for a time; eventually, I climbed down and led the beast up the trail. Sometime around midnight, the two of us slogged back into Palo Grande. I'll swear I heard that old nag sigh as a *campesino* led her away.

THE HARDEST PART OF LIFE that spring was getting around. I spent most of my time trekking from clinic to clinic and could devote less time to patient care than does an average American doctor. The dysentery only slowed me down more; sometimes I was too weak to ride, much less walk the trails of Guazapa.

During one such bout of fever and diarrhea, I spent several days of light duty in Palo Grande. It had been fully three months now since I'd come to Guazapa, and I still had little understanding of how things were organized beyond my contacts with Jasmine, Salvador, and the village committees.

One night, I was asked to visit a bedridden patient in the community, but missed her house in the dark. Off to one side, I saw a kerosene lantern burning through an open door and decided to inquire within for directions.

The small yard was deserted, but I could hear a number of male voices as I approached the door. With no other way of announcing my presence, I coughed a couple times and then walked in. There before me around a rickety table was a circle of *compañeros*. Among them, Comandante Raul Hercules, the chief of all military operations in Guazapa and the anonymous intruder whom I'd dispossessed from my litter that night in Salitre.

So this was their secret command post. It was a nondescript adobe hut with pitted walls, dirt floors, and a tattered newspaper photo of the slain Archbishop Romero nailed above the single open window. Much later I would learn the command post was moved every fortnight.

Raul Hercules and his officers looked up at me as nonchalantly as if this was their weekly poker night, and I was the pizza delivery boy. They said nothing and went on with their discussion. As I backed out, a *compañero* came sauntering up the path. He took little note of me, but I still felt I should offer some excuse for wandering into a session of the guerrilla general staff.

"They told me at the clinic to come here," I said. "I'm sorry to interrupt the meeting."

"Oh, it's just their weekly meeting," he said and sat down to roll a cigarette.

The comandante and I met again some weeks later. His sister-in-law, Rosa, was pregnant for the fourth or fifth time.

She had never been able to carry a child past seven months, and I now had her confined to bed in the hopes of coaxing a few extra weeks of gestation before she delivered again.

It didn't help much. In her thirtieth week she went into labor, and I was called in the late afternoon to attend her. The birthing was uneventful, but her baby was born functionally dead. There was no spontaneous heartbeat or respiration. Though the infant had no chance of surviving, I stroked his tiny chest with one finger to revive his heart and got his lungs working for a while with mouth-to-mouth resuscitation. This was the closest Rosa had come to bearing a healthy child. For her mental well-being, I felt it wise that she hold and suckle him for a few hours.

Raul Hercules stayed up through the night with me. He was a big man, broad-chested, with a crooked smile that revealed several broken teeth. Like Salvador, he was shy—which probably accounts for his meekness the night in Salitre when I evicted him from my blankets.

He remembered the incident, but not his tormentor; I'd confronted him with a flashlight that had obscured my face. Now I timidly admitted to the deed and was relieved when he smiled and said to think nothing of it.

It certainly had been an easy mistake to make. Raul Hercules, the storied commander of Guazapa, went around in a battered cowboy hat and blue jeans. His house consisted of one room he shared with his wife, two daughters, a brother, and his wife. They had a table, three chairs, two beds, and a few pots and pans. His sole modern appurtenance was a cheap transistor radio. Their only measure of wealth was a few scruffy chickens in the front yard.

We spoke on through the night as Rosa nursed her dying infant. Raul Hercules' wife, Carmen, snored in her chair beside them. The comandante wore the weariest expression I've ever seen.

"Camilo," he said in slow English, "we are very grateful to have you here. I apologize that you were sent with the column to San Antonio Abad."

As he explained it, Comandante Paco had freelanced the

entire mission. No one above him in the guerrilla organization even knew of the trip, and no one below him had questioned its advisability. Paco's adventuring had brought Raul Hercules a severe reprimand from the national guerrilla leadership.

He confirmed much of his life story that I'd heard from the *compañeros*. He was not yet thirty, a native of nearby Llano Rancho. His formal education had stopped at the sixth grade. His father, a leader of the local Federation of Christian Peasants, was hacked to death in his bed by a squad of National Guardsmen.

Raul Hercules joined the Federation, too. With Salvador, his civilian counterpart in Guazapa, he'd also worked in the National Union of Day Laborers and helped found Buena Vista, one of the earliest peasant cooperatives established on Guazapa.

As it had prospered in the 1970s, Buena Vista became the focus of harassment and terror directed by a local warlord named Fabián Ventura. A member of the paramilitary *Organizacion Democratica Nacionalista* (ORDEN), Ventura maintained his own small band of thugs, a death squad whose intimidation of the Guazapan *campesinos* was coordinated with periodic National Guard incursions against their villages.

Ventura operated out of a small fortress located in the farm country north of Zapote, near San Antonio. Backed by his army and the threat of the National Guard troops he could call in at will, Ventura forced a yearly tribute from the Buena Vista cooperative as well as the many small farmers of the area. Resistance meant death; by 1980 he was thought responsible for dozens of murders in Guazapa, including that of Raul Hercules' father.

That summer, Raul Hercules, his two brothers, and a group of about twenty others stormed Ventura's headquarters. Armed only with pistols, a few shotguns, bolt-action rifles, and a single G-3 automatic, they overpowered his guards and killed the warlord. It was the first act of revolutionary violence in Guazapa, and it served as a catalyst for *campesino* mobilization.

As Raul Hercules told me this, I noted the small crucifix around his neck. I asked if he was religious.

"No," he said, "not anymore."

His voice softened.

"Camilo, I was raised on the message of Father Alas and Father Grande. Though others said we would never bring change without guns, we thought it was possible. We demonstrated, we organized, and we said 'no' for the first time in our lives. You know what it brought. You've heard the stories."

I nodded and he went on.

"Alas was kidnapped, drugged, beaten, and left for dead. Father Rutilio was machine gunned. My own father was cut into pieces."

Raul Hercules paused.

"That man Gulliver," he said to my infinite surprise, "you know him?" Apparently the comandante had heard a version of Jonathan Swift's adventure story.

"Gulliver went to a land where all the people were very small," he said. "When he stood up, he ripped apart the threads that they used to imprison him. Now we have stood up too."

Raul Hercules was as adamant as anyone I'd met on the question of Cuban or Nicaraguan intervention in El Salvador. He was affronted at the suggestion the *compañeros* needed outside help.

"We don't need Cubans, and we don't need Nicaraguans," he insisted. "And we don't need the *norteamericanos*. This is an authentic revolution as yours was. We know what we're fighting for."

He wasn't sanguine on the prospects for negotiating a peace, principally because he believed that the United States was committed to a military solution: extermination of the rebels.

That, Raul Hercules said, was impossible.

"You *norteamericanos* will not control our country, and neither will the Soviets. If we must fight to victory, we will. It is only a matter of time."

CHARLES CLEMENTS, M.D.

*   *   *

ROSA'S BABY DIED NEAR DAWN. As the morning sun began inching up the doorframe, I watched Raul Hercules console Rosa and thought how he, too, was living on borrowed time. I marveled at his certainty. He didn't seem to understand that historical forces far stronger than the FMLN/FDR agenda may shape the future of El Salvador. Military might beyond his reckoning could reduce his dreams to rubble. He told me that he accepted his own probable death before the revolution was won, but he had no doubts as to the struggle's outcome. Raul Hercules and the rest of the *campesinos* had stood up; nothing could push them back down on their knees.

The feeling of this common cause was very strong in Guazapa. Five separate insurgent organizations, the National Resistance (RN), the Armed Forces of Liberation (FAL), the Popular Forces of Liberation (FPL), the Revolutionary Army of the People (ERP), and the Revolutionary Party of Central American Workers (PRTC), were subsumed under the FMLN/FDR and all were closely coordinated in the general defense of the Front as well as in any major offensive actions. After several years of factionalism, this level of cooperation among the "tendencies," as they are called, has made the whole much more formidable than the sum of its parts.

I inferred from my conversation with Raul Hercules that the high price of this unity was the everlasting meetings, since no one was about to grant uninformed consent on strategic or tactical issues. My impression, however, was that he fully endorsed this time-consuming process. I chuckle to think what a U.S. general would say if his every command decision were put to a vote of five political blocs within his ranks!

I never did work out their system of rank. From all that I could gather, one was either a *compañero* or a comandante—nothing in-between. I was never certain if there was a formal rank of column leader. Some of the officers wore hip weapons and a beret with a little red star on it—"the Guevara look"—but many others did not. About the only reliable indicator that someone of importance was in the neighborhood would be the appearance of *compañeros* with sophisticated Israeli assault weapons such as Galils or Uzi machine guns, which experience told me were reserved for the leaders or their escorts.

All the columns were extremely mobile; rarely did they even pass through villages, but kept on constant patrol throughout the zone. These were the same patrols that in conjunction with fixed outposts provided an early warning system. I was impressed with their ability to keep track of one another with nothing more than a few radios and the use of the young *correos*.

They had little use for sophisticated communications among themselves. The need-to-know rule was extremely important; the more information a single *compañero* had, the more potential value he was to the enemy if he was caught. The few radios the insurgents did possess were of far greater utility as a means of monitoring the enemy's movement. Except in actual combat situations when they used code, the government soldiers were practically magpies. I listened once with a group of guerrillas as a government soldier bragged by radio to his counterpart in another unit about his latest *campesina* rape. On another occasion, a soldier boasted at what he and his buddies had just done to a captured guerrilla. It wasn't difficult to figure out where they d been, where they were, or where they were going.

The insurgent columns were usually, but not always, drawn from the local population. Raul Hercules told me that in the early days of the civil war the fighters didn't stray too far from home. By 1982, however, casualties and increasing mobility between controlled zones meant that a person from Guazapa might serve across the country in Usulután Province or vice versa.

The militias were a different matter. These irregulars, basically older men and younger boys, were responsible for local protection. As fighters, they were of lesser value; their weapons were old and barely functional. But they served a more important role as coordinators of the many *guindas* as well as a force that, if necessary, could be called upon to augment the guerrillas themselves. They also provided transport because of the shortage of horses and mules. When there was no responsibility as militiamen, most would either work in their own fields or in agricultural cooperatives.

THE ALL-NIGHT CONVERSATION with Raul Hercules had given me some sense of events, especially the "lost column" fiasco. Not only had he provided my first sense of the guerrilla organization, but his frankness and confidences mitigated my feelings of isolation. Salvador and Jasmine, while always cordial, were far too busy to sit down for a leisurely chat. So was I for that matter.

It wasn't homesickness that bothered me. Home, to me, has always been wherever I happen to be. What I missed were common points of reference. It was as easy to sympathize with the peasants as it was important, as a doctor and a Quaker, to work among them. But I would always be the outsider. Language was one barrier to a closer rapport. It would have helped a lot if I could have made myself better understood.

Yet the true distance was cultural. Almost nothing of my past, or my prospective future, meant anything to these people. Likewise, I did not share their bond with the land. They, in turn, had never taken an ice cube for granted, or made a long-distance phone call, or voted against a scoundrel without fear it could cost them their lives. A Huey they understood; a microwave oven was beyond their world.

I was probably closest to the old men there. One group especially, the elders of Copapayo, held me in the highest esteem because I was able to fix their radio. The operation was nothing much; I only soldered a broken circuit to restore the receiver to life. But in the eyes of Miguel and his pals, I was a miracle worker. Old David welcomed me warmly every time I came to El Zapote, and I was to make still another fast friend in the aged Chepe.

The occasion was a clinic in Tenango, Chepe's village.

So we improvised a birthing chair.

Her family's two beds were pushed together. We placed her between them, one knee on each bed and a board with a pillow on it for her to lean back against between contractions. She could steady herself with two ropes we rigged on either side.

Mariá took some fluids and followed my breathing instructions. I showed the midwife how to massage her perineum and her uncle rubbed her back. The baby's head began to emerge and Mariá started to scream.

I thought I heard some dogs barking and mules braying outside, but her screams drowned them out. Besides, my attention was focused on the child. Her color was good. There was no cord wrapped around her neck. The midwife was skillfully manipulating a shoulder through when, all of a sudden, the room began to shake!

"It's either B-52s or an earthquake," I thought. At twenty-two minutes past midnight, a shock registering 7.4 on the Richter scale rumbled under Central America. It lasted for thirty-seven seconds. At least a dozen people were killed and hundreds more were injured in mudslides.

In the adobe hut in Los Gramales on the slopes of the Guazapa volcano, Mariá's baby was fully born just as the quake hit. I quickly placed a clamp on the umbilical cord, pulled mother and newborn onto one of the two beds, and then we pushed them under the hut's single roof beam. Mariá was totally oblivious to it all. She lay there cooing to the child as adobe bricks fell around us and the other bed jumped around the room like a Tinkertoy.

The first tremor passed. I placed another clamp on the cord, cut it, handed the baby to the midwife, helped Mariá to her feet and then we all ran outside into the mud before the aftershocks could trap us in the house.

The earth continued to sway beneath us as the midwife helped Mariá deliver the placenta and I applied Merthiolate to her daughter's navel stump. It began to rain. We crouched under a poncho and waited for the earthquake to be over.

When we were at last able to go back inside, Mariá took

her first close look at the baby girl. The long labor had temporarily misshaped the infant's head and Mariá was concerned.

"Why is my baby's head pointed?" she asked.

Everyone laughed with relief.

WE SAW THE FIRST A-37s two days later. On a rare, bright morning—the summer solstice—I stood with Chepe in his cornfield, watching the sun glint from the jet cockpits as they circled and dove on Chaparral, to the northwest.

Chepe said nothing for a few minutes. He only looked far off toward Lake Suchitlán then back at the attacking fighters.

"It is the sky of the long day," he finally uttered cryptically.

I answered that it was going to be a long day and a long night for the *sanitarios* of Chaparral.

"No, abuelito," he said, "the sky of the long day is the Pipil way of saying summer is here."

Chepe had never seen a jet fighter attack before. The planes looked like toys to him. Later, when he had known the fury of an A-37 sortie, I reminded him of his words that first morning. The sky of the long day became our term for a heaven rattling death down on Guazapa.

The A-37 "Dragonfly" provoked superstitious awe in Chepe and the rest. Watching an attack from afar, they could see a pilot pull up after a strafing run before hearing the thunderous report of his 7.62-calibre Gatling gun. I tried to explain to them that light travels faster than sound, but they chose to believe that the pilots had eyes in the backs of their heads, that they could shoot backward even as they flew away from a target.

I feared the aircrafts' destructive potential as much as any of them; the A-37 is the combat version of the trainers we flew in flight school. I knew what the jets could do in the hands of an able pilot.

When they began their predictable bombing approaches, I could tell at a distance where they were headed. If their

Scenes of Quipurito:

Comandante Ramón

Nico addressing his *correos*.

Infants in Guazapa were often tended by the elderly. Their drawings reflect their reality.

Selvin and Lia from Copapayo with their infant boy, Frederico's and Isabel's only grandchild.

A "Delegate of the Word" conducts a funeral service.

A military wedding of two combatants.

A review of the Ramón Belloso battalion.   CINDY KARP

A collection of homemade booby traps.

The versatile Huey helicopter that resupplied the volcano-top garrison from which life in Guazapa was constantly monitored.
CLAUDE URRACA/SYGMA

The principal means of transportation along with prized, captured equipment.   IAN

A training session.   DON NORTH

Ramiro was afraid to come out of his bomb shelter/cave long after the airplanes had gone.   DON NORTH

War From the Skies:

The spotter planes and helicopters seldom missed an opportunity to kill livestock caught in the open.
RICHARD CROSS/ARCHIVES

After the air attacks by A-37's intensified, every home, clinic, or school was encouraged to deepen and strengthen their bomb shelters.   DON NORTH

Door gunner in a Huey helicopter scanning a guerrilla controlled zone with an M-60 machine gun.
CLAUDE URRACA/SYGMA

An A-37 "Dragon Fly" jet fighter bomber. The wings can carry a variety of ordnance including fire and demolition bombs, guns, and rockets for a total of 5,680 lbs. A six-barrelled 7.62 minigun installed in the forward fuselage fires 6,000 rounds per minute.   US AIR FORCE PHOTO

Remnants of a cannister which contained a napalm-like substance dropped near the village of Delicias in December 1982.

Battlefield Medicine:
Dorita cleansing a mortar fragment from a wound.
The main ward of Jasmine's hospital.   DON NORTH

A *compañero* recuperating at home in "Salvadoran ambulance." CINDY KARP

Antonito (front) and the "Christmas Choir" with an elderly couple at the hospital.

Jasmine changing Fredi's dressings. Five-year-old Fredi suffered extensive burns when a white phosphorous rocket struck his home. His older sister died in the same attack.   DON NORTH

Lines of trenches formed part of the defensive perimeter and early warning system in the controlled zones.
RICHARD CROSS/ARCHIVES

Women spent long hours each day washing, boiling, grinding, and cooking corn or sorghum into tortillas.
LORRAINE GUAY

The volcano Guazapa as seen from the sugar cane fields near Delicias.
DON NORTH

Guazapa's Civilians:

After David's death, this man was one of only two ropemakers in the Guazapa front.
DON NORTH

A day's catch from the fishing cooperative.

Guazapa's Military:

Comandante Raul Hercules was born and raised on the slopes of Guazapa.

A guerrilla confronting his former neighbor, now a prisoner-of-war.
DON NORTH

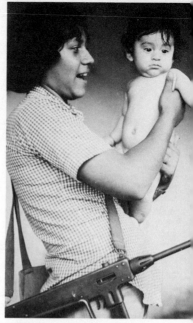

Magdaleno, age 61, was Guazapa's oldest combatant. FRANK CHRISTOPHER/ PAN AMERICAN FILMS

A Guazapa guerrilla holding up her infant.   ANNE NELSON

Arlena, nicknamed *"La Chinita"* (far R), and other women combatants before the election-day offensive.
FRANK CHRISTOPHER/PAN AMERICAN FILMS

Chepe from Tenango still in shock after his home was demolished by an A-37 attack. DON NORTH

The last photo of Frederico (second from R) and his family. Isabel (far L) and Janet (center) holding Noe.

Several thousand civilians were in the *guinda* of February 1983. Forced to flee in daylight, many were killed. DON NORTH

El Salvador

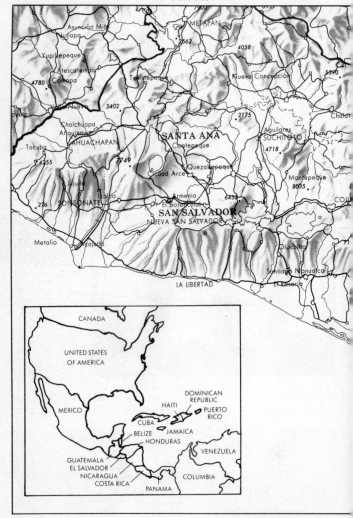

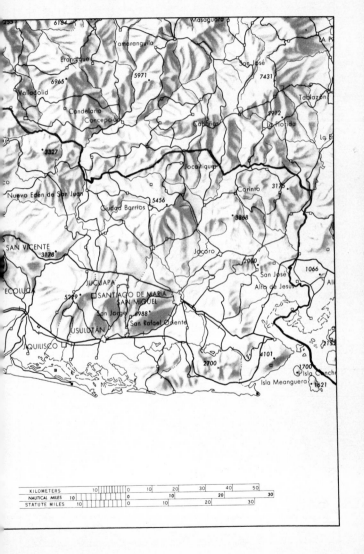

KILOMETERS	10	0	10	20	30	40	50
NAUTICAL MILES	10	0	10		20		30
STATUTE MILES	10	0	10		20		30

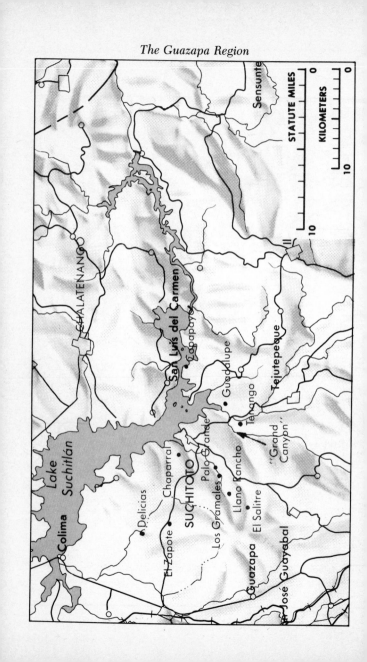

The Guazapa Region

flight attitude indicated they were coming directly toward me, I would take cover. Otherwise I stood and watched the attack as the *campesinos* all dove for cover. Not understanding this, the peasants thought me very brave.

In truth, the A-37s were very badly piloted. Once in a while, I would see a lead jet go into a series of maneuvers called "jinking" in pilot slang, dives and rolls designed to avoid surface-to-air missiles (SAMs) or anti-aircraft fire. The pilot clearly was much more skilled and daring than the Salvadorans who usually flew over us. I assumed he was an American or a mercenary, and I could imagine him radioing back to say, "Watch me, boys, and see if you can do it."

Generally, they could not. Typical of their raids was one on Palo Grande and Llano Rancho that I watched from the clinic in El Zapote. A propeller-driven spotter plane accompanied the flight of A-37s, marking their targets with white phosphorous incendiary rockets. All the markers came down on the villages, not on military targets.

The jets stayed ridiculously high; there was no weapon in Guazapa capable of reaching them and their high altitude made bombing accuracy impossible. More to the point from a military perspective, the pilots could have made out the guerrilla camps by watching where they drew the ineffective ground fire. Instead, they bombed the civilians. Anything could invite attack from clothes hanging out to dry to a cooking fire. Outdoor gatherings of people were always an invitation.

When the attack ended, I hurried back to Jasmine's hospital fearful of what I'd find there. To my infinite relief, all the bombing and strafing hadn't killed anyone and had wounded only five people, four *campesinos* and one guerrilla. In fact, the most serious damage had been done by a *sanitario* who had neglected to clean a foot wound before he sutured it. When I opened the incision the next day, I found bits of dirt and leaves inside.

Raul Hercules called several anxious consultations to which I was invited. Not only were the A-37 and Huey attacks increasing in intensity, but we also began hearing an

American C-130 flying over us each night, loaded with ordnance and bound for San Salvador's Ilopango Airport, where the rockets and bombs were placed aboard the fighters to be dropped on us. The urgent military question was could, or should, the Guazapa guerrillas try to shoot these planes down?

My opinion had been solicited once before when the *compañeros* came back from a raid with an 81mm mortar they had captured. They had also come away with a dozen "papayas," as they called the mortar rounds. Gleeful at securing their prize, they were troubled by just one thing—they didn't know how to use it.

Raul Hercules was aware that I wouldn't serve as a military advisor; he restricted himself to asking only if I would translate the manual they had captured with it. On that point I could plead ignorance. As far as I knew, a mortar is fired by dropping a round down the tube and then plugging one's ears. That is about all they knew, too.

He asked me, for instance, if "mils" on the range chart meant "miles." When I allowed, with an unintended smirk, that I had no idea, his pride must have been wounded.

"We know how to work a mortar," he said. "It's just the details."

I refused to counsel them on these matters, but I listened to their debates over the merits of acquiring hand-held surface-to-air missiles or other such arms to counter the air attacks The sentiment among them clearly was in favor of blasting as many A-37s and C-130s from the sky as they could. But the risk such a course would entail—the use of Soviet-made SAMs, and the retaliation that their successful use might bring—persuaded Raul Hercules against requesting the weapons. Although SAMs are available from a wide variety of free market arms dealers, it would be too easy for the United States to charge they had been given to the insurgents by the Russians.

Such as it was, their single weapon against the warplanes was an old .30 calibre machine gun. After the air attacks began, I saw it criss-crossing the Front, bowing two or three *compañeros* under its weight. They had about as much chance of hitting an A-37 as bringing down a flying duck with a bow and arrow, but they persisted. For a while everyone agreed the best place for the .30 calibre was Los Gramales, near where I delivered the baby on the night of the earthquake. Then it was moved to Palo Grande, El Zapote, and down to the farm country near Chaparral. I don't think they ever did position it in the right place at the right time.

Few people were actually killed in the air raids, but their advent ratcheted up the level of tension and fear. We already knew what was happening to the north. One night I picked up "The Larry King Show" on my radio and listened to phone callers discuss with the host the recent attacks against Chalatenango in the north. They debated a *Washington Post* story detailing charges of massacres in the province and the Salvadoran government's denials of atrocities. I was in a mood to phone King myself and share a few of my observations.

We saw the reinforcement of the government's volcano-top garrison and heard reports of troop concentrations in Suchitoto and other towns around our perimeter. Roberto d'Aubuisson, now President of the Constituent Assembly, announced on the radio that the guerrillas would all be exterminated in six months. He specifically indicated that the Ramón Belloso Battalion was being sent against the "subversives" in and around Guazapa.

PREPARATIONS FOR A *guinda* began. Families secreted their few valuables in *buzones* (underground hiding places) that might escape the soldiers' detection. What little corn was left from the previous crop was turned into easily transportable tortillas and packed for departure. All around the Front, the clinics prepared hammocks for the evacuation of the wounded and very ill.

We would survive only because the Salvadoran military was a fundamentally inept organization. They had the Front practically surrounded and vastly outnumbered. They controlled the skies and enjoyed limitless supplies. The few defenders were ill-equipped, practically starving, virtually cut off from any possible source of aid, and had 9,000 civilians to protect.

Yet the FMLN comandantes and their shabby little army outfoxed the enemy at every turn. Just as the Belloso Battalion was poised to sweep through the northern villages, the guerrillas launched a diversionary assault across Lake Suchitlán. A freshman cadet at the Air Force Academy wouldn't have been suckered by such a tactic, but the Belloso Battalion was. To our great delight, the entire unit turned around and headed off into the Chalatenango highlands in search of the insurgents. The move bought us precious weeks.

Then a daring raid was launched on the garrison in Suchitoto. Using small arms and grenades, a commando detachment struck quickly in the night and with lethal effect. According to sympathizers in the town, the government hospital was crowded to overflowing with wounded soldiers.

In eastern El Salvador, a rebel offensive was begun in Morazán Province. To relieve government pressure on these attackers, the Guazapa guerrillas cut the Suchitoto highway in half and practically invited a counterattack from San Salvador. The government soldiers stayed in their barracks.

I've heard it said that there are no bad soldiers, only bad officers. Whatever the truth of that saying, this former officer found much wanting in the deployment and use of government soldiers.

But "bad" does not necessarily equal inept. Leadership, no matter how inexperienced or stupid, can inspire heroism. The British proved this in the Crimea, the Sudan, and in Galipoli. If today the Salvadoran soldier is a question mark, it is largely, I believe, because of the venality and corruption of his officers.

In 1976, Colonel Manuel Rodríguez, then Salvadoran armed forces chief of staff, was convicted in the United States for plotting to sell 10,000 U.S.-manufactured sub-machine guns to American gangsters. Egregious as it was, the attempted sale was no surprise in El Salvador, where colonels are rewarded for loyalty with posts in which they may amply provide for their old age. One is the postal service, which processes all foreign money orders. While I was in El Salvador, it was announced that its chief, a high-ranking officer, committed suicide after disclosures he'd "disappeared" several millions of dollars in stolen money orders.

Under war conditions, the opportunities for graft multiply. Salvadoran commanders maintain phantom payrolls, a practice that was common among South Vietnamese military leaders, too. The army commanders have incentives for keeping their troops out of the field. The officers receive allotments to feed their men. It is much cheaper to do so in a garrison than during operations. The soldiers can dodge hazardous duty with a few *colones*, I was later told by POWs. Guazapa, known among them as "the graveyard," is one zone where ten *colones* tendered to the right sergeant can excuse you from a night patrol along the Suchitoto highway.

AT LEAST FOR A WHILE, Guazapa was out of danger. People dug up their *buzones*, the guerrilla columns scaled back their state of alert, and we all turned to preparations for harvest.

It was early July, and the corn was almost ready. Every day, teams of workers went into the fields to fight back the weeds. It was heavy work with their crude implements, but the slow passing of the rains and the promise of food put vigor into their labor.

Then came the harvest itself! All of a sudden, the gardens and plots yielded their bounty. Above all, now corn was king. The ears were boiled, broiled, baked, and steamed. There was corn soup, corn bread, corn candy, corn on the cob, corn tamales, corn underfoot, corn everywhere. Guazapa became a corn utopia.

The children's bony arms and distended bellies disappeared in a matter of days. The chickens and livestock perked up. Everyone beamed their pleasure at full stomachs and filling granaries. I gained five pounds in a week.

I hadn't realized how hungry and sick I was; feeling miserable was the norm. Even though my feet finally had healed and my weight had stabilized around 125 pounds, the dysentery had been a constant drain on my strength. Before I cured it, I was intimately familiar with every type of leaf around Guazapa.

The mosquitoes flourished in the rainy season and there was no escaping them. I was used to the fleas by now. The first time I found nits of lice in my hair I was almost indifferent. As vermin go, they're more or less benign. Sometimes I was wet for days, causing fungi to appear randomly on my body. I was resigned to the itch forever. This was rural El Salvador in the rainy season.

I also developed a common local condition the *campesinos* call neuritis. By June, every time I sat down or leaned against something or even rested my arm on a table my muscles would go numb. If I rested on my side, half my body would stay asleep for hours after I rose.

It's hard to say what caused the condition, although I believe it was due to the lack of fatty acids in our diet. One day in early July, I was given an egg and a bowl of broth with a drumstick in it. Within seventy-two hours, the numbness disappeared.

The food couldn't cure the rest of my ailments, but at least it restored some of my strength and buoyed my sagging spirits. Moreover, it relieved, for a time, some of the grosser, endemic medical problems among the civilians. The stronger the children became, the less susceptible they were to childhood illnesses like measles, which can be fatal to a malnourished child.

The best, however, was yet to come. One day in Palo Grande, around sunset, as many as fifty militiamen arrived from several directions at once. Since I knew of no current military emergency, I assumed they had some other purpose. But what?

I got my answer the next morning. After gathering out of my earshot, the militiamen had quickly filed off toward the southeast. They returned about 5:30 A.M., each carrying a large nylon sack. One by one, they brought these bags to the hospital, set them on the ground, and then walked off. I couldn't for the life of me figure out what they were doing.

Then Jasmine appeared and greeted me with a broad smile.

"Good morning, Camilo," she said cheerily. "Today, we have much to do."

I'd never seen her so animated.

"Your North American friends have sent us a great present," she announced with a gesture toward the pile of bags. "Those sacks are filled with medicines!"

Indeed they were. As I would later learn, several United States medical support committees had contributed to this bonanza, maybe $10,000 worth of critically important medicines. The gesture made a deep impression upon Jasmine as well as the health workers—a message of life, of hope, from the American people, compared to the daily messages of death we were now receiving from the United States government.

Like children on Christmas morning, we gleefully set about opening the sacks and inventorying their contents. What a trove!

There were lots of IV solutions, analgesics from aspirin to Demerol, antibiotics, anti-psychotics, and tranquilizers. I found a store of Dilantin for the many epileptic patients. Head injuries, a common cause of seizures, were frequent in the zone. We found two blood pressure cuffs, six stethoscopes, many reusable syringes, plaster for casts, splints, tubing, and sutures.

One bag contained a precious supply of anesthetics; another yielded antihistamines, antacids, and even a few birth control pills that were an especially welcome sight. Menstrual irregularities were rampant in Guazapa, and the pills would help cycle so many of the women concerned about losing their periods.

These supplies had been assembled with great care; someone who knew something about tropical medicine had helped plan it. He or she had made sure to include antibiotics as well as anthelminthics, remedies for our specific types of worms and parasites. Dysentery, mine as well as a lot of other peoples', could be treated now. They had laid on a good supply of anti-malarials. We even found iron tablets, material for treating burns, anti-parasitics, and some asthma medicine

After so many weeks of frustration and dashed hopes, the events of July seemed too good to be true. The enemy had been checked, the weather had cleared, we had plenty of food, and now Jasmine and I had the wherewithal to truly practice medicine, at least for a while.

I confidently plotted an expanded public health program for the zone If the peasants knew we could dispense pills, they were much more amenable toward cooperating with our preventive health measures. These initiatives—the sanitation programs, the use of natural remedies, the training of the *sanitarios*, the broadening of the *campesino* diet—would now have time to take effect.

Jasmine was a key to my aspirations. Besides myself. she was the only person on the Front with anything approaching a formal medical education. She, and Dorita, supported every one of my ideas and spared me not only the responsibility for military medicine but also the many hours of presenting and defending the programs before the bureaucracy. Without her endorsement and support. I would have been at the mercy of Lupe as well as every skeptic on the Front

I guess I took this protection for granted, just as I saw no reason to question how long our luck would hold out. Something in me refused to dwell on what might go wrong. But go wrong things most assuredly would. And the unraveling of all my great expectations began on July 31, 1982. the day I was informed that Jasmine had vanished

GUINDA

AT FIRST, I WAS TOLD THAT JASMINE would be gone only for a few days. This presented no immediate problem. My attention at the time was focused on the completion of the new civilian hospital in Palo Grande.

It was their pride, a tangible symbol of community and the peasants' determination to build their new society even while the Salvadoran government sought to destroy them. Unlike any of the other facilities, which were nothing more than converted houses or sheds, the new hospital had been planned as a medical building. Its main ward was large enough to accommodate up to eight beds, or as many as twelve hammocks. There was an examining room with a fixed table that would double nicely as an operating room. We had a secure storage area and a pharmacy that was even fitted with a window from which medicines could be dispensed.

Keeping the supplies under lock and key would be a big step toward drug control; one of the more serious medical problems on the Front was tranquilizer abuse. In a month when I might personally prescribe forty tablets in all, seven or eight times that many were consumed. Now we could preserve them for when they were really needed.

Each village on the Front contributed to the hospital's construction. The men of Zapote, for instance, cut rot-resistant eucalyptus trees and shaped them into roof beams. The women of Chaparral fashioned the clay tiles for the roof. A crew of artisans from Delicias put up the adobe walls. A militia column ventured outside the Front to an abandoned village near Suchitoto where they salvaged boards to build the examining table, window frames, and doors.

All seemed well except for the curious and continuing absence of Jasmine. I knew she wasn't dead or wounded, and I knew her sense of duty was too strong for her to have abandoned her responsibilities. After a week with no sign of her, I went to Raul Hercules. When I asked just how long the head of military medicine would be absent, he turned his palms up, shrugged, and said that I would be taking over her duties. His posture discouraged any further discussion.

No one ever did give me an explanation for Jasmine's disappearance; apparently it was a matter of security. Weeks and then months passed before she returned. By then, most of the public health initiatives among the civilians had collapsed from neglect. Keeping my wits as de facto head of all medicine on the Front was challenge enough.

The first of the new demands was physical. I was forced to suspend clinic rounds and then to move my base from the new hospital to Jasmine's smaller, less convenient facility. The two structures were separated by a wide, deep ravine: siting them too close together, it was reasoned, would only invite attention from enemy aircraft. Now I found that every time a military casualty, black or green, was brought to Palo Grande, I had to climb a mile up-and-down through mudslides and brambles. They always seemed to come at night.

Reluctantly, I took up residence at the old hospital. By now, it was somewhat more capacious; a small surgery annex had been added and the sleeping porch covered over. As many as eighteen patients could be accommodated.

But it was no more sanitary than the first day I beheld it. Margarita, the head nurse, took personal offense when I requested the piles of debris be cleaned up. The first night I slept there, a call came to assist a midwife with a complicated, double-footling breech birth. I was up most of the night. When I returned at dawn, someone was sleeping in my hammock. Mindful of my gaffe with Raul Hercules, I decided to let the intruder slumber on, and took myself to the annex where I curled up on the floor.

"Lazy gringo!" I heard Margarita bark a few hours later. "With Jasmine gone, he sleeps all day! You must move so we can do examinations."

Margarita, who somehow thought me responsible for Jasmine's disappearance, proved to be even more hostile and nettlesome than Lupe. The situation was impossible enough without her gratuitous sniping. The only person for whom she harbored greater enmity was Marco, a curt and self-important military surgeon who came onto the Front just as Jasmine vanished.

Marco was a macho caricature. His hair was cut very short. He affected a razor-thin mustache, aviator glasses, expensive boots, and freshly laundered shirts. His snug Levi's completed the ensemble and, to my amusement, caused him no end of discomfort. As Lupe and Francisco had experienced in Quipurito, the fleas were drawn to tight-fitting spots. Marco cursed them when we operated together, scratching his legs against the table as we worked.

City-bred and, from what I could see, a very well-trained surgeon, he made it clear that operating on *campesinos* wasn't a priority. Even I, his professional peer, didn't warrant much collegiality. Marco called me "gringo" in a tone that translated "ptui."

Our first consultation came the day of the A-37 attack on Palo Grande. The peasant with the shrapnel wound in her foot had suffered a severed Achilles tendon as well and was in danger of a life-threatening infection from the sloppy suture done by a *sanitario*. I would have preferred to watch Marco operate on her, but he refused to scrub. As I fumbled through this delicate surgery, he mixed helpful directions with pointed comments at my awkward use of surgical instruments.

At least Marco was even-handed; he treated everyone as his inferior. On another occasion, he deigned to assist me and my untrained assistants as we desperately tried to save a *campesino* who had accidentally been injured by a guerrilla landmine.

The device was one of many homemade booby traps that the guerrillas had sown around a citrus orchard just outside the limits of the Front. Enemy soldiers repeatedly came through the orchard, tearing off all the fruit and ripping up many of the trees. Before they could come through again, this farmer had stepped on one of the mines and literally shredded himself.

His right leg had been torn off, and he had sustained several minor abdominal and thoracic injuries. The blood loss alone was mortal, but he had somehow retained consciousness right up to the time we put him on the table. The entire hospital staff gathered at the door, listening and weeping as he told me that he knew he would die but that he appreciated our care. He was humble and very dignified.

I couldn't begin to stop his hemorrhaging nor, at the time, were we equipped to do transfusions. As he bled, the dirt floor beneath our feet turned to red mud. I slipped several times as I tried to adjust the IV. Before he died, we put fully three liters of saline solution into his arm; his heart was circulating little more than salt water by the time it gave out.

Though the best trauma unit in the world might not have saved his life, that didn't deter Marco from complaining all during and after the surgery. He was imperious with the *sanitarios* who I believed were ready to turn the scalpels on him at any moment. So furious was Margarita that she dropped her personal hostility toward me to concentrate on Marco.

* * *

HE MADE HIMSELF A FURTHER NUISANCE when it came to the distribution of the medicine. Among the three staples of life in Guazapa, food, arms, and medicines, the last was easily the chanciest to procure. Rifles and bullets, while hardly abundant, were nevertheless available. With the coming of the harvest, there would be food enough for everyone for the foreseeable future. But medical supplies were becoming rarer and rarer everywhere in El Salvador.

One way of procuring them was from the army itself; for a price, the soldiers would rifle their own infirmaries. While there was always the possibility that they would sell and tell, it wasn't necessarily any riskier to deal with them than a pharmacist.

Many newspapers and occasionally television stations in El Salvador advertised a convenient telephone hotline for reporting "subversives." A store owner, or employee, or one of the ubiquitous *orejas* ("ears" or informants) could expect a reward of up to several thousand dollars if his or her information led to the apprehension of an important enough guerrilla.

Our guess was that Camilo, the *sanitario* from Salitre who was Lupe's companion, fell victim to this civic-mindedness. He and a group of *compañeros* went to San Salvador in search of general anesthetics as well as specific medicines like digitalis and diuretics for our many elderly heart patients. Somewhere along their return route, they were "disappeared."

Among the many items declared contraband by the government was gauze. Word that someone had bought even a small quantity of it was sufficient to start the *orejas* dialing for dollars.

Once, during the late spring, Jasmine asked one of the peasant women if, on her bi-monthly trip to San Salvador, she would bring back some cloth diapers—our gauze substitute. On the bus trip back, or so several witnesses later said, the woman was asked for her identification card. She produced it, but the card lacked an election stamp. Several soldiers pulled her off the bus. As the rest of the riders looked on, they searched her bag, found the diapers, and then marched her away. She was never seen again.

A similar fate befell one of Miguel's nephews. One afternoon, the old man told me, his arthritis had twisted him into knots of agony. Seeing his uncle suffer so, the twelve-year-old took it upon himself to walk outside the Front to a small town where he bought a bottle of one hundred aspirins. In El Salvador, it is common to buy aspirin as few as two at a time; the bulk purchase of mild analgesics raised someone's suspicions. Several days later, the boy was found dead.

At the first of our conferences called to hammer out the division of the medical supplies, one of the *sanitarios* told how a woman from his sector was sent out for a one-hundred-tablet package of the anti-malarial chloroquine. Her mutilated body was later discovered, the package of pills stuffed in her mouth.

I also discovered in these meetings that if exigency, or the common need for defense against government invasions, helped unite the five tendencies, or factions, in Guazapa, a stroke of fortune could create an opposite, divisive effect.

The divisions, in part institutionalized, were a result of the spectrum of attitudes and experiences among the five rebel tendencies. The FAL, for instance, became the military arm of the old Communist Party. It was among the smallest tendencies and had been the last to take up arms. The FPL and RN, both strong on Guazapa, enjoyed broad support among the peasants and trade union members. A principal difference between their tactical outlooks was reflected in one's emphasis upon organization by taking over leadership of various unions, while the other sought to build a base at the worker level. The ERP, the most militaristic of the five, fielded the largest number of combatants, but was slowest to be concerned with popular organizing. The PRTC had begun in the mid-1970s as part of a regional organization, which looked at issues from a Central American perspective. In 1980, however, its national units separated into distinct parties.

As components of the FMLN, they all agreed on the necessity for armed revolution and nominally subscribed to Marxism-Leninism. But subsumed as well under the political platform and leadership of the FDR, they made common cause with groups as diverse as the Association of Slum Dwellers, the Popular Social Christian Movement, and a professional association of doctors, engineers, and lawyers known as the Independent Movement of Salvadoran Professionals and Technicians, to name but a few of the member organizations.

Marco, for instance, came to the conferences as the representative of a tendency with few civilian adherents in Guazapa, but several military columns. He wanted one-fifth of all the medicine for his faction's *compañeros* and argued that the other *tendencias*, two of which included thousands of civilians and very few guerrillas, should also each receive one-fifth of the total.

He defended this disproportionate allocation by frequently using buzz words such as "heroic combatants" and the rest of the revolutionary jargon he seemed to favor. In the same wooden tones, William, *campesino* from Guazapa, who was the representative from a *tendencia* that would get short shrift under Marco's plan, declared, "That is an extremely important point of view. However, those heroic combatants to whom you refer have wives or husbands and children, mothers and fathers, whose well-being is on their minds. It is those *campesinos* who grow our food. Therefore, we cannot say the priority for distribution of medicines is to the combatants."

This speech-making and posturing went on for several more meetings. We usually gathered in an old coffee *finca* (farm) near Palo Grande where, ironically, our usual liquid refreshment was tea from Marco's private supply. While it would seem logical to drink coffee on a coffee plantation, such was not the case.

To Marco, who placed great store in the perquisites of rank, the hospital collective was being arrogant and impertinent for refusing to provide fresh coffee to lubricate his orations. Margarita reminded him that the beans had to be picked, dried, pounded in a huge mortar to remove their shells, then roasted and ground before they could be brewed. If he cared to help the *sanitarios* in that work, they would be happy to produce more than the small amount of coffee given to the patients.

I had no difficulty siding with her on this issue or with William on the ultimate distribution of the medicine. Argue as Marco might, he and his one ally at the meetings were voted down. The medicine would be shared as needed.

To my surprise, word that I had opposed Marco spread throughout the community and put me in great favor among some of the *campesinos* whose pride he had injured. While I regarded the two-week confab as a necessary, but irritating exercise in administration, my role in defending the rights of the peasants even impressed the vinegary Margarita. While she still resented me as Jasmine's replacement, she did stop calling me lazy.

Marco could have cared less what the *campesinos* thought. He was the first and only of the guerrilla leaders I met who seemed to view the farmers as either too naive or too slow to comprehend the grander sweep of the revolution. Undoubtedly his opinions were heavily influenced by his military as well as his medical responsibilities.

Still, for all his drawbacks as a person, he was of undoubted value to the Front. As angry as I could get with him, I also respected Marco for putting his life on the line to tend the *compañeros*. He came from the privileged class against which this insurgency was being fought. Life would have been far easier and far safer if he had remained in San Salvador and treated the rich.

I found out about Marco's background from one who understood him well. Salvador possessed diplomatic skills far beyond mine. Without his help we might not have steered those medical meetings to a satisfactory conclusion.

"We are creating a new society," he told me during one of our frequent evening conversations. "Everyone must contribute and everyone must be heard. It is unfortunate that people like Marco do not as yet know how to talk to the people, but the important thing is that he is here with us."

Salvador, like Ramón and Raul Hercules, was remarkably free of cant and sloganeering. Not one of these men was out of his thirties, yet they each had enough political and social maturity that I could easily envision any of them—should they survive—assuming important roles in a future government. Not only were they plotting military strategy, trying to protect the lives of the *campesinos*, and raising their own families, but they were also seeing to the foundation of Salvadoran democracy.

FAR LESS ACCESSIBLE, and far more mysterious, was the redoubtable Pedro. I was curious about Pedro from the moment I met him. He was my size, fair-complected, and about thirty years old. Judging by his soft hands, small paunch, and limited physical endurance, I assumed he was from the city.

Pedro came into the Front in June and was assigned as my assistant even though I had not asked for one or been asked if I needed such a helper. He accompanied me everywhere, helping with the patients, socializing with the people, and twitting me for overworking the both of us. My compulsiveness, he said, was a product of life under voracious capitalism. I replied that it was probably laziness, not the benign influence of socialist thought, that took him to a hammock each afternoon while I continued to see patients.

We got along quite well. Pedro was a very quick student and a great help in aiding the *campesinos* to understand the doctor's orders. Everyone looked forward to seeing him as we made our rounds of the villages. But he was no simple patriot. Like everyone else, Pedro was secretive. I never learned his real name, and his only concession to my curiosity was that his home was Costa Rica. Even that shred of self-revelation wasn't necessarily true.

He didn't bother to tell me where he learned so much about medicine, or how he knew the best way to prune tomato plants, or his technique for lancing a boil on a horse's back. He also didn't explain his skill with weapons.

One night, as we crossed the "Grand Canyon" on our way to Copapayo, a rattlesnake began clattering in the dark ahead of us. My old horse bolted and nearly pitched me off the trail and into the chasm. Pedro took charge immediately. Shouting for us all to be still, he flipped on his cigarette lighter and located the snake. He coolly produced his .45, and by the lighter's glow and from a distance of several yards, he blasted the rattler's head off.

Not until Pedro was ready to tell me would I learn the true nature of his mission; until then, I contented myself with light conversation. One tack was to open up some of my life to him in the hopes that he would reciprocate.

I told him of my Vietnam experiences since he was very knowledgeable about Vietnam, and of the months I spent at Wilford Hall. He was surprised but very understanding when I explained how the psychiatric discharge had left me feeling as ashamed as I was bitter about the Air Force. My lone foray into the anti-war movement, an attempt to try draft counseling in Austin, went badly. I suppose my haircut was a dead give-away, because I had barely explained who I was, when a militant sneered at me and accused me of being a "baby-killer trying to atone for imperialist war crimes." I didn't seem to belong anywhere. I felt I needed time for reflection and to think through my future. Most of all, I wanted to get away.

An opportunity to do this came in the form of an old, three-masted tall ship cruising the Caribbean and scheduled to become an excursion vessel in the South Pacific. Its owner had placed an ad in the *Los Angeles Times*: "Crewmen wanted, no experience necessary; meals, travel, and a dollar a day." I'd always wanted to learn to sail, and I'd never been to Tahiti. That spring, I signed on.

In some ways, recalling my days as an ordinary seaman had a sort of tonic effect upon me. It was my unspoken assumption that Pedro knew most of the ports I recollected and could follow with his mind's eye some of the more remote scenery I talked of. I realized in the midst of telling the saga that I truly missed the company of people whose horizons stretched beyond El Salvador. Maybe I just needed to talk.

"Have you ever been to Punta Arenas?" I asked Pedro, knowing that if he was a Costa Rican he should be familiar with this port city. Besides, one of my first adventures had been there.

"Por cierto, Camilo," he answered.

"Do you know the Three Sisters of Virtue?"

This was my little test. The Three Sisters of Virtue was an infamous waterfront bar in Punta Arenas. I remember it well because it was there in the late spring of 1971 that my shipmates held me down while a prostitute pierced my ear and inserted a gold ring in it—my seaman's insignia.

Pedro described the bar in convincing detail; if he wasn't Costa Rican, he had certainly spent some time there. He was also very good at always shifting the conversation back to me and my exploits. And I was only too happy to keep on talking about them.

I told him how we lurched on to Los Angeles and then headed southwest across the Pacific toward Tahiti. I was fine for the first five days, but spent the next thirteen in isolation under a little tent atop the galley; somewhere in Mexico, I had contracted hepatitis.

Worried about catching hepatitis, the captain and my crewmates were happy to leave me on the island of Nukahiva in the Marquesa chain, where I spent most of the summer of 1971 convalescing. It really wasn't so bad there. I had a pile of books and the view of the Pacific from my rented thatched hut was terrific. Because you cannot eat fatty foods with hepatitis, I became a vegetarian. Actually, I'd contemplated vegetarianism ever since Vietnam; the stench of burned or rotting flesh had been so common there that a steak could make me queasy. As I studied non-violence, I found a further, spiritual motive to confine myself to fruits and vegetables.

It took two months for the hepatitis to clear up. Then I left Nukahiva for Tahiti aboard a passing banana boat. In Tahiti, I took a job as a tractor driver for a Tahitian farmer, and spent several weeks as a salvage diver near Bora Bora.

Pedro urged me on in these reminiscences. In a rainstorm one night, I told him of the time a flying fish had leapt into the hood of my jacket. He was reduced to convulsions of laughter when I explained that this had happened while I was on watch and that my first fear had been of some giant squid grabbing for my neck to pull me under.

There were other bizarre stories. For a time, I served as a cook aboard a leaky plywood sailboat that had been built in Brooklyn. Its owner, a man in his twenties whom I'll call Bill, had finished the craft at just the time his draft notice came. Instead of going for his physical, he launched himself out into the Atlantic. Now he and I and another refugee sailor from New Zealand decided to head for a tiny atoll in the Cook Islands where, we understood, a hermit by the name of Tom Neal lived. Tom had not been heard from in three years.

We found him all right, the emaciated lord of an islet in the Pacific, no bigger than a football field at high tide, where Tom tended his garden, fished in the lagoon, and very occasionally welcomed a stranger to his realm.

He was very happy to see us. I fixed Tom a breadfruit pizza, and Bill rolled him a couple of cigarettes. I had fixed a special treat for all of us—a chocolate cake. I passed the small eight-by-eight-inch pan to Tom, and we watched in awe as he slowly consumed the entire cake! Living alone, we decided, didn't accustom him to the social graces.

We told him that a man had stood on the moon, and he introduced us to coconut crabs, immensely strong beasts that feed exclusively upon coconuts, which they are able to open with their claws. We caught one of them, placed it under a tin can, and then secured it with a twenty-five-pound stone. The crab pushed the apparatus off him as easily as he might have snapped my femur.

By July of 1972, I was in Fiji and applying for a teaching post at the University of the South Pacific.

With supplemental income from part-time employment as a private pilot, I taught physics at the University until December. It was in Fiji that I began seriously to consider studying medicine. The notion had been with me ever since Vietnam, where I felt the only positive roles were played by the medics and physicians and those pilots who rescued and ferried the wounded.

I had a broader motive for seeking a medical degree, however. The vivid images of disease and hunger I had seen during my first brief stay in India had remained with me, and the misery I saw among the Vietnamese civilians only reinforced the sense that much of the world lived in deprivation. I did not think in political terms about the enormous gap between haves and have-nots, nor did I feel guilty about the advantages I enjoyed as an American. I was deeply disillusioned by our involvement in Vietnam, but questions of imperialism and exploitation didn't interest me nearly as much as the perceived opportunity to alleviate suffering.

My upbringing had predisposed me to equate career with duty; it was a mode of thinking—a conditioned approach, if you will—that even my ordeal with the United States Air Force couldn't undo.

From Fiji, I wrote to a number of medical schools in New Zealand, my next stop. When I got there, however, I was told that twenty-seven was considered too old to start medical school. It was a tender age at which to first experience age discrimination.

Nearly broke, I took a job as an orderly at a geriatric/psychiatric hospital in Auckland. I also put my business education to use as a consultant to a badly disorganized warehouse owner there. He was thrilled to learn that inventory could actually be accounted for. In the meantime, I'd been encouraged by an old Air Force friend to try applying to the University of Washington medical school in Seattle; maybe they would enroll an old geezer. On the strength of that suggestion alone, I flew from New Zealand to Seattle in the spring of 1973 and managed, after no small effort, to gain admission to the University's School of Medicine.

Charlie Clements, ex-warrior and former inmate, was going to become a doctor.

I finished recounting my Pacific odyssey on one of the last circuits Pedro and I made around Guazapa.

One afternoon, as we crossed an isolated stretch between Zapote and Delicias, we happened upon a dozen or more vultures hopping around a corpse they were consuming. They were among the few wild creatures that prospered in the zone; there was always plenty for them to eat. Often, it was their presence that alerted us that something, or someone, had been killed by air attacks or ambush.

Hideous, disgusting beasts with monstrous flapping wings, the only way to kill them with a single shot is to put it in their heads. This Pedro accomplished at the instant we found them. Three lay dead around the faceless body of a young woman as we buried her.

We saw little of each other after that; Pedro would stop into one of the Palo Grande hospitals from time to time, or I would see him talking with one of the comandantes. It wasn't until a month later, after an all-Front congress held near Llano Rancho, that we spoke privately again.

THE CONGRESS WAS EVERY BIT as startling and illuminating as the *balances* of April. The first topic was the death of a military *sanitario* named Mario. I had a vague acquaintance with this medic, and I had not taken to him at all. He seemed to be a chronic complainer and a disruptive influence. Several times, he had been caught trading medicine for food.

But Mario was much more than an irritant. At the meeting, several *campesinos* came forth to denounce the story of his supposed drowning. Mario, they said, had died of a bullet to the back of his head before being dumped in an unmarked grave. They wanted to know why Raul Hercules and the rest of the leadership covered up the execution

"Yes, it was a lie," Hercules conceded to the meeting. "Mario was a traitor. It was decided for morale purposes not to reveal his true identity."

The explanation pleased no one.

"We are not fighting and dying to be lied to!" exclaimed a *compañero*. "We will not win our struggle just to replace killers and liars with more killers and liars."

I was disturbed for quite another reason. In revealing the truth about Mario, Hercules had said: "With *compañero* Pedro's diligence, we captured the spy."

So, my supposed friend was an agent, and I had been his unknowing accomplice. I sought Pedro out at the back of the crowd and pulled him aside

"You've known all along that Mario didn't drown, haven't you?" I said.

Pedro looked away. "I knew something about it." He wasn't smiling.

"Camilo," he continued, "there are some things we cannot talk about. I had nothing to do with the decision to conceal Mario's death."

"This isn't a matter of security," I replied. "I know more than three-fourths of these people about security here; I'm the only one who travels the Front day and night. Don't use that bull with me!"

I reminded him that we were supposed to be friends.

"You were checking me out, too, I suppose?" I asked. "Was it you and not the enemy who fired at me last month?"

He laughed. "You've seen me shoot. Would I have missed you?"

I knew that much to be true. But it didn't make me any happier to have been used as Pedro's cover.

"I never lied to you," he said. "It's just that sometimes I didn't tell all the truth. I am a medic. I spent time with the *compañeros* in Nicaragua. But I came to the Front to find a spy, and what better way to travel around without causing suspicion than to be with the gringo doctor!"

According to Pedro, Mario came under suspicion because he asked too many pointed questions of the *compañeros*. Besides selling medicine, he told the civilians that the guerrilla commanders ate steak every night. He even, or so Pedro now insisted, told my patients that I was sleeping with women in every village.

"Can you imagine!" Pedro laughed. "Camilo the monk!"

This wasn't the first time Pedro had mocked my sexual restraint. He and others thought me unusually distant from the women. While true, it was not from any aversion to relations with the opposite sex. An intimate relationship automatically tied a man and woman, in a semi-official way. The couple was known as *acompañado* (practically married). It was an unspoken code among the guerrillas that protected women from machismo attitudes. Even if my libido could have risen above the fatigue, hunger, and dysentery, I wasn't ready for the responsibility.

Mario was also identified by a *campesino* as the man who tortured him in one of the government's clandestine jails. Armed with this information, Pedro had confronted him. The interrogation was taped. I later heard it and instantly recognized Mario's voice. His tone was thin, but calm; he already knew he was a dead man.

"I'll make your job easy for you," he told Pedro. "I have been a torturer myself, and I do not wish to go through what I have caused other people to experience. I will tell you everything if you will only execute me."

Pedro's openness had its limits. He switched off the tape before I could hear Mario's confession.

"Do you understand now?" he asked. He didn't seem to expect an answer.

AUGUST WAS A NIGHTMARE for me, as black a period as I had yet been through in Guazapa. Jasmine's disappearance, the hassling with Marco, the forced suspension of my clinic rounds, Pedro's revelations: Fate was correcting its indulgences of July with a vengeance.

Then I learned of Salvador's death. He and several of the Front's senior guerrilla and civilian leaders had gone to the capital for a clandestine meeting. Scattered throughout the city in safe houses, the comandantes were betrayed by an informer who had given the government security forces the safe house addresses, then publicly declared his true identity as a spy.

It was Paco!

The supercilious, macho comandante—the one who had argued we should walk back from San Antonio Abad—had been a traitor all along. The damage he caused was enormous. In San Antonio Abad, at least thirteen guerrillas were killed as a result of his treachery, and twelve more seriously wounded. A half dozen of the organization's leaders were captured with Salvador. Paco was intimately familiar with the Front and all security measures, information he now shared with the enemy. Plus Salvador was dead.

I now understood Raul Hercules' indifferent response to Jasmine's disappearance. His organization had suffered two serious breaches of security, and he was lucky to be alive; the same dragnet that caught Salvador nearly captured him too. But even more startling news was to emerge from the congress.

Several *compañeros*, members of the column from Quipurito, had entered the Front in June after the Belloso Battalion razed their village. They and others from Quipurito regrouped in Salitre and there, perhaps at Paco's instigation, were told a string of outrageous lies about Raul Hercules and his staff. It was unclear to me if Mario, Pedro's target, had been part of this plot or if he and Paco were even aware of one another. However it was organized, it very nearly succeeded.

Many of the *compañeros* from Quipurito blamed Hercules, at least in part, for the devastation of their community. During the May military alert, they felt, too much attention had been given to the defense of Chalatenango and the planting of Guazapa, thus neglecting the fate of villages like Quipurito. This discontent was inflamed by unnamed provocateurs who told the *compañeros* that Hercules and his aides all had battery-powered televisions and drank wine each night with their sumptuous dinners; there was the strictest prohibition against any alcohol of any kind on the Front.

These and other stories prompted a cabal. A few of the

Quipurito *compañeros* began recruiting malcontents for a death squad of their own. A five-man team would sneak up to Palo Grande and murder the entire leadership. Jasmine, had she not left, would have been one of their targets. Having taken over her responsibilities, I never knew if I might have been designated for termination too.

When the plot was discovered by a loyal *compañero* who reported attempts to enlist him in the murders, the dissidents were not arrested, but were invited to come up to the congress to air their complaints. Led by the two chief instigators, *compañeros* Daniel and Esteban, they arrived under armed escort and proceeded to excoriate the entire leadership.

Daniel, a fire-breathing rhetoritician, charged that Raul Hercules was an uneducated rube too ignorant to be a comandante and too stupid to appreciate the principles of Marxism-Leninism. Esteban, his partner, complained that the leadership had cut the Quipurito *compañeros* out of the decision-making process. Moreover, he accused Raul Hercules of womanizing as well as of corruption and ineptitude.

Some of the *campesinos* at the congress were for executing Daniel and Esteban on the spot. Many spoke angrily in defense of Raul Hercules and denounced the plotters as bloodthirsty adventurers. Yet Raul Hercules himself argued against killing them. It was a solution, he said, no better than the intended crime. Moreover, he admitted that his leadership might have been too rigid, too closed. How else, he asked, could previously loyal *compañeros* like Daniel and Esteban begin to have the suspicions they did?

It took the better part of two days to resolve the case. I was fascinated as first a minority of *campesinos*, then a small majority, and finally every one of them endorsed a temporary demotion for Daniel and Esteban, plus a sentence of six months' labor in one of the agricultural cooperatives.

The whole affair was handled in such a decidedly civilized way that I found myself forgetting that these two had recently planned murder. Just as he had fearlessly denounced Raul Hercules, Esteban now bowed to the sense of the meeting and seemed practically eager to get back to the land. He expressed his hopes that a few months of hoeing and raking would re-educate him to the values of the revolution. But Daniel was adamant and would not offer his weapon. It had to be taken from him before he was led off, scowling, by an escort.

At its most basic level, the congress was a reaffirmation of the *campesinos'* sense of democratic control. In one exchange that particularly amused me, a comandante spoke for what seemed like hours about solidarity with oppressed people around the world. He made several references to Cuba and Nicaragua.

When he sat down, a *campesino* stood up and agreed that it was important to remember brothers and sisters in other lands. Then he eyed the comandante and said, "We should also remember that we are not Cubans or Nicaraguans. This is our revolution. Comandante, if Ché himself were to appear here tomorrow, he wouldn't understand our reality any better than we do."

The speech was given a round of applause.

Among the many measures put forth or endorsed during the congress was a resolution to amplify the Front's educational programs; ignorance, it was decided, lay at the heart of the plot to kill Raul Hercules. He, in turn, took his lumps for being too independent in his decision-making. Taking their cue from the peasants, the guerrilla leaders caucused and announced a command reorganization wherein Raul Hercules would share power with two other comandantes, Misael and Mauricio.

Then it ended with a watermelon feast and the singing of the Salvadoran national anthem. The music, taken from Giacomo Meyerbeer's opera, "The Prophet," is much admired by Salvadorans. I thought it sounded like a dirge.

"Why can't you people think up something a little more stirring?" I asked one of them as the anthem concluded. "The Sandinistas have a better song than you do."

I was partially joking, but this *compañero* was not amused. "We do not sing the song for you, gringo," he said. "We are Salvadorans and patriots. It is our country's song, that is why we sing it."

His words had the unintended effect of synthesizing several strands of thought and emotion that had been developing in me since Jasmine's disappearance. Until then, I had avoided bearing arms, or suffering them to be carried in my personal defense; I was a letter-perfect pacifist. Spiritually, however, I'd slipped from strict neutrality to an "us-versus-them" view of the conflict. Events overtook me. In a matter of weeks, I had been drawn perilously far into the rebel counsels. I had discovered there was a conspiracy that could have cost me my life, and I had learned from Pedro that all was not as it seemed.

We do not sing the song for you, gringo.

Suddenly, it was essential that I back away from their revolution. The principles that had brought me there in the first place had to be reasserted. Having long since lost any illusions about my own mortality I decided if anything happened to me, it would be as a Quaker and physician, not as a revolutionary.

THE DISENGAGEMENT WASN'T to be easily accomplished. As the congress closed, we received urgent radio messages from several villages around the San Pedro volcano, some sixty miles to the south in San Vicente Province. According to the reports, government troops had slaughtered over a thousand civilians there. Few of the bodies had been buried; many were dumped in wells or springs. Typhoid and cholera had broken out. There was no medicine.

Pedro and I and several *sanitarios* rushed back to Palo Grande, where we put together a medical-relief package that included a third of our total medical supply. The two weeks of wrangling with Marco seemed particularly pointless to me at that moment.

For a couple days, there was talk of sending me, and a priest, to San Pedro to document the massacre. Using parish records and my own clinical observations of the dead, we hoped to bring back forensic proof of the atrocity that was constant news on Radio Venceremos, but nowhere else. Neither National Public Radio nor the Voice of America mentioned a word of it. Foreign journalists, I was told, were being prevented from visiting the village.

We were just about to leave, when another urgent radio message arrived. The military had re-entered the San Pedro zone, cordoned it off, and was now burning and burying the evidence. All that was left was to wait and hope to help treat whatever refugees made it the sixty miles to Guazapa.

Few did.

I treated one old man whose right calf was nearly destroyed by shell fragments. He had made it from San Pedro, I was told, under his own power. His was a very complex operation, done under general anesthesia. In essence, I built him a new calf muscle, then placed him in a homemade traction device we called "the helicopter." Similar in shape to a medieval torture rack, it was in fact an artfully engineered wooden table outfitted with a long box and a wooden blade with which we could stretch straight and immobilize the calf as it healed.

Next, I was taken across the Suchitoto highway to a temporary camp set up for the San Pedro evacuees. There I met Toño, a seven-year-old whose story was harrowing even by Salvadoran standards.

According to what he and several of the other refugees claimed, the government had mounted a hammer-and-anvil action against the village. Less battle-hardened than *compañeros* elsewhere, the San Pedro guerrillas had fallen for the maneuver and evacuated their civilians straight into the waiting soldiers.

The government troops didn't fire at first. They told the villagers to gather in a ravine where they would be safely out of the line of fire during the expected counterassault by the insurgents. There was no choice but to obey, and nowhere to run when the soldiers opened fire.

Toño had been standing by his mother. He took an M-16 round through his collarbone as she shoved him to the ground and fell on top of him, dead. His brothers and sisters were slaughtered in the ravine, as well.

The troops then walked among the bodies with their machetes, finishing off the few *campesinos* still alive and mutilating others. Toño, silenced by trauma and physical shock, felt his mother's body shift violently. Through glazed eyes, he then watched as a soldier hacked her wedding ring from her finger.

For several hours he lay there under the pile of bodies, then crawled out from beneath his mother and made his way up to some bushes. The next day, peasants from a neighboring village found him shivering and sobbing on the edge of the ravine.

Toño didn't utter a word for two days after they brought him, hastily bandaged, to Guazapa. He was mute with me as I coaxed him to take a codeine tablet before trying to remove his dirty dressings and examining his wound.

While the pill took effect, I walked outside and struggled for composure. The little boy had yet to confirm what the others had told me, but the stark sight of him sitting in the examination room, covered with dirt and blood-soaked bandages, had truly unnerved me.

"Why," I asked no one in particular, "is it always the children?"

We soaked his bandages with saline solution to soften them, but they nevertheless tore at his flesh no matter how careful we were in removing them. The M-16 slug had shattered his clavicle, but luckily it had ricocheted straight up, leaving his lung intact. It was an ugly but clean wound.

As I dressed it again, I gently put a few questions to Toño, and he answered in monotones. When he was ready to be evacuated across the highway to Palo Grande, there was no friend or relative to accompany him except for a cousin, also a small boy, from a nearby village.

I was still haunted by Toño's look of blank terror when several days later Pedro summoned me to examine another casualty—a prisoner.

Prisoners present special problems in any armed conflict. Not only must they be housed and fed and guarded, but they are accorded certain rights guaranteed under the Geneva Conventions.

In El Salvador, the government gets around these problems by the simple expedient of shooting all but a handful of their prisoners. It is a policy that has appalled their American advisors and has led to several embarrassing threats by the International Red Cross to quit the country unless it is stopped.

The guerrillas, however, have many reasons to be extra-sensitive to POWs and their rights. For one thing, the government soldiers are told that they, like the rebels, will be tortured and killed if captured. As far as my experience with the guerrillas went, such treatment is rare. I saw or heard of no torture, and to my knowledge the only summary executions of POWs during my time in Guazapa were the killings of the two soldiers following the assault on San Antonio Abad. As I noted, these acts were roundly criticized at the ensuing *balance*.

Once prisoners learn they are not going to be abused, the government soldiers then worry about their release; some had been known to return to their units only to be killed for supposed cowardice. Of course, the government also does not want it known that the rebels enjoy a qualitative edge in humanitarianism and civility.

The POWs obviously know of this policy, as well. If, as is often the case, they are invited to join the guerrillas, they might accept as a matter of personal safety. But then, of course, their families are jeopardized by the death squads as relatives of subversives.

The best possible solution from the rebels' standpoint is usually to hand over their POWs to the International Red Cross, which at least will vouch that it received the prisoners in satisfactory physical shape. Since the IRC is not always in a position to take custody of POWs, the guerrillas must often hold and guard them for weeks.

The prisoner I was taken to see was a twenty-three- or twenty-four-year-old lieutenant and the first captured officer I'd seen. He was brought to me at an old shed in a sparsely populated region west and north of Salitre, an area where I had established no civilian clinics.

His guard wore the officer's blood-stained uniform shirt, and he had on the guerrilla's ragged shirt. He was sullen and stiff, and his left arm was in a sling.

At a glance I could tell that he had taken three light hits of automatic fire. One had ripped through his thick latissimus dorsi muscle. A second had lightly grazed his upper arm. The third went straight through the bicep and apparently nicked his humerus. They were painful but slight wounds, and I told the lieutenant he'd been lucky.

He said nothing.

I was irritated; San Pedro had occurred only a few days earlier. Undoubtedly, officers such as he had directed the massacre. "Lieutenant," I said, "I am also the liaison to the International Red Cross here. I am not a guerrilla, and I take no side in this war. All I want is some information from you so that I can begin contacts with the Red Cross to arrange for your release."

I received several curt responses to my questions, and then more silence. He asked for and received a cigarette. After a couple puffs, he looked up nonchalantly and asked if I was a Communist.

"No," I answered, and then I took a chance. His manner had been so formal, so by-the-book, that I guessed that he had been to a military academy. "As a matter of fact, I'm an academy graduate like you, a former U.S. military officer, and I was a pilot in Vietnam."

He didn't conceal his surprise. "How do you know I went to a military academy?" The word *vagabundo* (bum) was added to the query.

It was my turn to be silent. As I gazed at him, I saw

traces of my former self sitting there. He was young, rigidly educated, patriotic, and probably ambitious to be a general. Had I been captured under similar circumstances during my first weeks in Vietnam, I'm sure I would have been equally impenetrable and equally hostile.

After a pause, I told him that the enlisted POWs I'd met in El Salvador reminded me of the South Vietnamese soldiers I'd seen in Vietnam. Their morale was very low, and they did not like to fight.

"You have talked only to cowards and collaborators," he replied.

"And you are a POW. Are you a coward as well?"

Infuriated, he snarled, "I was captured because my cowardly soldiers deserted their positions, gringo."

"Speaking of cowards," I shot back impatiently, "do you know of the military operation against San Pedro?"

He warily acknowledged that he did.

"Do you know of the hundreds of civilians murdered there?"

"No," he answered.

I told him about Toño.

"I do not believe this story," he said haughtily. "Why should I? The boy is probably a guerrilla. We know women and children fight with the Communists."

The interview had taken a definitely unprofessional turn.

"How long," I shouted, "do you think your military can go on committing atrocities against civilians before the U.S. Congress gets fed up and cuts off your aid! How long?"

The lieutenant looked me straight in the eye and then flicked his cigarette butt onto the dirt floor.

"Your government will never cut us off," he said. Pointing to his chest with his good right arm, he added, "We are anti-Communists!"

I HAD MET THE LIEUTENANT in the middle of September, several weeks after being asked to become the Front's liaison to the IRC. It was a responsibility that I embraced with enthusiasm. Treating POWs was perfectly consistent with medical neutrality and the contact with the IRC—a possible source of medical supplies—could be helpful for the civilian population. Meeting POWs would also give me a chance to explore their attitudes, and perhaps answer a lingering question: How were they capable of such brutality?

The first three POWs I met were conscripts. Rafaga, eighteen, and Moreno, fifteen, had enlisted at the urging of a truckful of troops who had met them with guns as they walked out of a movie theater. The third prisoner, Monterosa, seventeen, claimed that he reluctantly answered his draft notice after his village priest had reminded him that failure to do so would mark him and his family as "subversives." All three names were pseudonyms, chosen by the prisoners to protect their true identities, in case an *oreja* reported the circumstance of their captivity to the government.

Each told me he had been terribly afraid when first caught. They had been told by their officers that the guerrillas were Communist monsters who lived in caves, ate roots, and sometimes even barbecued their prisoners after torturing them. I could well imagine the young lieutenant saying something very similar to his men.

None of them showed any interest in joining the guerrillas, just relief that they were not going to be sliced up and boiled. On the other hand, they were extremely nervous about being repatriated. They knew that returning POWs faced prospects similar to those who answered the government's infrequent offers of amnesty. One such case, a boy from a farm village in the northern sector of Guazapa, had gone to the garrison in Suchitoto to give himself up. He stole the rifle of a *compañero* and surrendered it too, hoping this act would further validate his change of heart in their eyes. According to what the sympathizers in Suchitoto later reported, the youth was flogged for hours in the marketplace, then dragged off to a secret prison where he died.

My first scheduled meeting with the IRC was to be on September 3. Moving at night so as to shield ourselves and the POWs from the lookouts on Guazapa's summit, we hiked down from Palo Grande, past Salitre and out of the Front to a pre-arranged meeting place.

As we neared the zone's border, it occurred to me that being the designated IRC liaison carried more than an important responsibility with it. It was dangerous. The prisoners, our armed escort, and I would be out of the Front in broad daylight at a location that the Red Cross had to disclose, beforehand, to the government. What better opportunity could there be for the soldiers to ambush and kill us all? They could blame the murder of the IRC representatives, who weren't particularly welcome anyway, on the guerrillas and then announce that, alas, they had come to the Red Cross' rescue too late to do anything but avenge the murders by killing all the guerrillas. Condolences, perhaps, might be sent to the families of the prisoners who unfortunately but bravely died in the skirmish. After nearly six months in Guazapa, that scenario didn't sound farfetched at all to me.

As it turned out, nothing happened one way or the other. We got to the rendezvous point two hours before the scheduled meeting and waited the pre-agreed five hours before giving up and heading back toward Salitre. We did hear on the government radio that an IRC representative had been detained by the security forces that day, but it was impossible to know if he had been on his way to our meeting.

FOR THE NEXT SEVERAL WEEKS, we would continue to ferry POWs around Guazapa; sometimes IRC representatives would appear at the designated time and place, more often they would not. Frequently, the trips took us past Salitre and a nearby adobe hut, half destroyed by a five-hundred-pound bomb. I grew accustomed to seeing two small boys there. They often greeted me with a happy "Ola, doctor." One afternoon after yet another failed rendezvous with the IRC, we were trudging by the house when the two youngsters came bounding out like a pair of puppies.

"Camilo, Camilo!" they shouted. "Did you hear about our father? He captured two rifles last week!"

This was a feat of great distinction. Liberating a brace of M-16s carried with it far more cachet than simply killing their owners.

"¡Qué bueno!" I called back. "Your father must be very brave. What is his name?"

"He is called Magdaleno," they answered, "and he's in our home."

Magdaleno—El Anciano, the ancient one—was something of a legend in Guazapa. His grandfather had fought in the great *matanza* of 1932 and now he, at age sixty-one, had also become a rebel. Magdaleno was the oldest *compañero* on the Front.

El Abuelito meets El Anciano. I spotted him stooped over an old, homemade children's wagon that he evidently was trying to repair. Magdaleno rose at the sound of our approach and offered me a calloused hand as firm as a rock wrapped in leather. Short and spare and weatherbeaten, his sharp brown eyes appraised me quickly before softening. When he smiled, his face exploded into wrinkles.

"You are Camilo, the gringo doctor?" he asked.

"Sí, Magdaleno," I replied, "and I am honored to meet you."

"No, amigo," he answered, "we are fortunate to welcome you."

He invited me in for a cup of coffee. It was prepared by his plump wife, Ursula, a woman in her early forties, I guessed, whose own ready smile was distinguished by the absence of one upper, and one lower, front tooth.

The coffee was hot, black, and heavily sugared; the *campesinos* would consume it no other way. When we sat down, I raised my earthen mug and toasted Magdaleno on the capture of the two weapons. He nodded in modest acknowledgment and counter-toasted to the day of victory, of peace.

Maybe the reason I got along best with the children and

old men of Guazapa is that they were the least circumspect with me. Unlike the *compañeros* or comandantes or even the average villager who took security matters very seriously, the very young and the very old were too innocent or too at ease with the world to care as much about protecting personal secrets. I could actually have conversations with them.

Magdaleno, for instance, freely explained that his course toward "incorporation" began at a local meeting of the Federation of Christian Peasants, the same organization in which membership had cost Raul Hercules' father his life.

The outlawed national Federation, founded in 1965, was very strong in Guazapa. An amalgam of several rural unions, it aimed to be a force for defending *campesino* rights against usury and unfair wage practices. Radical only if viewed from the perspective of the fanatical right, the Federation had called a couple brief strikes in its history and had aligned itself with several center-left organizations that were looked upon with equal horror and hatred by the landowners and their governments. They saw it as another seed-bed for "subversives."

Magdaleno had not joined; he only attended a meeting out of curiosity, he said. Nevertheless, the soldiers came for him that night and then kept him for three days of questioning. They wanted the names of the forty other people who had come to the meeting. He hadn't known most of them, but figured that official interest in the gathering meant only one thing—their lives were at stake if he gave their names.

El Anciano said nothing more at that point about his time in detention. Relaxing at his table with me, enjoying a cigarette, he recounted that upon his release from custody he knew he was marked and that the next arrest could be his last. Thus, he moved Ursula, the boys, and an older daughter and grandchild to Guazapa, then went himself to San Salvador to seek an audience with Archbishop Romero. This was in late 1979, several months before the death squads assassinated Romero as he said Mass in a hospital chapel.

"Father," Magdaleno remembered saying, "I am very

troubled. I can no longer feed or clothe or educate my children. I may soon be arrested and 'disappeared.' I feel it is just that I join the people's struggle, but I am also a Catholic."

According to Magdaleno, he asked the Archbishop if a Christian could resort to violence in such a situation. Was killing justified in the face of so much misery and oppression?

Romero, said Magdaleno, was anguished by his questions. The Archbishop told of his own internal struggle with similar dilemmas. In such circumstances, how does one best defend the sanctity of life?

He told Magdaleno that it was also a crime to let his children starve. As I understood him, Romero hadn't endorsed bloodshed; he had only said it was no sin to defend his family from starvation.

"That," explained the old man, "is when I joined the struggle."

Several days after our conversations, Magdaleno appeared at the Palo Grande hospital. He had contracted a painful condition on his groin, something the Salitre clinic hadn't been able to successfully treat.

He was very reticent about the examination.

"Camilo," he said, "can't you give me the medicine I need?"

I answered no, at least not until I'd diagnosed the problem.

With great reluctance, he lowered his trousers to just the level of his pubic hair where I could see an angry rash. It did not appear local, so I pushed his hand away to examine the area more generally. He resisted me, then let his trousers drop.

Magdaleno had been castrated.

"I did not mean to embarrass you, *compañero*," I said quickly.

I completed the diagnosis. He had a case of scabies, a mite infestation for which I gave him a salve.

Like David, he had waited to be my last patient of the day. Since we had some time, I asked him if he would tell me how it happened.

"They kept me three days, Camilo," he said. "When I wouldn't talk, they put a plastic bag filled with white powder over my head to make me choke. They held me upside down and dripped water up my nostrils. I didn't tell them a thing!"

The questioners' last abuse, he went on, was to attach weights to his testicles. More and more weight was added until his scrotal anatomy was destroyed. Then they released him.

Magdaleno made no mention of the agony he must have endured. He simply explained that he went to a clinic where the doctor told him the damage to his testicles could not be reversed and that his only option was surgical castration.

"He told me I needed the surgery," Magdaleno said, "but that it was complicated, and I would have to spend a day there. They could not endanger their lives by treating someone who had been tortured by the security forces."

It was several days before a physician could be found who would take that risk.

Like so many of my patients, what Magdaleno had suffered seemed so enormous as to set him apart. Whether it was torture or mental trauma or war wounds, the ferocity of what they bore up under—and sometimes overcame—invested these people with a sense of superhuman resolve and endurance.

That was not, however, the way they saw themselves. In their view, decades of oppression had robbed them of something far dearer than physical well-being, a stabbing of the spirit more dreadful and abhorrent than a machete or M-16 slug in the heart.

As he prepared to walk back to Salitre that night, I asked Magdaleno why he became a *compañero* instead of a militiaman, an equally honorable way of contributing and one perhaps more suitable to his years. In a country where the median life-expectancy is forty-seven, there was no shame at age sixty-one in taking time to hoe the *milpa* and tell stories to one's grandchildren.

"Camilo," he said, "death in some ways has more meaning than life. We have lived as slaves here. Now we have awakened to know that this was not the law of God; only other men determine that we should live as second-class people. One more day of that life is impossible for me. Even the old ones, like me, who won't see the victory are impatient for their children and the unborn generations."

MY UNINFORMED ASSUMPTION about the weather in Guazapa was that the monsoons of that June were the norm. It was a rainy season such as I had experienced in southeast Asia, and it seemed therefore unextraordinary, albeit inconvenient to work in.

In truth, some sort of meteorological quirk was responsible for the constant deluges. Much of Central America was inundated for weeks. Normally, the rains come each afternoon, gradually subsiding through the July harvest and into early August. A second, smaller crop is planted then in the hope that the earth has retained enough moisture to allow another growing season.

In Guazapa in 1982, August brought a short dry spell that worried the peasants as much as June's overabundance had disrupted the usual scheme of things. The uncommonly clear days also abetted the government's plans.

In July, units such as the Ramón Belloso Battalion had been thwarted or outmaneuvered, but they certainly had not been defeated. The threat of invasion was always imminent. The massacre around San Pedro volcano was a lightning stroke that could hit us at any time.

Our moment was coming—soon.

But before the ground troops began their assaults, the A-37s stepped up their terror attacks on the villages, sometimes killing or injuring, but usually achieving with their bombs a secondary objective of heightening fear and stress throughout the Front.

Meantime, the garrison atop the volcano itself increased their mortar fire. This tactic of "random fire" was used by the

United States in Vietnam to terrorize and confuse peasants thought to be sympathetic to the Viet Cong.

Unless I was scheduled to meet with the IRC, or more rarely, a civilian emergency required my presence, I was more or less restricted to a few hours' walk from the vicinity of Palo Grande. From there, I could hear the mortars or see the warplanes wherever they were attacking.

I had at first been amazed at the small number of civilians bearing scars from these attacks. Many of the guerrillas had a wound or two at least, but few of the *campesinos* did. Evidence of head, chest, or abdominal wounds was very rare. The reason for this, I now came to understand, was not that the peasants didn't suffer injury, it was that they were much less likely to survive one. During invasions, the guerrilla columns had the minimal service of their *sanitarios* and could, at least occasionally, remove their wounded to a safe haven.

Not so the civilians. To begin with, they were generally less fit than the fighters and consequently less capable of surviving a wound. Secondly, they often received their wounds at point-blank range. Thirdly, they were far less likely to receive medical attention, meaning many otherwise survivable injuries resulted in death.

The guerrillas were safe, too, from A-37 attacks. Even when the guerrilla columns were engaged with the government troops, neither the jets nor the helicopters ever, in my experience, provided close air support for their side. On more than one occasion such support would have, in my judgment, turned the tide in favor of the soldiers. Instead, as they fought at close range with the *compañeros*, their aircraft were visible over other parts of the Front, bombing and strafing the villages or occasionally the guerrillas' rear positions.

As the intensity of these aerial assaults increased, so did the odds that the Salvadoran pilots would do some damage. At the same time, they began to employ a new tactic. Instead of coming behind the spotter planes (whose appearance in the sky served as an evacuation alarm), the A-37s now attacked pre-selected targets. That targeting information was provided, we assumed, by Paco or Mario. They would fly in over the top of the volcano and drop their bombs with no warning. Among the successes of this new tactic was a direct hit on an evening catechism class in El Roble. Six children and two adults were killed.

Another victim of an A-37 strafing run was Manuelito, a ten-year-old boy. As he and his elderly uncle ran for a bomb shelter, the old man was killed instantly and the youngster took a machine gun bullet fragment that entered through his chest, perforated both his lungs and diaphragm, then ripped through his stomach and intestines.

We spent four hours operating on him by flashlight. Besides Manuelito's enormous loss of blood and the physical damage to his internal organs, the injury put him at great risk of developing an infection.

Since the operation used up the last of our batteries, his vital signs had to be checked by candlelight. I thought the *sanitarios* understood that they could take his pulse for thirty seconds, multiply that number times two, and then enter the answer on his chart. Apparently I'd overestimated their math background, for when I returned to the operating room at first light, their notations of pulse rate ranged up and down between 38 and 172. The record was useless.

Manuelito awoke with two surgical drains running from his abdomen, IV lines attached to his arms, and a nasogastric tube coming out of his nose. Until his bowel could function normally, the tube was necessary to clear the several liters per day of fluid that normally is produced by the stomach and small intestine.

If he was frightened, he did not show it. Nor did the little boy ever complain about the pain he surely was suffering. But we couldn't keep him still on his bed, an old piece of lawn furniture. He pulled out his IVs several times as he tried to find a comfortable position, and he yanked the irritating nasogastric tube out twice.

The nasogastric tube was by no means a proper apparatus to begin with. Lacking a suction device to force the fluid up from his stomach, we connected a semi-rigid but collapsed IV bottle to the tube. As it slowly expanded, to regain its shape, it provided a weak vacuum. The process had to be repeated every ten minutes.

Still, Manuelito had survived his initial surgery, and I permitted myself an ounce of hope that he would pull through. He even found the strength to talk with me a bit that day. He said that if he hadn't so many responsibilities at home, he would like to come work as my assistant. But his father had been killed a year ago and now, with his uncle dead, he had to take care of his mother and four younger brothers and sisters. He wanted to know if I thought August had been too dry to ensure a good second crop.

The next day was his last. In the morning, he told his mother that he was going to die; in my experience, seldom does a patient say that without it happening. She sat outside the operating room as we went back into him early in the afternoon. I could see that infection had begun. A fistula, or artificial sinus, had opened between his lung and stomach. He was hemorrhaging again. In the fourth hour of the second surgery, he died.

Outside, when his frantic mother heard the activity cease, she knew her boy was dead. She wailed, "No! No! No!" and, in her anguish, cried for him, for the husband she'd lost a year before, for herself, and for her remaining children. As they carried Manuelito up the hill and away from the hospital, I could hear her at the side of the stretcher.

"Manuelito, no! You cannot leave. Who will cut the wood? Who will plant the corn? God! God!"

A failure in surgery, even one for which a doctor cannot logically hold himself accountable, can lead to a state of mind known familiarly as "knife-shy"—fear and doubt rob the physician of the self-confidence that is absolutely necessary if you are to cut into another human's body.

I became knife-shy after Manuelito's death. I kept turning the procedures over and over in my mind, dwelling on the loss when I should have put it behind me. I reminisced about the failed amputation and other failures, ignoring the successes. Such preoccupations, if carried too far, only endanger the next patient.

She was Camela, a thirty-seven-year-old mother of four who had been grinding corn on her front porch when a random fire mortar from the volcano-top garrison exploded in front of her. I knew her casually and remembered that she had reported a number of childhood ear infections that had left her a little hard of hearing. She had missed the warning WHUMP! as the mortar left its cannister, a few yards away.

After Manuelito's death, I went to the military and asked for one of their two small generators used to power the radios. I explained that I needed a reliable source of light, not just flashlights, to operate by. I also reminded them that the lives they saved by giving me a generator might include their own. They agreed that this was a good idea.

Thus, when Camela was brought in on a bamboo slung hammock, IV already running in her arm, I was able to operate under a weak, but constant, sixty-watt light bulb. A *sanitario* with some training in anesthesiology had arrived in Palo Grande that night. She would assist, together with a full team to hand me instruments, sterilize the ones we needed to use twice, and help brush away the flies. This was first-class health care we were about to provide.

Camela was still conscious when she arrived, but rather than ask me about the severity of her wound, she was only interested in knowing if it would prevent her from having any more children. After eighteen months of amenorrhea, the absence of her menstrual period, a condition not uncommon on the Front, she was worried that this injury would mean the end of hope for future children. I assured her it would not, and she lay back in repose as the general anesthetic took effect.

Knife-shy or not, I knew there was no time for hesitation. We opened her and found four perforations of her small intestine. Ordinarily, I might have resected, that is, removed sections of the bowel, then re-attached the severed ends, but

under the circumstances the procedure seemed too complicated and would have prolonged her recovery. So I clipped
and sewed, removing pieces but not whole sections of the
organ. After operating on Manuelito by flashlight, the glow of
the sixty-watt bulb seemed brilliant. The surgery went
smoothly, and we closed her with her life signs all strong and
steady.

This time, however, I was going to personally supervise
her post-operative care. I stayed up two nights with the
sanitarios as they rotated their shifts. I taught each of them to
take precise blood pressure readings, pulse rates, and
temperatures. Before sleeplessness brought me to the brink
of incoherence, they all were expert at these duties, as well
as at changing our nasogastric suction bottle and monitoring
the IV rate.

Camela recovered. For four days, we watched her constantly, pitying her because we had no injectable painkillers
left, but also admiring her incredible strength and will to
live. As soon as she began to pass wind, meaning that her
bowel was again functioning, we relieved a little of her pain
with spoonfuls of willow bark tea, the only available analgesic.
After ten days, she was strong enough to be moved and was
carried off home in a hammock, surrounded by her children.

Her husband returned the next day. He brought a pair
of socks. During those two weeks of recovery, Camela had
noticed my bare feet through the gaps in my boots. It had
been almost three months since my feet knew anything other
than the touch of the wet leather of my boots. As I thanked
him I sheepishly recalled my remarks about the purchase of
women's underwear and socks for the *sanitarios* back in March.

OCTOBER 8, 1982: the fifteenth anniversary of Ché Guevara's
death.

There is perhaps no one symbol that better illustrates
the polarity of perceptions between North and Latin Americans than the career of Ernesto ("Ché") Guevara. In the

CHARLES CLEMENTS, M.D.

United States, he is popularly known as a leftist revolutionary, the friend and confidant to Fidel Castro, who was killed while trying to stir up a civil war in Bolivia.

Throughout Latin America, however, his memory is cherished. For guerrillas in Central America and elsewhere, his life has become a sacred example. For the millions more with no thought of taking up arms, he is more than that, he is mythic. They remember him not as an ominous threat to liberty, but as the passionate doctor who once spoke before the United Nations General Assembly, challenging the northern industrial nations to share just one percent of their gross national products with the Third World. Even in the remotest villages in regions as isolated as Guazapa, the children sing songs in honor of his words and deeds. What Longfellow did for Paul Revere, the poets of South America have achieved for Ché Guevara.

For me, the eighth of October was important for different reasons; as suddenly as she'd disappeared, Jasmine returned to Guazapa to resume her duties as head of military medicine. I was too happy to see her to ask where the hell she'd been, and knew she probably wouldn't tell me anyhow. My only thought was of resuming the clinic rounds that had been suspended since early August.

That morning, I woke up in Delicias to the sound of speeches, revolutionary songs, and the sight of captured weapons displayed for everyone to admire. My impression was of a Fourth of July in small-town U.S.A.

At 4:00 P.M., after having seen about seventy-five patients, I started walking back to Palo Grande. Along the way, I wandered near the tiny hamlet of Platanares, which was no more than a collection of five or six houses situated near an abandoned hacienda. I heard guitar music and remembered that some sort of festivity had been planned that day. Since I had very little experience with the guerrillas at play, I decided to take a detour to check out their party.

It was being held under the canopy of several ancient oak trees in the hacienda's courtyard. A four-piece band consisting of two guitars, a bassist, and a violin player were sawing away on a succession of dance tunes while a crowd of some two hundred dancers shuffled back and forth to the music.

They weren't real lively. Each couple swayed together, nearly at arm's length, their hands resting lightly upon one another's shoulders or waist. Never roaming more than a few feet in any direction, they would swing their hips a bit, dip a shoulder, and then shuffle on. Many had their weapons slung over their backs and the rifles bounced and clacked together to the beat.

Their demeanor toward one another was as chaste as that of an Air Force Academy ball where a "public display of affection" (a peck on the cheek) could earn you several demerits.

I had been drilled at the Academy in about every dance step but this Guazapa cha-cha-cha, so I moved on to the food and refreshment stands. There, I found vendors hawking *refrescos* (tepid mixtures of fruit juice, sugar, and water) as well as the last of their corn cakes and *quesadillas*, a delicacy for which the *queso*, or cheese, no longer was available. They were a bit tastier than a day-old tortilla.

A government spotter plane circled high overhead a couple times and then left as I sat enjoying a cup of sugary coffee and a couple corn cakes offered me by a heavy-set woman. She refused my money and suggested, instead, that I dance with her daughter. When I declined to make a spectacle of myself she laughed and asked if *norteamericanos* were taught to dance.

We chatted for maybe half an hour and then I rose to continue my hike back to the hospital. As I left, a *compañero* with an audio tape appeared and shooed away the musicians. It was the latest "Top Twenty," taped from a broadcast by a Los Angeles station, and its effect on the dancers was instant. As the New Wave rock came blasting out of a cassette player, they dropped their restraint and began kicking up some dust. The day the revolution is won, I thought as I walked away, even the Marxist-Leninists of the Farabundo Martí Liberation Front will dance in celebration to the sounds of Boy George or the Talking Heads.

I had made the deserted village of San Antonio, about halfway between Platanares and Palo Grande, when the A-37s came screaming in on Guazapa. They were everywhere at once, like a swarm of angry hornets. I stood stock still, as if mesmerized, as two of the jets hit Platanares behind me and another peeled off to strafe Zapote ahead and to my right. Another A-37 began bombing Palo Grande and still others hit Salitre on the other side of the volcano as well as the eastern village of Tenango and Guadalupe. It was an all-out attack.

A half-hour on a dead run brought me to the hospital, which was still under attack. In the twilight, I could see thick smoke rising above Platanares, Zapote, Tenango, and several other villages. Everywhere, there was the rattle of M-16 fire, the guerrillas' pitiful and pointless response to the impervious jets. Only nightfall would bring the attack to an end.

We prepared the operating room and began our wait for casualties. Around 8:00 P.M., I learned that one *campesino* I knew had been caught on horseback near Zapote and had been decapitated by machine gun fire.

An hour later, the radio reported that a family of twelve, including the woman who had served me coffee and cakes that afternoon, had been crouched in their slit trenches near their house in Platanares when the structure took a direct hit. The walls exploded outward and down upon them, crushing and suffocating all of them.

By 11:00 P.M., we were informed that there would be no casualties brought to Palo Grande that night. The local *sanitarios* were to do their best for the injured while every able-bodied person spent the night digging through the rubble in search of survivors.

I was furious at the attack's wantonness. My Quaker principles might easily have been cast aside had an M-16, or better yet, something powerful enough to drive the marauders from the sky, been at my disposal.

Then came the long wait, interrupted only by radio

reports of death and destruction. I grieved and silently raged at the news. Not only was I helpless before the enormity of what was happening around me, but if neutrality was measured by feelings as well as actions, I had lost it.

We do not sing the song for you, gringo.

What good were these abstractions in such circumstances? Who, besides myself, cared or understood or would even remember the scruples of a dead gringo doctor in an unmarked grave somewhere on the slopes of an extinct volcano that now was erupting in blood?

I lay down on the operating table unable to cry or sleep. Manuelito had died here, under my hand. His blood, and that of dozens of others, had caked and hardened the dirt floor beneath me. Those whom I'd saved to walk, laugh, and celebrate Mass once more remained candidates for the table again.

Jasmine found me there that night. Unaware of my distress, she announced a messenger would leave for the capital before dawn. Would I prepare a list of our most critical needs for the civilian sector? It took all of five minutes to do so, time in which I decided to express my turmoil on paper. Along with the list of medicines, I would enclose a letter to be sent to Salinas.

For the next three hours, I banged away on our aged typewriter. It was an appeal to those who saw the Salvadoran civil war for what it wasn't, a Communist conspiracy to engulf freedom-loving people in godless slavery. Revolting conditions create revolutions, I explained. I took Ché's anniversary as my occasion to describe the appalling inequities of *campesino* life in El Salvador and explained, as best I could, the critical difference between terrorists, which is what the *compañeros* were being called, and guerrillas, which is what they are. Without the support of the people, I pointed out, this and any revolution is doomed to failure. With their support, as I had personally witnessed it, the rebels must eventually win.

I called it a "necessary struggle for human dignity" and thanked, somewhat presumptuously, my unseen audience "on behalf of the people of El Salvador."

By the time the courier left, I was exhausted. When morning came, my anger, too, was spent. I recalled another image of Ché when he faced a similar turning point. In the first hours of the Cuban revolution, Guevara along with Castro and his tiny rebel army were pinned down by government troops as they tried to infiltrate the island by sea.

Only a quarter of the band survived a suicidal charge past the troops and up into the Sierra Maestra mountains. As Castro gave the order to advance, Ché saw before him a bag of medicine and a satchel of ammunition. He could take only one of them.

He left the medicine behind.

I won't presume to judge the moral correctness of that choice or its historical significance. If Ché Guevara hadn't existed, perhaps some propagandist or poet might have invented him. All I knew was that I would not decide similarly. It was clear now that I didn't want the song sung for me or about me.

Writing the letter purged me of my anger and frustrations. It had been a delicate balance, but the experience helped restore my perspective. I would continue as a healer and witness.

I CONTINUED AS THE IRC liaison for the Front. Before the gathering violence made contact impossible, we managed one meeting with them in September, and another in the second week of October.

I remember that first rendezvous vividly. A group of *compañeros* and I were standing in the rain, pondering the wisdom of waiting much longer, when we heard the sound of a motor and then saw a white Jeep painted with a large red cross come slowly up the trail and stop.

In it were two Swiss nationals, both males, who apologized for their tardiness by explaining that the dining room at their hotel didn't start serving breakfast until six. I gritted my teeth as my stomach growled ferociously.

They were surprised to find an American, and wanted to know if I was a guerrilla. I explained that I, like they, was medically neutral. Wasn't being among the guerrillas an endorsement of their cause, one asked. Did he signal approval of civilian massacre by cooperating with the government, I asked.

These exchanges weren't as tart as they sound. They were more curious than accusatory, and I felt a mixture of joy at seeing someone from the outside and envy at their well-groomed and well-fed appearance.

Little was accomplished. They explained that they had brought no medicine and could only promise that which would be earmarked for care of the POWs. Not even vaccine for whooping cough or polio, which I'd seen active cases of recently, could be brought in.

By then we had six prisoners. We gave the IRC the data to verify who they were as well as letters from the POWs to their families to prove they were still alive. In return, they promised another meeting, said they would do their best to bring medicine, and left me with an out-of-date copy of *Newsweek*. Short of a hot dinner or a new pair of boots, I couldn't imagine a greater personal treat.

At the October rendezvous there were three of them, including a young woman doctor, who sported a large white bib with a red cross on it. Of course, the bib was meant to ensure her safety as a Red Cross worker, but it was also a convenient target for the snipers on the Guazapa heights. As we walked closer to the Front, where they would examine the POWs, I was glad the bib kept others from walking near us. It gave us the chance to converse in English, which would otherwise arouse suspicion.

Except for the lieutenant, our prisoners were ambivalent about being repatriated; they still feared what might happen when they rejoined their units. Rafaga, for instance, reacted with little apparent joy when told by the IRC that his wife had given birth to their first child. I couldn't understand his reaction and asked why he wasn't happier about the news.

When he was away from the lieutenant, Rafaga told me that he seriously considered staying to join the guerrillas, but fatherhood made that decision much more difficult.

When possible, POWs in Guazapa were kept under guard in the homes of families belonging to base Christian communities. Exposure to their religious services, it was felt, along with the chance to watch the schools, clinics, and cooperatives in action, would give the prisoners a deeper appreciation for what the revolution is about. Most of the soldiers were conscripts from rural towns not unlike Copapayo or Delicias. Most were just as poor as the Guazapa *campesinos*. Most had never seen anything like the sense of community and hope they saw during their detention.

They also would learn what it was like to live through an A-37 attack. Rafaga and the others told me it scared the daylights out of them. Several *campesinos*, veterans of the headlong dive for shelter, were amused by the POWs' mad panic each time the scream of a jet was heard overhead.

The second meeting was a success. The IRC delegates brought some supplies such as gauze, injectable antibiotics, and anesthesia to replace the medicine we used to treat the prisoners. They offered me no hope, however, that there would be vaccine available soon since the government would not permit it.

A time and place for the actual POW transfer was not yet worked out. But the soldiers were nevertheless elated to receive letters from home and food packages. When the three Red Cross workers left, all of the prisoners, except the lieutenant, shared their food with us. He stayed to himself, frowning at the fraternization and spooning smoked oysters into his mouth.

IN A WAY, THE LIEUTENANT'S BRITTLENESS epitomized what I had come to see as a chief obstacle to resolution of this conflict. Ignorance, mistrust, and fear characterized nearly every relationship I encountered.

The POWs, for instance, were extremely relieved to learn that the guerrillas didn't eat prisoners for dinner. *Compañeros* Daniel and Esteban were easily persuaded that Raul Hercules watched TV each night and swilled wine with his officers.

Perhaps the paranoia on both sides was understandable; the daily prospect of sudden death from any quarter does not promote a trusting nature. It leads to mad acts, such as the 1975 murder of poet Roque Dalton. A romantic and a visionary, Dalton had devoted his life to the revolution. Yet it turned on him when a splinter group of left extremists ordered his assassination as a "Cuban-Soviet CIA agent."

The fact that Dalton's killers could actually believe such a thing is no crazier, however, than the presence of Roberto d'Aubuisson at the head of the Salvadoran Constituent Assembly. The virulence of d'Aubuisson's anti-communism would have made Joe McCarthy envious.

Imagine in the United States if the Speaker of the House or the Majority Leader of the Senate were known to spend his private hours ordering the murders of opposition congressmen, the leadership of the AFL-CIO, or the hierarchy of the Presbyterian Church. Imagine if the instruments of this terror were rogue elements of the FBI and the Pentagon. Imagine further, as a United States citizen, if some foreign power such as France or Great Britain publicly condemned this state of affairs but still provided the funds for it to continue.

This is one reason why guerrillas such as Ramón, an otherwise prudent and thoughtful man, could regard Ronald Reagan as a fascist. It is also part of the explanation for the rebels' preoccupation with the CIA. Whatever this agency does in furtherance of U.S. foreign policy, or in the name of national security, its true influence on world affairs may reside more in what it is suspected, or thought capable, of doing.

On Guazapa, more than a couple of *compañeros* suggested to me it was highly suspicious that Nicaragua, of all

Central American countries, was hardest hit by the freak storms of June. Was the U.S. spy agency now manipulating the weather?

Then there was the dengue fever outbreak.

Civilian health care around the Front had lapsed in the many weeks I was unable to visit the village clinics. There hadn't been time to make the various programs self-sustaining, nor opportunity to adequately train the local health workers. As a result, when hundreds of people came down with malaria symptoms during the late summer, they were routinely given chloroquine tablets, or the *quina* tea, for their illness.

No matter what the *sanitarios* did, however, the incidence of malaria rose alarmingly. Comandantes came to me with reports that fully a third of their fighters were down. The disease swept whole villages. I had expected an upturn in the incidence of malaria once the rains provided the mosquitoes the opportunity to breed. But the size and persistence of this outbreak were baffling.

An examination of several sick guerrillas, as well as radio consultations with some of the abler *sanitarios*, revealed diagnostic inconsistencies with malaria. But for a microscope, I could have known in thirty seconds! The patients I examined lacked the symptomatic splenic enlargement of malaria and the periodicity of the fever. Otherwise they all had the right symptoms: headache, high temperatures, photophobia, malaise, and the rest. It had been easy to misdiagnose dengue fever.

A radio alert was broadcast throughout the Front, explaining the differences between these two mosquito-borne diseases, and giving details about the treatment for dengue; no chloroquine or *quina* tea, just plenty of fluids, rest, and aspirin for pain and fever. Aspirin's natural counterpart, the willow bark tea we made, suddenly was in heavy demand. And just as suddenly the Front's ample number of willows stood bare of their leaves and bark, looking for all the world like shorn and forlorn poodles against the now-lush mango or eucalyptus trees.

The *compañeros* first thought that the C-130s were dropping vials of dengue virus on Guazapa each night as they approached San Salvador. Even after I persuaded them that the true villains were the squadrons of their own mosquitoes— two to lift your covers, one to attack you, I joked—they still suspected a CIA plot.

How, I asked in astonishment, could the mosquitoes know only to bite *compañeros* and their sympathizers?

"That is easy, Camilo," someone would answer. "The CIA is very clever. What is training mosquitoes compared to putting a spaceship on the moon?"

In one regard, the United States did have some indirect responsibility for the increased incidence of both dengue and malaria around the Front. Bomb craters that scarred the landscape quickly filled up with stagnant water and began producing mosquitoes. Likewise, the civil defense measures taken against these bombs, the construction of village shelters, and the excavation of caves along the trails helped expand the mosquito population.

It seemed to get worse every day. Not only did the A-37 and the mortar attacks increase in frequency and intensity, but the government then brought mobile artillery pieces up the highway and from the far side of the volcano would lob 105mm shells in on us.

We were, as well, victims of geography. The jets were sent not only against us, but also to continue attacking villages to the north in Chalatenango Province. If they did not unload all their ordnance there, they would swing by Guazapa on their way back and randomly dump whatever was left on us.

The psychological toll of this constant bombardment was high. After one particularly heavy artillery attack, I spent several hours coaxing an elderly woman out of her bomb shelter. She had stumbled blindly into the pit, and sat there shivering in the mud and darkness, too frightened to move. Only a tranquilizer and the lure of a hot cup of coffee finally brought her out.

I began seeing a broad range of psychological effects of

the air war. Peptic ulcer disease increased; patients came to me with complaints of black stools or vomiting blood. I treated more depressives and saw cases of acute anxiety converted into physical impairment, the classic sign of hysteria. One man went blind with fright for several days. A teen-aged girl lost motor control below her waist. She had to be carried home and catheterized for a week.

UNLIKE THE GOVERNMENT OFFENSIVE of July, this campaign could not be finessed by the guerrillas. It was well-planned, well-organized, and part of a nationwide strategy to dislodge the insurgents and their supporters from nearly all their strongholds. On Guazapa, we knew that the weeks of aerial bombardment were a prelude to something, but we couldn't be prepared for when and where it would come.

The first phase was to bolster the garrison at Suchitoto. Then the patrols along the highway were increased. Since this had happened many times before, no special note was taken of the fact that reaching the eastern villages had become more perilous. Several groups of civilians were killed or wounded trying to cross the highway in the night.

I made the crossing myself in the third week of October, close to three months since I'd last visited any of those villages. Once again I could hear the government soldiers' radios not fifty yards away, but since it was nighttime, we had little to fear from them.

My first destination was Copapayo, where there was a happy reunion with Miguel and his old buddies. They played their radio for me and thanked me again for fixing it. One, an elder with whom I was unacquainted, announced that "we missed our old American, el viejo norteamericano!"

Old, huh?

"Just how old do you think I am?" I asked them.

After a moment's ponder, Miguel replied that "judging from your gray hair, you must be at least fifty, Camilo."

At last, the *real* secret of my popularity with the old guys. They all thought I was one of them!

In Copapayo, I again stayed with Frederico's family. He had suffered from an infection in his eyes, which I had vainly tried to diagnose and treat long distance by radio from Palo Grande. His arthritis kept him from venturing there.

The various salves applied by the *sanitarios* had done nothing to stop the infection. By now, it had cost him total vision in one eye. Had we not just received a supply of chloroamphenicol drops, Frederico would have been totally and permanently blind in a matter of days.

At supper that evening, Frederico and Isabel gingerly broached a subject they had long wished to discuss with me. Their youngest child, Noe, the one with Down's syndrome, was probably the most-loved of all their children. Yet his condition perplexed them. They had been told all sorts of superstitious nonsense about why he looked the way he did and why he was retarded. When I explained in a simplified fashion that Down's syndrome was not uncommon when women over forty years of age conceived, they were immensely relieved.

Isabel also had news of her friend, and my patient, Blanca, a seventy-six-year-old widow, who suffered from chronic angina. Her condition, said Isabel, had improved greatly since I'd been able to give Blanca propranolol, a so-called beta blocker that, among other things, governs against over-exertion of the heart. Blanca had rejoined her women's farm collective and could be seen daily bringing water to the workers in the fields.

Isabel and Blanca were part of the feminist vanguard on the Front. The former, as head of the local Association of Salvadoran Women (AMS), promoted health and sex education among the women in order for them to better understand their bodies, particularly when it came to childbirth. This was a small step that showed that many of the women of the Front were taking a more active part in shaping their own destinies.

Blanca, who had no immediate family left, was more the activist. She had refused her widow's full-share food allotment in favor of contributing her labor to an agricultural cooperative. No free hand-outs for her! Tiring of the men's comments about the women's slowness and awkwardness in the fields, she formed a women's farm collective, where she could contribute along with the rest. That summer, their field outproduced all but a few of the many others, mostly men's collectives, a point of great pride with Blanca.

Isabel and she harbored few illusions over the time it would take to bring female equality to a macho society. There were centuries of custom and habit to undo. Yet the *compañeros* had already adjusted to fighting the *chuchos* alongside women; depending on the "tendency" from which they were drawn, the columns now included from five to thirty female combatants for every hundred males.

Women also moved into politics, teaching, medicine, and communications. Village government, as well as guerrilla structures, had women leaders in increasing numbers. Men could occasionally be seen doing traditional female work, such as gathering wood, bringing water, and grinding or washing corn. The door was opening a bit.

FROM FREDERICO'S HOUSE that night I was summoned to the village radio room. Guadalupe, they said, had been attacked and overrun by the enemy. The *guinda* had begun. We could expect the survivors by dawn.

The government strategy now began to unfold. They probably knew from past experience that the eastern part of the Front was the most lightly defended. More than anywhere else in the control zone, it was vulnerable to surprise attack from the lake or from the highway. It was also the easiest sector to isolate and surround, an important consideration for Raul Hercules and his officers when they deployed their fighters.

What forces he could devote to the eastern sector (the exact number of guerrillas stationed in the various parts of the Front was never known to me) had further been deprived of fresh ammunition and supplies by the government patrols on the highway. They were too few and too poorly equipped to effectively counter a large assault.

Guadalupe, among the southernmost of the eastern settlements, was the first target. Before daybreak, the first of her citizens had made it due north to Copapayo. We found surprisingly few had sustained physical injury; the Front's early warning system of radios and messengers had given most of them time to flee before the soldiers came to raze their village. There were a few wounds to treat, mostly from mortar fragments.

Copapayo began to prepare for its own *guinda*. The women got busy grinding corn for making tortillas, the only portable food we had. A supply to keep the village fed for at least two or three days' marching was prepared in addition to the amount needed to feed the evacuees from Guadalupe, numbering two hundred people.

The men took most of the livestock out into the hills where the animals would be hidden from the invaders. The corn and bean seed stocks were buried. Children were made responsible for gathering and stashing family possessions in *buzones*. Everything they treasured, from primitive, hand-operated sewing machines to the children's favorite toys, went into these underground caches.

In the midst of the preparations, the Guadalupe refugees began returning to their village. The enemy had attacked quickly and withdrawn. Barely an hour before the first of the villagers would have made it to Guadalupe, the soldiers came back hoping to trap them. Instead they were ambushed and suffered heavy casualties.

A day later, I went to Tenango, which was a bit west of the midpoint between Copapayo and Guadalupe. There, the citizens had also evacuated and had only just returned from two days' hiding in a cavern on the eastern slope of the "Grand Canyon." They were cold and tired and hungry. Many of the children were ill from exposure to the constant dampness; everyone was covered with mosquito bites. They were understandably extremely tense.

During that night and throughout the next day, we could hear small-arms fire, machine gun chatter, and the explosions of mortars as well as the distinct sounds of the guerrilla land mines. The *compañeros*, with very little at their disposal, were trying to keep the beast at bay.

They used several tactics. Since the soldiers withdrew to their bivouacs each night and refused to fight, rebel teams would salt the trails leading away from the camps with their homemade landmines. We could usually hear them detonating in the morning as the enemy officers drove their troops out and down the trails.

The soldiers would half-heartedly contest a rifle or other piece of equipment that the guerrillas tried to seize. But they could be ferocious when trying to protect or retrieve the body of a fallen comrade. I do not know why this was so, unless they believed the insurgents desecrated corpses the way they did. Perhaps it was a matter of pride. In time, the rebels learned it was easier and more effective to booby-trap a body than to waste ammunition fighting for it. Those *trampas* (booby traps) were larger than the small landmines, and we heard several of them as well that day. Most of the fighting seemed to be taking place between the "Grand Canyon" and the highway.

There was no hope of actually repulsing the enemy; they were too numerous. But like a bull in an arena, a battalion could be driven one way and then the other with picador-like strikes to its back and flanks. Small detachments of heavily armed *compañeros* kept these skirmishes going constantly. More than once during the day, I was later told, they succeeded in totally disrupting the troops' deployment, actually drawing the enemy into firing at each other.

Waiting for me in Tenango was a sixteen-year-old called Ricardo whose left forearm and hand had been seared through by white phosphorus from a spotter plane rocket. His wound was a horrible, stinking mess, so ugly that at first Janet was ill at its sight.

There was no question of saving it. The burns, I knew,

would soon infect, and if Tenango had to be evacuated again, gangrene would be inevitable after several days in the bush. Crossing the highway during an offensive was out of the question. To save his life, we would have to amputate—now.

Here, more than usual, the problem was equipment. I had a few scalpels with me and a small amount of suture, which I had almost exhausted in Copapayo. What I lacked was a bone saw, bone wax to seal off the exposed marrow, and general anesthesia. As Janet sterilized the clinic's six instruments in boiling water, I achieved a local block with lidocaine and dug out my Swiss Army knife.

I wanted to leave the humerus intact, if possible, but I couldn't immediately tell how much of the tissue had been damaged by heat and shock. We cut into him at the elbow and removed the traumatized forearm before realizing we hadn't gone far enough to ensure a margin of safety. We would have to amputate a couple of inches above the elbow.

Ricardo had passed out at the start, but fainting didn't prevent him from yanking and jerking throughout the operation. We had him on a low bench with one person sitting on his legs and two others pinioning his upper body. They could barely restrain him.

My knife's saw worked well. Janet, who overcame her nausea once the burned portion of the arm was cut away, then incised the "fish-mouth" flap of skin and muscle to cover the stump. Having used all the suture to tie off blood vessels, we boiled some dental floss that I carried in my pack and loosely closed the flaps. It was clumsy, but Ricardo would survive.

IN THE AFTERNOON heavy fighting began near the southern approach to Tenango, where it was easiest to cross the "Grand Canyon." For the first time that day, an A-37 appeared in the sky. As usual, it did not support the ground troops but came in on the village with its gattling gun roaring. It came down the solitary dirt road that led to the clinic where I was seeing patients. The only casualty was a cow, which three *campesinos* instantly dragged off to butcher. It didn't take an hour for the entire carcass to be cut up and distributed.

The guerrilla radio warned that the soldiers were pressing in our direction, so the inhabitants of Tenango evacuated again at nightfall. I packed my gear and with Janet hiked north and east back to Copapayo.

The next morning, we learned that the Ramón Belloso Battalion, only months out of advance training at Fort Bragg in North Carolina, had cut a diagonal swath east to north through the eastern sector. By noon, they were headed toward Copapayo.

In all, about 350 *campesinos* and militias were trapped on the Copapayo peninsula. At our backs was Lake Suchitlán and more government soldiers on the Chalatenango side. We would be easy targets from the A-37s or spotter planes if we tried to escape by boat. Air power was the anvil.

The hammer, the Belloso Battalion, would either drive us into the water, or surround and slaughter us in the village. A council was held, and it was decided that a nighttime *guinda* straight back up the peninsula and through the enemy lines was our only chance. Janet would go with the mass of civilians as soon as darkness fell. Héctor, the male *sanitario*, joined the thirty-five or so militias who were trying to slow the battalion's advance.

I spent the day helping to prepare the hammock cases for evacuation and readying what medicine we had. In the village's tiny schoolhouse, Janet's sister carefully wrapped her three texts, the students' notebooks, and a few pencil stubs into a plastic bag and then buried it.

The villagers' calm was remarkable. They were not surprised by an afternoon radio broadcast from San Salvador that announced that the Ramón Belloso Battalion had surrounded a large group of guerrillas and was closing in despite heavy resistance.

My diary entry for the next day was brief. "Thank God," I wrote, "that the government has a nine to five army."

In truth they had worked overtime the previous afternoon, dropping mortars until a few minutes after dark. Then Janet and the *campesinos* with their drugged children made their way silently up the peninsula past the soldiers' camps.

I remained to tend a wounded militiaman while several others kept firing from time to time to help preserve the myth that we were all waiting in Copapayo for our deaths. Before we, too, sneaked north through the lines, they lit a couple of campfires and tied several dogs to their front porches. We knew they would bark all night.

I assumed that Miguel had evacuated with the pregnant and elderly women; there was no sign of him as I and the others prepared to leave. One of his friends, a militiaman named Gerinaldo, asked me if I wished to carry an M-1 that night. The only temptation at that instant was to tell Gerinaldo all the reasons why I did *not* wish to carry a weapon. It had been two weeks since the anniversary of Ché's death; time to consolidate my attitudes and to prepare myself for their possible consequences.

I had come back from the precipice. If nothing else, the cumulative force of events on Guazapa had taken abstract principles into the realm of the concrete.

"No, Gerinaldo," I answered as politely as possible. "It is better that a fighter like you carries the rifle."

I left Copapayo just in advance of Gerinaldo and the five other militias. Inching along with a wounded *compañero* who leaned on me for support, we spent many hours in silent, slow progress past the soldiers. Not a guard was posted. There were no patrols. Fifteen hundred of the Salvadoran army's most elite, U.S.-trained troops allowed 350 peasants to walk right through their cordon.

We waited two days before returning. Well-hidden up in the hills to the south and east of Copapayo, we listened to the government's announcement of a great victory and counted the hours until it would be safe to return. In one of the strangest interludes of my life, I listened to two-quarters of a Notre Dame football game and struggled to understand how

60,000 people could get so worked up about a game. Then I closed my eyes and imagined what a beer and a hot dog would taste like.

The march back to Copapayo was solemn. We could see from far off that the village was still smouldering. At a mile's distance, we could already smell the beginning rot of the dead animals.

The soldiers' fury at missing us was directed at the village. They had killed all of the livestock that they could find. The dogs had been shot, too. We found them still leashed to their posts—stiff, bloated, and covered with flies.

No one spoke as we examined the devastation. Some of the houses were blackened shells. The clinic was totally demolished as was the schoolhouse. In all of the residences, we found cups and plates with bullet holes shot squarely through their centers; even the forks and spoons were broken in half. A photo of Archbishop Romero was scrawled with obscenities.

The silence was eerie and went unbroken for several minutes until we heard an anguished moan from one of the wrecked houses. I ran to Frederico's door to find Isabel wailing before an alcove beside her kitchen. On its tiny shelves, her collection of religious figures—saints, Mary, a sacred heart of Jesus—had been smashed. On her wall, a dead cat was nailed through a religious picture.

We found Miguel. He had crawled some distance before bleeding to death. Gerinaldo worked his friend's arms into a more natural position, and we covered him with a cloth. Painted on a wall near where he died was a message: "This is what happens to those who live with subversives. Ramón Belloso Battalion."

The silence returned. As I squatted in the dust next to Miguel in his shroud, Gerinaldo hunched down beside me. After several minutes, he rose and whispered.

"They taught them well in your country, Camilo," he said with no emotion. "They are more thorough than the others."

WHITE FIRE

I LEARNED FROM VETERANS of past government offensives against Guazapa that this one of late October, 1982, was inconsequential. They numbered the offensives like Super Bowls, Guazapa I, Guazapa II, and so on. Guazapa IX, which had come the previous February, had inflicted major damage; it was the main reason for the near-famine of May and June. This one was not considered up to Super Bowl quality and was not even numbered. Though it cost the Front a good deal of livestock, there were only two deaths and three injuries. The Ramón Belloso Battalion had managed to kill Miguel and one *compañero*.

Besides Guadalupe and Copapayo in the eastern sector, the only other village to be hit was El Roble. Nearby Palo Grande had been evacuated successfully except for the loss of our medical records, a couple of notebooks with penciled entries. Slight as their loss seemed then, it soon was of tragic importance to me.

Most of the people saw the invasion as a defeat for the enemy. Forty soldiers were killed, nearly one hundred were wounded, and many weapons were retrieved. From what I saw, this ratio of dead, ten or twenty to one, was typical of government actions against Guazapa. Even with the A-37s and the effective isolation of the eastern sector, the government still was unable to score a significant victory over the *compañeros*, or even to match their earlier successes against them. And despite the constant military pressure on the zone, its population had swelled by a thousand refugees since the previous spring. Harrowing as our lives were, the situation must have been even worse in other parts of the country.

The offensive did, however, seriously disrupt communications; it was several days before radio contact was reestablished throughout the Front and the *correos* could be dispatched to Palo Grande with full assessments of the destruction.

During this interim, I left the stunned but physically whole population of Copapayo and hiked back to Palo Grande. Our little party arrived there unannounced and provoked considerable joy in the village.

For the first several months I was in Guazapa, I had no permanent or reliable shelter. If I didn't sleep in the open, I bedded down among the health workers at the various clinics or, very occasionally, with a family I'd befriended. In Zapote, for instance, I often stayed with David and his wife. Nearer Palo Grande, my hosts were usually Rutilio, David's nephew, and his wife, Ita. They had "incorporated" after many years of working with Archbishop Romero and Father Rutilio Grande, the priest from Aguilares who, along with Father José Alas, had been instrumental in organizing the local peasants. As was the custom among the people there, Rutilio had taken his pseudonym in honor of Rutilio Grande. His wife, Ita, chose hers for Ita Ford, one of the four American churchwomen murdered in 1980 by the National Guard.

My many long conversations with Rutilio and Ita taught me much about the uses of terror and oppression. They were both devoutly Catholic, which was not unusual for El Salvador, and they both had long experience with the peaceful approach to change. The establishment and spread of base

Christian communities, they both had felt, was an evolutionary process, one that might correct injustice and deprivation without recourse to armed revolt. But just as Magdaleno had explained about his own conversion to the guerrillas, Rutilio and Ita had also been radicalized by the extremes of the right. Attending Romero's funeral at the San Salvador cathedral, Rutilio and Ita heard the bombs go off and watched the snipers firing from atop the buildings. One of their children, a son, was crushed to death by the crowd as it surged for cover. After burying their child, Rutilio and Ita "incorporated."

My contact with these friends was abruptly curtailed once Jasmine left the Front and I moved my gear into her hospital. I stayed there until shortly after the *compañero* congress of late August. Then came a more permanent arrangement.

Paco's betrayal of Salvador and the other guerrilla leaders at the safe houses in the capital had been a heavy blow to civilian administration on the Front. This tall, rather quiet man, my advisor during the negotiations with Marco, had coordinated almost all of the social welfare projects in Guazapa. His common sense and good counsel had been instrumental in keeping and maintaining the elementary school system, the literacy classes for adults, and many of the other programs that lent the community cohesiveness as well as a sense of purpose and permanency.

His wife, Flor, was devastated. Caught between rational acceptance of Salvador's probable fate and her hope that, somehow, he might survive arrest, she fell into a deepening depression. When their fourteen-year-old son, Aurelio, left the house to "incorporate," Flor became even further distressed.

Her forty-five-year-old aunt, Fernanda, feared for Flor's health. At her insistence, and with the concurrence of everyone in the household, I was asked to come live with them. Since I had been Salvador's friend, Fernanda said, I was practically "family" anyway. It might take Flor's mind off her fears, and it would be good for the children. Compared to life around the hospital collective. the idea of living with a family was very appealing. I readily accepted the invitation.

As I mentioned earlier, Guazapan households were not strictly defined. There was a constant shifting and sorting to make sure people had a roof over their heads. Flor was now head of a fourteen-person household, all contained in a single room. Its door and two windows opened south onto a small porch and a kitchen; the military hospital stood across the way. Besides herself and Fernanda, her unmarried cousin Remata lived there, as did Uncle Magnífico, Meme, a niece, an unrelated oldster named Gastón, seven children, and me.

The oldest child, sixteen-year-old Maribel, was in charge of the education of the other kids. Sometimes, they read their lessons to me. Sometimes they made great sport of the gringo who happily fell for their jokes and pranks.

Uncle Magnífico would set out each morning with a couple tortillas and a gourd of water to wage war against the weeds and worms in his corn patch. In my small amount of free time, I sometimes accompanied him for a couple hours. He didn't say much; then again, he had only three teeth.

Other times, I could be found learning to grind corn on the porch. Flor tried to offer advance instruction in tortilla-making, but I was hopeless in mixing and shaping them.

I was closest of all to the youngest boy, five-year-old Antonito, the ablest slingshot artist of my acquaintance. Most young boys in Guazapa were good with a slingshot; bringing down a single mango from a distance of fifty feet was considered minimally proficient among them. But Antonito was special. In the time I stayed with the family, he brought home an opossum, a rabbit, an iguana, and numerous birds for the supper table. His proudest kill was also the saddest for me. A bird of great beauty, *la tijera* (the green scissor-tail). had the ill fortune to be resting high up in a eucalyptus tree one afternoon as Antonito happened by with his slingshot. He conked the poor thing dead, then plucked, gutted, and skewered it for the two of us. Two mouthfuls, and that was it. I felt terrible about consuming something so rare. It was worse still that Antonito didn't have a little boy's leisure to appreciate. rather than eat, a thing of such beauty.

Antonito and the other kids were not without their instincts for art and self-expression. I remember him coming to me one afternoon and asking for a sheet of paper from my notebook. As precious as paper was, I couldn't refuse him. Since he was just then learning to read and write, I considered the donation my contribution to the future literacy of El Salvador. But the moment he had it, the rest of the children clamored for sheets of their own. I had no choice but to be equitable.

An hour or so later, back they came with their individual creations—not letters or numbers but drawings of surprising skill. It was their subject that bothered me. Each child had recreated war scenes. The pages were full of diving jets, burning houses, explosions, and broken human bodies. Each was also covered with pictures of flowers and of children playing—realistic interpretations of the two truths they all knew.

I later tried to get enough paper for the whole village to make drawings. I hoped somehow to get them back to the States. As it was, the best I could do was to get a couple pieces of chalk from the IRC. Antonito and his siblings used them to decorate Flor's house with the same menacing rockets and graceful hibiscuses, dead *campesinos* and dance scenes.

WHAT I AT FIRST TOOK to be a dose of dengue hit me in the first week of November. I had caught it once before in the Pacific. There dengue is called "bone break fever" for the agony in the joints it causes, and I assumed with the onset of ferocious headaches that I had contracted it once more.

As we were once again totally out of aspirin, I treated myself with the willow bark tea and set my mind against dengue's customary seven-day siege. Soon my fever rose precipitously and any sudden noise from the children made me cringe with pain.

I took to my bed in the corner of Flor's house and

wished for sleep or darkness or at least some silence. What I got were patients, dozens of them, who weren't satisfied to be treated by *sanitarios* when they knew the doctor was nearby. I saw a couple of them at my bedside before Fernanda chased the rest away.

On the fifth day, I was called to perform a delivery. I remember walking to the woman's house, and I remember that we successfully delivered the child. I think I recall being carried back to Flor's. I may have dreamt that the children had to carry me to the air raid shelter after an attack the following afternoon.

Dorita, officially my superior, consulted with Jasmine and Pedro over my deteriorating condition, and the three decided I should be removed to a more remote, quieter household where prospective patients couldn't besiege me and there would be less chance of an air raid. They loaded me, half-conscious, onto a horse from which I promptly slumped to the ground, injuring a rib and raising chuckles from the group. Pedro hadn't cinched the saddle tight enough. I clearly remember lying on the ground under the horse. But I have no recollection of Pedro realizing I was indeed quite ill or of him lashing me to the horse and then walking the animal high up above Palo Grande to my retreat.

Most of the next several days is very mixed up in my mind. It wasn't dengue, but malaria's fever and dehydration that set me hallucinating, again and again, that a giant bottle of Coca-Cola, all frosty and foaming, stood just inches from my grasp. Intermittently, I would become semi-conscious and open my eyes to darkness. There were whispers and then a candle glow by which I could make out pictures of Mary and the Sacred Heart tacked to the wall above me. Then more darkness and the sound of murmurs and incantations.

I struggled to clear my mind. What is this? I remembered the Salvadoran custom of holding ten nightly services for the deceased before a final wake. Did they think I was dead?

"Ola!" I tried to shout. "Camilo está vivo!"

Someone patted me on the arm.

Another lapse of consciousness before the sensation of being carried somewhere. My bearers were in white. "Angels?" I asked, then fell back and out.

As my periods of wakefulness lengthened, I asked to listen to the radio; it was the only sure way of learning how long I'd been delirious. They found the Voice of America for me. It was November 12, nine days after the onset of my headaches and fully three since Pedro had taken me from Palo Grande.

I was as weak, limp, and helpless as a newborn lamb as I lay there on my pallet in the dark, listening to the dedication ceremonies for the new Vietnam Veterans' Memorial in Washington. I dimly recalled that such a memorial had at last been undertaken, and I listened intently as an announcer described the scene there that day. I heard about the flowers and the weeping relatives. The reporter spoke of vets in wheelchairs and fatigues and of the little American flags that children carried. The Vietnam vets finally had their parade.

An ache started up in my chest as the program shifted to a church. Organ music was audible in the background as someone began reading the 57,000 names of the Vietnam War dead.

I listened intermittently over several hours.

"Max Anderson," the speaker intoned over my radio.

Max Anderson. My friend whose remains I'd stumbled over in a body bag at the rear of my C-130.

"Dennis Pugh."

Dennis Pugh, a fellow member of the Academy track team. Died when his F-4 was shot down.

"Kenneth Svanoe."

A well-liked wrestler from the squadron next door, whom I used to help with aerodynamics classes. Lost to anti-aircraft fire over Laos.

The dead were visiting me on my pallet in a dark room somewhere on the side of the Guazapa volcano. Their faces returned to my memory as sharply as if I'd seen them only days before. I moaned at the sound of each familiar name. So much of this had been buried deep, deep in my unconscious.

I fought for years not to individualize the war, to keep the personal losses aside from the issues. But now I couldn't help crying for my friends and so many others.

Everything seemed so hopeless. They had died useless deaths, and here I was in the middle of another savage, pointless conflict. The exact same stupidity and arrogance that had killed Max and Dennis and Kenneth was about to be repeated. At the same time their names were being chiseled in stone, their government—my government—was wading deeper and deeper into another senseless war. A whole new generation of clear-eyed Air Force cadets and regular Army grunts were trained and ready to die for U.S. credibility.

I turned off the radio and tried to let the silence calm me, but constant stress and the malaria had disposed me toward melancholy; the radio program from Washington was only the catalyst for my paralyzing fear that history was about to repeat itself.

It wasn't just fever, however, that underlay that fear, nor was the situation in El Salvador an abstraction to me anymore. It was more real, even, than Vietnam had been. There, I'd flown C-130s, heard and seen a lot, but had little firsthand experience of the war as it was being waged on the ground. In El Salvador, I bore personal witness to the character and capabilities of the rebels. I had seen atrocities—so many of them. I knew how competent the government fighting forces were.

If the Reagan administration really meant what it said when it dedicated itself to the defeat of the *compañeros*, this goal was not going to be achieved by the Salvadoran military. How long would it be, I wondered, before the United States dispatched its own forces to take over the government's fight?

On the tenth day, I arose from the dead, or at least that's the way it felt. My wits returned, and I came to understand that the candlelight services had been nightly rosaries—prayers for my recovery—in the home of the base Christian community to which I had been carried. As soon as the word spread that my fever had broken, there were nearly constant visits by *campesinos* bringing eggs, cooked bananas, and *atol*, a hot and sweet children's drink made from corn mush.

The women of the house politely accepted the food and kept it until I could eat. For the next several days, they kept me confined to my pallet, feeding me drinks of *quina* bark tea and expertly rehydrating me with a variety of fruit-flavored liquids.

Rarely had they seen a malaria attack as severe as mine, and never have I been prostrate for so long. I can only reason that I was struck so hard because I had developed no immunity and was physically spent to begin with. I now appreciated how an episode of malarial headaches could reduce the toughest *compañero* to sobs.

Against the women's protestations, I insisted upon returning to Palo Grande and Flor's house before I had fully convalesced. The disease was more debilitating than I'd thought. Every mile or so on my walk back down the volcano, I'd have to stop and rest for at least half an hour.

Shaky, and still afflicted with intermittent headaches, I tried to force my recovery. The third night at home, I believed I was strong enough to answer an emergency call.

JULIA WAS THIRTY-SEVEN and this was her twelfth pregnancy; there were seven children at home, three had died at birth, and she'd suffered one miscarriage. Her husband, Dimas, was among the bravest and most popular of the guerrilla comandantes. A true swashbuckler, Dimas was the *compañero's* equivalent of Francis Marion, the "Swamp Fox" of our revolution, or Colonel Mosby, the "Gray Ghost" of the South in the Civil War. He even looked the part of the romantic rebel, down to the cowboy hat, black boots, and snow-white horse he rode throughout the Front.

Julia's life was not as romantic. She was a frequent patient at my pre-natal clinics. She had only eight teeth and hands horny with calluses from chopping wood. All the pregnancies had left her chronically anemic, and her diet was too iron-deficient to replenish the iron she lost. In short, she was in no condition to have another baby.

She was brought to the civilian hospital after hemorrhaging most of the day. When I got there after ten-thirty that night, I found her very pale, her pulse at a weak and thready 150. She was nearing shock. The fetal heart tones were weak and slowed considerably during and after each contraction, which was not a good sign. A gentle vaginal exam revealed what felt like a spongy placenta in the way of the child's head—placenta previa, in medical terms. This was a true obstetric emergency. We had to operate.

We lost time carrying her in a hammock down the ravine to Jasmine's hospital, our surgical facility. When we got there, I found that all the blood-typing chemicals had been used up. Only the Rh reagent was left. She was positive.

Since our notebooks of medical records were lost, I turned to the nurses and *sanitarios*, asking each their blood type. We needed at least four units of blood, and we needed them fast. The staff blinked sheepishly at me. No one could remember if they were A or B or O, positive or negative. Though this was important knowledge, they'd taken my constant reminders as another gringo peculiarity and quickly forgot their own types.

There was no time for anger. Knowing myself to be O positive, I quickly asked Dorita to draw two units of my own blood and then began administering it to Julia. More time wasted, and the doctor hoped he wouldn't have difficulty standing up.

We got the baby out in four minutes. There was no heartbeat, no respiration, no cry. Her tiny body was stained green with meconium, fetal excrement, a sign of severe stress. Try as we might, the child could not be revived.

Meanwhile, I closed Julia's uterus and abdominal muscles and was suturing her skin when she went into cardiac arrest. For a half-hour more, we tried to resuscitate her. None of us wanted to stop the effort, but it was to no avail.

It was a horror for me as a doctor, a double tragedy. I looked down at her dead figure on the operating table and made the usual clichéd observation that she looked very peaceful. But I knew she left seven children in an adobe house in Chaparral. Feelings of incompetence, uncertainty, and guilt flooded over me. As weak as I was, the call to another emergency in Salitre was a welcome chance to flee this scene, my blackest ever as a physician.

I started out on foot at first light. Stumbling, cursing, feeling faint from time to time, I marched for maybe an hour when Dimas, astride his white horse, suddenly towered over me on the trail. I was speechless.

"Camilo," he called down to me, "I received a radio message. What is the emergency? How is Julia?"

As steadily as I could, I told the comandante that he was a widower, that Julia and their infant daughter had died under my knife. Humbly, I said I was very, very sorry.

Ever the consummate leader, Dimas betrayed not a trace of shock or grief at my news. I mumbled something more to him, but he only dismounted and strode over to me. A single note of reproach might have crushed me just then. Instead, he asked me to look up.

"You must not let this tragedy defeat you," was all he said, but even then I could see tears welling in his eyes. As if to encourage me by example, Dimas hastily remounted and rode on to Chaparral to see his children.

I stood on the trail for a few minutes, marveling at his stoicism. The man's wife and infant daughter had just died on the operating table, and he was consoling their doctor! Perhaps he wasn't being purely selfless; what good was I to the Front if I retreated into remorse? Whatever his motives, however, Dimas' few words checked any possible surrender to self-pity.

I traveled on to Salitre, light-headed from the malaria and blood loss. Pedro was there to welcome me. Together, we treated the emergency, a forty-six-year-old man who had fallen from an orange tree and suffered some broken ribs and a dislocated shoulder. Then we talked until I fell asleep.

* * *

CHARLES CLEMENTS, M.D.

THANKSGIVING CAME TWO WEEKS LATER. All day, the U.S. Armed Forces Radio Network and VOA tormented me with talk about food. The announcers repeated recipes for stuffing and roasting turkeys. They discussed pumpkin pie. They recounted how savory their own meals were that day and how overly full they were. I listened until I could bear no more, then shut them off.

At midday, we shared our usual meal, beans and tortillas. I looked down at my plate and out of boredom counted my beans. There were seventy-nine of them. Counting my blessings worked a little better. My health had improved; the malaria had subsided into sporadic headaches. And the Red Cross had agreed to hold a one day *consulta* (clinic) for our civilians.

Four days later, as I was listening to the radio again, the announcer happened to mention the date; it was my birthday. For months, I had measured the time of day by the sun; I cared about my watch only for its second hand. Likewise, the day of the week seemed unimportant, or even the month.

A far more vital measure than time was that of wear and tear; specifically, the relative state of my boots. Would they last a trip to and from Delicias? Did they require repair before I essayed the "Grand Canyon"? On my thirty-seventh birthday, they didn't look as if they would take me to the latrine.

I had stitched them back together a dozen times with every imaginable material. Nylon, I found, was good for two weeks before it snapped. Heavy fishnet line was a bit more durable; it held together for three weeks. From the wreckage of a government tank, I salvaged some radio wiring, but it must have been a cheap radio. My boot soles were flapping again in seven days. So I attacked the problem with the copper wire that the *compañeros* used to lash machete blades to their wooden handles. It was stiff and unwieldy to punch through several layers of hard leather and rubber. But by using my forceps and clamps, I closed the wound, as it were, in four hours. This time, the boots stayed sewn.

As I admired my handiwork, I heard someone calling the

"medico norteamericano." I looked around to find a *compañero* walking up the trail with a package.

He had just arrived from Quipurito after spending six weeks dodging government raiders in the hills of Chalatenango to the north. During all that time, he had gamely hung onto a letter and a package for me. Only by the sheerest coincidence, he at last was able to deliver both on my birthday.

I thanked him and opened the package with a good laugh. It was a book entitled *How to Train Community Health Workers*. The volume had been sent down to me by friends in Salinas back in June.

The letter, also from my friends, was the greatest birthday treat of all. Although several months out of date, it was filled with glad words that were all news to me. My parents were fine. They had received my somewhat cryptic farewell note from Mexico and seemed to have accepted my reasons for going, even if they weren't at all sure just where it was I'd gone.

Since neither of them enjoyed great health, it was a relief to know they were doing well. I didn't want them to worry, and I didn't want that worry to have a physical effect. In the past, they had made the very difficult adjustment to my anti-war sentiments and the acutely felt taint of my hospitalization. That they were now safe and reconciled to yet another unsettling move on my part made me very happy.

My pleasure at the letter extended even to the familiar hand in which it was written. It was partially in code and deliberately kept vague, since possession of a more explicit note could have cost a messenger his life. Nevertheless, each nugget of news I could infer or decipher was a single, separate joy to savor.

I further realized, while reading it, what a circumscribed being I'd become among the guerrillas. Except for the rambling recollections I'd shared with Pedro the previous summer, I had altogether ceased to be Charlie Clements. Nobody on the Front knew anything more about me as an individual than I knew about them, much less, actually. So complete was this loss of self that if someone there had addressed me as

"Dr. Clements" or "Charlie" I might not have recognized the name.

As Camilo, the gringo doctor, I had very little dimension. People came to me with their ailments, discussed practical matters, or talked about the whys and wherefores of their revolution. Nothing else was shared. Nothing else seemed germane. Though I was shown much care and warmth, gratitude and generosity, it was my contribution to the commonweal that was mightily appreciated. I, like everyone else with their pseudonyms, existed only as part of something, not as a whole unto myself.

I had to accept the situation and the unbridgeable culture gap between me and them. When I failed to observe these twin perimeters on my behavior, it caused a considerable degree of distress for everyone concerned.

One night at the old hospital, I looked up from an emergency bullet extraction to see one of the *sanitarios* opening a bottle of tranquilizers. A couple hours later, I inspected the bottle and discovered it was at least two hundred tablets short.

As previously mentioned, tranquilizers were the single most popular medicine on the Front. Everybody wanted one or more to help them sleep or to cope with stress. From the nightly sounds of combat to the squeaking and scurrying of the rats in the roof timbers, there was more than sufficient cause to make every single one of us a junkie.

One of my reforms as de facto head of civilian medicine was to place the tranquilizers on our "control" list. Whereas before they were dispensed by anyone in any of the health cooperatives, now they could only be given under Jasmine's or my direction. The supply was strictly accounted for. At the same time, I constantly tried to encourage the use of natural sedatives brewed from mock orange leaves or petals of the *pita* flower. This was not a popular initiative. Although it helped to stretch our tranquilizer supply for those who really needed them, the hysterics, patients being prepared for anesthesia, and the children during *guindas*, it angered some of the population. To them, the restriction was a matter of gringo arrogance and nothing more.

When I questioned the *sanitario*, he told me he had taken the tablets for a depressed friend. He also admitted to lifting a few for Dorita, who wanted them to help deal with the recent combat death of a close friend. I exploded, accusing the medic of violating his trust, of taking advantage of a surgical crisis, and of favoritism. The next day, I upbraided Dorita as well.

My anger backfired. Instead of becoming contrite, the *sanitario* was indignant. He quit the hospital, as did Dorita. The rest of the staff also threatened to leave, and treated me as if I were a pariah.

Utterly confused by this response, I went to Jasmine. Gently and firmly, she informed me that my campaign against tranquilizer abuse had gone too far, that I was imposing my own values on their system rather than dealing with the *campesinos* and medics on their terms. Jasmine also reminded me that everyone in all the cooperatives was an unpaid volunteer.

"They are not your employees," she added.

The only way to deal with the crisis was to call a meeting. I coaxed Dorita and the offended *sanitario* back to the hospital and then in front of the entire staff I apologized for my temper. Swallowing hard, I spent a full half-hour in self-criticism. I admitted that my behavior had been inappropriate and that I was trapped by *norteamericano* ways of thinking.

Following the speech, we all sat down and discussed the issue some more. No one regarded the theft itself as serious. What had bothered them most was my response to it, especially the suggestion that Dorita had taken tranquilizers for herself. That she had was beyond question, but it was very bad gringo form to actually accuse her of it.

In the end, I was forgiven, even though it was many weeks before I could once again regain their trust and confidence. Everyone agreed that in principle I was trying not to impose my own point of view, but in practice I often did.

At first it rankled me to have to soothe a thief's wounded dignity. Still, the affair was a valuable object lesson in humility. It wasn't within my purview to issue reprimands or to help guide them in their ethical development. Having lifted themselves out from under the *dueño*'s boot, they were not about to take orders from the gringo.

To a person, they were phobic on this issue. Arrogance of any sort was squashed as quickly as it arose. Even Raul Hercules exercised only minimal discretionary powers. Just the suggestion that he and his officers enjoyed a privileged life had been enough to help spark a plot against him.

AS UNREALISTIC AS THIS rigid egalitarianism seems, it was honored in practice as well as principle. It guided the development of their social order and, for a community of peasants, it made for surprisingly effective organization.

A group of fishermen, for instance, formed themselves into a cooperative that not only enlarged their total daily catch but also led to a fish-salting facility where more portable food for the *guindas* was produced. Another group raided a government-controlled apiary and came back with hives to start their own bee farms. In time, they produced enough honey for the militias to begin packaging it and burying it in barrels as emergency food supplies around the Front. After Guazapa IX, the guerrillas organized a rustling party that came back with several head of livestock to replace those killed by the government troops.

More impressive still was an all-night raid on a chicken farm just outside the Front. The farm, owned by a Salvadoran army colonel, was surrounded and secured by the guerrillas, who then established a five-mile cordon stretching back into the Front. Along it came over a thousand *campesinos* who grabbed as many chickens as they could and then carried them back through the secure cordon. Some of the men brought poles on which they hung as many as six or eight of the birds. Others, like the children, struggled back with one or two of the hens squawking and flapping in their grasp.

Stealing the chickens, however, was only the beginning. The animals had been raised according to modern farming techniques. They had been kept under shelter; their exposure to light was regulated; and their special antibiotic feed was distributed in carefully measured amounts. There would be no such luxuries for the birds in Guazapa.

At first, they stood around like a tour group waiting to be shown the way to dinner. When they weren't fed as usual, most of them dropped their feathers and stopped laying eggs. They knew nothing about scratching around for worms or roosting in trees.

For several weeks, in fact, they represented a net drain on the Front's food stores. They had to be fed corn and shown where to go for water. They had to adjust to natural daylight, and they had to learn where to sleep so that the rats and skunks didn't eat them. The tougher and more practiced they got at country ways, the scrawnier and scruffier they looked. But they did finally settle into the guerrilla's life of air raids and *guindas*. They did not, however, attend many of the political meetings.

These civic ventures were as well planned as they were daring; no mean feat for a people with only the briefest experience with self-governance. But the severest test of their organization was the International Red Cross *consulta*. Once the Red Cross agreed, in principle, to hold a one-day clinic for the Front's civilians and was given tentative government approval to do so, the entire zone had to be mobilized.

At first, several of the *tendencias* opposed the clinic outright. Since the government would insist upon knowing when and where it was to be held, they argued it offered too great a risk of a massacre. They worried, as well, over the clinic's propaganda implications. It could be a public relations bonanza for the government. On the one hand, the enemy would demonstrate their generosity. On the other, they might show up the rebels as incapable of taking care of their own people. Several long meetings were held to discuss these objections, which were overridden by widespread popular support for much-needed medicines and treatment.

Next, the site for the *consulta* was selected. It had to be accessible to as many people as possible, while not too close to militarily sensitive areas. It had to be easily evacuated and defensible should the government launch a surprise attack. An abandoned schoolhouse just inside the zone and less than half a mile from the town of Suchitoto was chosen. After another round of meetings, it was decided that detachments of militiamen from several of the villages would clean up and refurbish the building, as well as bring tables and chairs for the clinic. They also set about digging latrines and bomb shelters to accommodate the one hundred or so people who would be at the schoolhouse at any one time. For the three days prior to the clinic, the militiamen and guerrillas would keep the site under twenty-four-hour guard in case the government tried to booby-trap it or set up an ambush.

The next problem was patient selection. We divided the Front into eight sectors and asked the *sanitarios* in each to screen their cases for the sixty or seventy who needed attention most and who could also be brought to the *consulta*. We estimated that with Jasmine and myself, along with the two doctors and a dental surgeon the IRC had promised to send, we could see a maximum of five hundred people.

Each village was then assigned a time for its residents to be seen. Zapote, for instance, was to send its patients at 9:45 A.M. Delicias' sick and lame were to come at 10:30.

Under the direction of the town councils, the agricultural cooperatives were organized to provide food for the day as well as horses to bring the very sick and to carry the IRC doctors up from the rendezvous point. The various women's associations volunteered to oversee food preparation, as well as register and direct the flow of patients at the site.

In all, the preparations required two weeks. My major contribution was to act as liaison between the Front and the IRC. We held six face-to-face conferences and exchanged many messages by way of radio or volunteers who carried our handwritten notes back and forth to San Salvador. Among the many problems that required delicate negotiation was the IRC's request for a detailed epidemiology of the Front. They needed the information to select the right medicines, but certain of the guerrilla comandantes feared such data could be of military value to the enemy. Dorita, who by now had forgiven me my transgressions against her character, forcefully contended that this was no time for such caution and carried the vote on behalf of providing the epidemiology.

At last we were ready. On the morning of the *consulta*, a squad of militiamen and I walked down to the Suchitoto highway and waited under a partially destroyed bridge for the IRC to arrive. It was a very nervous moment at a time and place tailor-made for a government ambush.

The IRC drove up in two Land-Rovers, and we quickly unloaded the medicine. As the militiamen hoisted the boxes onto their backs and headed up the hill toward the schoolhouse, I exchanged brief pleasantries with the three Red Cross delegates, all of whom were Swiss. I guessed that the oral surgeon was in his early thirties. The pharmacist was about my age. The third member of their group was the woman physician I'd met some weeks earlier.

As was true of our past encounters, I couldn't help noting how well-fed and well-groomed they all were. I, filled with worms and covered with lice, sporting a scraggly beard and clad no better than a Calcutta rag-picker, must have shocked and puzzled them greatly. Though they were too polite to say anything, I noticed none of them came too near me.

My overriding emotion was envy. For all their good work and the serious personal risks they ran in conducting a clinic such as this, they at least enjoyed hot meals, clean sheets and wide respect for what they were doing. I, for whom scroungy was a euphemism, was probably worth several thousand dollars if delivered dead or alive to the enemy.

It was a forty-five-minute journey to the schoolhouse; the IRC doctors rode a trio of skinny horses while I walked. Jasmine met us there and we instantly set up operations. The oral surgeon, assisted by a group of our *sanitarios*, began pulling teeth. By noon, they'd built a tidy pile of extractions. The rest of us went to work, too, examining draining ears or infected skin, listening with our stethoscopes to congested lungs and peering into pupils with our diagnostic kits.

In fact, we conducted more of an open pharmacy than a true clinic. There was little time for taking histories, consulting on diagnoses, or making complete examinations. Cases of chronic arthritis were dispensed full bottles of aspirin. Anyone who complained of weakness or tiredness received thirty vitamins. Stories of sleeplessness were handled with a dozen tranquilizers. The many malarials were given ten chloroquine each, plus fifteen primaquine tablets, which were effective in preventing relapses of resistant malarial strains.

Besides the crush of peasants who saw the clinic as a one-day "Great Medicine Giveaway," our other problem was with the local argot. The woman doctor had no idea what one *campesino* meant by a "nail cocktail" until I explained the regimen. Her colleague, who spoke excellent Spanish, was thrown by the Guazapan verb, *pavmada*, which means to be crazy in the sense that one could not make oneself understood. Another stumper was *patojo*, to limp, or the phrase that translates, "I've had a cholera." It means that the patient had been in a rage.

We worked around these barriers and nearly made our goal of seeing five hundred patients before three-thirty that afternoon, the agreed-upon stopping time. We might have gone on for several more hours, but the Swiss doctors were wary of a dangerous, nighttime drive back to San Salvador.

Our only rest period was during the midday meal, a blue plate special of beans, rice, and chicken prepared exclusively for us. I ate the food with gusto, grabbing it from the plate with my fingers and greedily stuffing my mouth.

My colleagues, however, declined to join in the feast. Maybe it was our manner of eating that put them off; knives, forks, and spoons were rarities on the Front. It might have been the condition of the plates, which obviously had seen no soap for quite some time. But I imagine it was the flies that took away their appetites. I hardly noticed them anymore, but they were swarming, as usual, on and around the food.

The *consulta* ended with a ceremony. A band of POWs,

which included the starchy lieutenant I'd treated earlier that autumn, was being released to the IRC that day. As any gathering of three or more was occasion enough for speech-making in Guazapa, I wasn't surprised to hear one of the comandantes go on at length about the fairness and care with which the prisoners had been treated. The lieutenant scowled as the speaker encouraged all the POWs to tell of their fine treatment by the guerrillas.

Then it was young Monterosa's turn. In a very moving address before the assembled crowd, the seventeen-year-old announced he wanted to join the revolution. Monterosa, who had an elderly mother left in his home village, had been so affected by what he experienced among the guerrillas that he believed risking retaliation against his mother was a small enough price to pay for joining in the liberation struggle.

"I am a Protestant," he explained, "but I have never known love and warmth like that among your base Christian communities."

He fibbed a bit when he said he had joined the army to serve his *patria*; Monterosa had received a letter ordering him to report for duty. There was no reason, however, to doubt his next words.

"I killed children because I was told they were the subversive seeds that needed to be eliminated," he said. "And I killed their mothers because I was told the *campesino* women were factories for more guerrillas. *Campesinos* recruited to kill *campesinos*. Will the army soldier gain? If I survive my year of duty, I become a *campesino* again myself. So, in the name of God, who gains? The *dueños* who have exploited us and their army and their policemen!"

Cheers went up not only from the *campesinos* but from Rafaga, the new father, who that day had decided to stay as well. Then we marched the remaining prisoners back down to the Suchitoto highway where they climbed into the Land-Rovers with the IRC doctors and drove away.

* * *

THE SOUND OF THE LAND-ROVERS' motors hadn't yet died in the distance when government soldiers descended on us from two directions. Strictly speaking, they had honored the IRC's neutrality and had permitted the clinic to be held without incident. But once the Swiss doctors and the POWs were en route back to San Salvador, it was business-as-usual in Guazapa.

The ambush, which succeeded in destroying one old horse and wounding two guerrillas, marked the beginning of yet another round of offensives against us.

Before I give the impression that the guerrillas of Guazapa fought an exclusively defensive war while I was there, I should point out that they were constantly active in harassing the Suchitoto garrison, the highway outposts, and all the rest of the government installations in the area. Usually, I knew nothing of these attacks until after they were over. Now that Jasmine was back I rarely treated any of the combat wounded, and news of the raids' successes or failures came to me second- or third-hand.

A major guerrilla objective was economic disruption. They would blow up trains, burn trucks, block highways, and cut power lines—anything to increase pressure on the government.

One of their targets with which I was familiar was the power transmission lines from the giant Fifth of November hydroelectric plant just up the lake from Copapayo. The lines came straight across Guazapa on their way to San Salvador.

I wondered about them every time I trudged up and down the steep slopes of the "Grand Canyon" en route to or from Tenango. In addition to enjoying their ever-changing "song" as they vibrated in the breeze, I admired the engineering feat of the gracefully arching lines strung across the chasm. Some of the pylons were perched on ledges that I could hardly scramble onto, much less imagine building a tower upon.

"Why," I finally asked Pedro one day, "haven't the guerrillas blown up these pylons?" I knew that they had sent numerous missions to destroy power lines in and around San Salvador.

"Camilo," Pedro grunted with good humor as we struggled up one side of the canyon, "now I know why everyone says the gringo asks the stupidest questions! Sure, we could blow up the pylons here. It would be easy. But you must remember that we have to rebuild our country some day. How many years, how much do you think it would cost, to replace these pylons?"

Cutting the lines nearer the city achieves the desired effect. Why smash the light bulb when you can turn off the switch?

Pedro's metaphor was somewhat more tangled. "You know," he said, "you have a saying, 'Don't throw the baby in with the bathtub,' right?"

After straightening him out on that expression, I asked if this economic sabotage wasn't alienating those they meant to help. Didn't the disruptions in electrical power hurt the working poor? Pedro admitted that some workers were hurt when the factories closed. He added, however, that the economic and social benefits of electrification were enjoyed disproportionately by those who owned the factories or could afford appliances in their homes. Pedro reminded me that very few among the poor had either running water or electric lights in their homes.

The government forces were less precise with their targets. In December, harassment by the A-37s kept the whole Front hunkered down in bomb shelters for long periods. They, as well as the spotter planes, now used white phosphorous rockets—the *campesinos* called phosphorous *fuego blanco* or white fire—as primary anti-personnel weapons, not as target markers. No matter what ordnance they brought, however, a single plane was enough to paralyze us all. Because the Front was so small, an A-37 could attack villages throughout its borders in a single, swift series of dives and rolls. The earth trembled constantly as if the human assaults on it were stirring the old volcano to erupt in protest.

One morning I thought it had done just that. En route to Salitre and enjoying the bird chorus greeting the sunrise, I was shaken out of my serenity by a series of enormous explosions. Like the night of the earthquake, the first impression that flashed through my mind was of B-52 carpet bombings I'd heard and seen in Vietnam. But since I didn't hear any aircraft, my next thought was that the guerrillas must have successfully attacked an ammunition depot in Suchitoto. Within fifteen minutes there were pauses between explosions, during which the roar of combat could be heard. It was coming from some place closer than Suchitoto.

I hurried to Magdaleno's house, where I found his family preparing for a *guinda*. The Salitre column, of which Magdaleno was part, had already left to meet the enemy—the Front was being invaded.

I couldn't believe it. The guerrillas had never been caught off guard before. Generally, sympathizers in nearby towns reported troop build-ups, a warning of impending action.

This turned out to be a new type of lightning attack launched against us from the highway. Small enemy units equipped with 90mm recoilless cannons, M-60 machine guns, and M-70 grenade launchers had all opened fire at once. In a matter of a few hours, foot soldiers behind the barrage had punched their way about three hundred yards into the zone at a spot perilously near the central hospital.

Three hundred of us waited out the assault for four days in a secluded ravine. Food arrived twice a day—a single tortilla each—but discipline was quite good. Since during the *guindas* no one ever carried more than a few possessions, there were no tools to dig latrines, only 'designated areas.' One afternoon a half-dozen militias arrived with a large burlap sack of oranges, which eased our thirst. Our situation wasn't serious yet, but we were poised to flee if the fighting came much closer. Of course, I had nightmarish visions of the casualties with the sounds of combat so close.

On the second day, Magdaleno came by to visit his wife and family. I was relieved to see him; rumors were rampant and my information was no better than anyone else's. He calmed me down, telling me not to worry so much because the *chuchos* never liked to fight during the holidays. He told his two boys with no uncertainty that they would see him late Christmas Eve after he got off guard duty.

True to his prediction, two mornings later the Front was peaceful. I rushed to Palo Grande in a panic, expecting all sorts of casualties. There were few. One guerrilla had been killed by an early A-37 sortie. An elderly man and his grown daughter had been caught gathering wood the morning of the barrage, their mutilated bodies left as a warning to others. Two guerrillas had been wounded in combat.

The government radio announced that a cache of seventy-odd rebel weapons had been found, that its troops were advancing splendidly, and that a clandestine guerrilla radio station had been overrun and silenced.

I asked Jasmine about the radio. She said they all had laughed about it and figured it must have been someone's transistor model left in one of the homes the soldiers overran. We both knew the "weapons cache" was a joke—there weren't enough arms to worry about having to hide any. Later that day I listened to the reports from San Salvador that declared the capital "safe" for the holiday because the "subversives" in Guazapa had been put to rout. This announcement tickled me because the insurgents had been proposing a holiday truce for weeks. The other government claims were just as spurious, but far more serious. There was a familiar pattern—weapons destroyed, radios silenced, and numerous guerrillas killed.

They were numbers. The kind of numbers that look good in reports. The kind of numbers that gain promotions for junior officers. The kind of numbers, I knew well, that had led to distorted news from Vietnam. I wondered if the Salvadoran generals could sustain such resounding successes as long as the many corrupt South Vietnamese generals had done.

The official Salvadoran army report omitted another important detail; napalm had been dropped near Delicias. Jasmine and I had been expecting it for some time, however, because intelligence reports from the FMLN in late November warned that longshoremen in the port of Acajutla unloaded crates which, according to decoded markings, contained white phosphorus and napalm. Besides, Roberto d'Aubuisson had called for its use as one of his campaign pledges.

There was very little Jasmine and I could do to prepare for the use of these horrible weapons. Through the town councils we re-emphasized the construction of covered trenches and bomb shelters near any place of work, school, or home. We explained to everyone that water was useless against napalm and phosphorus, that the burning could be stopped only by smothering it with sand or mud. Buckets were then filled with sand and dirt and placed near as many bomb shelters as possible.

I put out an urgent request to one of the medical support committees in the United States for a dermatome, an instrument not unlike a sophisticated cheese slicer with which a doctor can remove layers of healthy skin to graft over burns. Until it arrived, three months later, the only means for excising tissue for grafts was razor blades.

In February, just prior to my arrival, I had heard Radio Venceremos speak of napalm use in the government offensive against Guazapa. My own investigation revealed the "napalm" had been the fifty-gallon drums of gasoline with contact detonators that had been dropped from helicopters onto buildings. Now Jasmine was fairly certain one of the guerrillas in the hospital had been wounded by napalm near Delicias. I was not sure and asked to see the patient.

She was a nineteen-year-old woman named Elsi. Her wound was clinically consistent with napalm—a third degree thigh burn that had penetrated deeply, coagulating muscle, fat, and other deep tissue. Her description of the incident convinced me further. A sizzling substance had landed on her, she said, immediately setting her blue jeans on fire. When she tried to slap it off, part of it clung to her hand and seriously burned it. I decided to go to Delicias and see what I could discover.

There, I interviewed several witnesses who offered consistent accounts of the incident. An A-37 had made a low pass and dropped a short, cigar-shaped object that had tumbled end over end. Rather than exploding on contact like the other bombs from A-37s, it burst into a rolling ball of flame burning everything in its path. The smoke was heavy and black. Bits of the burning substance stuck to an adobe wall and kept burning. Several people asked me if I wanted to see the "bomb."

It was a thin aluminum cannister-like container. There was aluminum ribbing in the interior for stability, and it had an obvious filling port and what appeared to be a contact detonator. I took several photos. There was no crater. There was no other evidence to gather except charred plants, shrubs, and trees that had been in its path—the swath of burned vegetation was about 150 yards long and 25 yards wide.

"White Fire" is usually the igniting substance for napalm because it burns at extremely high temperatures. Medically, it has a unique feature that has been well-documented. Not only does it become embedded in deep tissue where it can continue smouldering long after initial trauma, but, on occasion, it spontaneously reignites. The phenomenon of reignition would explain the most macabre episode I encountered on the Front.

One afternoon in late November, a *campesino* was walking his mule with a load of firewood in a remote sector of the Front when he was hit by a white phosphorous rocket. From what I gathered, the man was wounded, but managed to mount the mule and direct it toward his home. Once inside, he collapsed from what must have been extraordinarily painful burns.

A while later, his wife returned home to find the mule in front of the house. When she walked in, she found her incinerated husband lying on the floor. Nothing else in the house was disturbed in any way. She looked in horror at the smouldering remains of her husband, then ran screaming into the village. The entire community and much of the Front was soon convinced the CIA had supplied some sort of secret ray gun that could locate and sizzle people even in the safety of their own homes.

CHARLES CLEMENTS, M.D.

* * *

IT WAS ALMOST DUSK on Christmas Eve as I trudged back to Flor's from Delicias. Since I had been shot at earlier in the year, I remained paranoid about trails, preferring them only to the open areas where the air attacks made me feel even more vulnerable. Nearing Flor's house, I heard a rustling ahead on either side of the trail. I froze, then screamed as they jumped me. It was an ambush!

The ambushers, Flor's children and the other kids from the house, screeched with delight at the success of their surprise attack and all yelled, "Feliz Navidad, Camilo," in their high-pitched voices. They had waited all afternoon by the trail worried I wouldn't return until the morning.

Some weeks earlier I had sent a few colones outside the Front with a messenger to purchase a few gifts. It was going to be their first Christmas without their father. I wanted to make it as merry as possible, but it is not easy to keep secrets when fourteen people live in one room. I had wrapped each present—a little comb, a barrette, a toothbrush, a pencil, a few pieces of candy—and then hid them away.

December 24, not Christmas itself, is the traditional day of celebration in El Salvador. Perhaps because they had lived with so much sorrow all year, or perhaps because they are such genuinely warm people, it was a time of great joy and sharing.

When I got home, Flor had laid out a chicken dinner replete with beans and rice flavored with her small and precious store of spices. Later, the adults drank coffee and listened to Christmas carols from a San Salvador FM station as the children opened their gifts. I looked at the little poinsettia plant that the kids had hung with strips of tin foil from cigarette pack liners and wondered what my parents were doing right then.

I have never seen children so elated. The combs and barrettes were a big hit with the girls. Pedrito, Salvador's ten-year-old son who had been withdrawn since his father's disappearance, lit up with happiness as he opened his toothbrush. He jumped up and down for several minutes, waving the brush and yelling, "Mom, mom, a toothbrush!" He'd never had his own before. Even Flor, who was so stoic in Salvador's absence, warmed up enough to laugh at their excited antics.

Afterward, I said I was going to go over to the civilian hospital to see the patients. Shyly, the children asked if they could come along. I was a bit puzzled since the hospital was the place where children got injections; they didn't go near it if they didn't have to. Besides, it was a mile walk in the dark across a deep ravine with no light. My caution was somewhat overdone; all of the kids had been on at least one *guinda*. What was a mile's walk to a child who'd trudged all night for two nights in a row? With Flor's consent, I told them to come along.

When we reached the hospital their reason for coming was quickly evident. Each had divided up his or her little store of Christmas candy and brought a portion with them for the six patients, four elders and two children. Then they formed themselves in a semi-circle and began singing. Their repertoire was quite broad—Christmas carols, religious songs, and lively revolutionary songs. The patients beamed at the chorus and an elderly couple began to cry. I knew that the elderly couple had two grown children in San Salvador whom they hadn't seen in over three years. I was a little misty-eyed too and had some trouble with my composure as we wished the patients a final Merry Christmas and headed home.

Mass was celebrated at midnight. Certain that the enemy would not fight on the holiday, the *campesinos* built an open bonfire that on any other occasion would have invited an attack. Over a thousand people came to hear the priests, to sing and to applaud Alma, Salvador's replacement, who spoke of how special Christmas was for children.

"For all the fear they feel, there also now is hope for them," she told the congregation. "This year for the first time, they all went to school, and they all had something to eat." The kids also had a doctor to look after them. And in a difficult year, they could all take pride in what they had accomplished and could look forward to the day of triumph.

I slept very peacefully that night, the first I could recall when not a single bomb or mortar or even rifle round was heard in Guazapa. Flor's old aunt snored blissfully on her pallet, and the children whimpered only once or twice in their sleep.

Christmas Day itself started in an ordinary way. Palo Grande and the rest of the villages seemed to return to their daily routines as if there was nothing special about the day at all. I had plans of lazing around a little, but they were scratched when a message came from Zapote. Why wasn't I there for a scheduled clinic?

I arrived by foot about noon and spent several hours seeing patients. Afterward I visited for a while with the villagers before striking out for David's house.

David's epididymitis had cleared up completely. For a time, he was restored to his *milpa* and to making rope from sisal hemp, a skill that only David and two other *campesinos* on the Front still practiced. But a more insidious, chronic condition was surely killing him. David suffered from congestive heart failure. His scrotum was swollen again but this time with fluids that had slowly accumulated from his feet upward.

Watching him die both angered and saddened me. David was perhaps fifty-five years old and for no more than five dollars' worth of digitalis and diuretics a month, I could have had his heart beating and his body free of accumulating liquids indefinitely. Hundreds of thousands of elderly citizens in the United States are maintained in this way, adding many years to their lives.

But we didn't have the luxury of such medicines in Guazapa. Doses of foxglove flower potion helped his heart somewhat, but there was nothing I could do to reduce the swelling in his feet and scrotum. Either his heart would finally give out from pumping against this pressure, or his lungs would eventually fill and he'd drown.

His wife, Ana Mariá, met me on the porch and showed

me inside. David was now bedridden and very weak. He opened his eyes at the sound of my voice and then whispered a few words I couldn't understand.

I slept overnight on their porch and awoke to the sound of children singing. There on the dusty trail in front of the house, kids from the nearby cultural collective had come at David's request to sing for him on his death bed.

I arose and went inside. David was now propped up on his pallet, a small smile on his lips. His eyes were closed.

"David," I said, "can you hear the children?"

When he didn't respond, I touched his cold hand and realized that he had died.

"He's not with us anymore," I told Ana Mariá as she came in. She crossed herself.

"It was a good death, Camilo," she answered after a few moments. "He wanted to be surrounded by the children."

The singing stopped and several of the kids began to cry softly. I went outside to comfort them and then returned to the dark room.

David's widow motioned me to her dead husband's side where she showed me a photograph he held in his left hand. Gently, she took it from him and gave it to me. It was a picture of David with the priest, Rutilio Grande.

"David said to thank you, Camilo," Ana Mariá said, "and to give you this after he died."

The picture was rumpled and soiled. On the back, the priest had scribbled a line from Psalms 9:18, the anthem of judgment. "Hope," he wrote to his friend David, "shall not perish."

WITH DAVID'S DEATH, I began reconsidering my own future in Guazapa. At no time had I seriously thought about leaving the Front, nor did his passing suddenly galvanize a determination to go. Rather, this most recent in a series of easily preventable deaths brought home the futility of doctoring without the tools of my scientific art. Somehow, medicine and equipment of sufficient quantities to meet at least mini-

mal health needs had to be obtained. Without explicitly
acknowledging what that necessity entailed for me, I did start
thinking beyond what I might achieve with what was at hand
to ways of bringing patients more meaningful medical aid.

It was almost New Year's, an appropriate time to look
ahead with resolve. For the *campesinos*, it was also a time to
look back, to celebrate achievement.

The occasion was *la matriculación*, the yearly graduation
exercises held for the children as they advanced up the lower
grades of the Front's elementary system. "The Guazapa String
Quartet," two guitars, a violin, and a bass who called themselves "El Grupo Insurrecto," provided lively music.

Eight hundred and forty-two children from forty-two
schools were honored around the Front that day. Schools
may be a misleading word. With constant air attacks, the
education system had been dispersed so not too many children were gathered in one place at any one time. The schools
themselves were often just the covered porch of a bombed-
out house.

I attended the graduation ceremony of the 152 children
from the Palo Grande school system, where Maribel, Salvador and Flor's oldest daughter, was headmistress. Antonito,
Pedrito, and the rest of Flor's children were among the
graduates. They stood at polite attention as Alma, their father's
successor as head civilian authority on the Front, made a
brief address. After her departure, the fun began.

The children put on skits and acts. They sang and recited
poetry. Everyone ate *tamales* and *quesadillas* and drank cups
of *refresco*. Near the end, they offered a moving recitation of
the names of their friends and classmates who had died or
been killed in the preceding year. It reminded me of the
Vietnam Veterans Memorial Service that I had heard over
the radio. Finally, they all proudly sang the Salvadoran national anthem—all four dirge-like verses. Meaningful or not,
to my ear it was still a dreadful piece of music.

Another holiday event was the release of several recently
captured prisoners. It was a gesture of magnanimity, but also
a practical move. One of the POWs was wounded, though not

critically, and was beyond our limited scope of medical care. He had taken a bullet wound through his face, shattering both bone and upper teeth. Without constant intravenous feeding, he would slowly starve to death. We needed to transfer him as soon as possible.

Pedro sent one of the older POWs, a man over forty who belonged to a civil defense unit, down the hillside a half-mile or less from Suchitoto. There he was provided with a bullhorn, and he called to the town to send a delegation to receive him and the rest of the prisoners.

Pedro and I listened to him via a walkie-talkie at the hospital in Palo Grande. He started out strong, calling in a clear voice to the town for someone to come for him and the others. He pleaded that he wanted to be with his family for New Year's Eve. This went on for about forty-five minutes. When no one came from Suchitoto or even replied, he grew frantic, imploring the mayor or the garrison commander to come. After two hours, he was sobbing.

Seeing this appeal wasn't going to work, the prisoner was then sent alone into Suchitoto itself. A simpler procedure would have been to just let the whole group of POWs walk down the hill to the town. The guerrillas, however, wanted an official delegation to come out and acknowledge that this was a release, not an escape. It was very important that the government not turn the gesture into a propaganda victory.

About three o'clock in the afternoon, an officer from the garrison radioed up that he would lead a delegation to receive the prisoners. Quickly, the rest of the POWs were sent down. Then we turned to the problem of the one who would require special transport.

Having taken bullets through both his face and buttocks, he could neither walk nor be carried in a hammock. His wounds were too painful. Our only recourse was a fireman's carry. First Pedro, then I, and finally his brother, who had also been captured, took turns carrying him from the civilian hospital across the ravine to Palo Grande.

Then his brother said good-bye. He had decided not to be repatriated and could go no farther. I wondered, as I'm sure they did, whether they would be firing at each other one day. I gave the wounded man a shot of analgesic and a group of guerrillas accompanied him down to the rendezvous point.

The commission from Suchitoto arrived as promised. Along with the garrison officer, a major, there was a priest, an alderman, and another officer. Back at the military hospital, Pedro and I listened intently to the exchange.

Much to everyone's surprise, the major embraced each of the *compañeros* as they brought down the wounded. He spoke of his hopes for peace and wished one and all a Happy New Year!

I was dumbstruck. Then the major asked if he could talk to the person who had made this occasion possible. The young *compañeros* at the transfer site handed him a walkie-talkie and told them that Pedro was his man. This was even more astonishing.

By radio, the major congratulated Pedro for making such a fine gesture and added his hopes that their country would soon be at peace. He was known to us as one of the ablest of the enemy officers, one of their few leaders whose troops could be expected to fight and fight hard.

He addressed Pedro with respect and was answered in kind. Mortal enemies, *chucho* and subversive, exchanged several expressions of mutual respect and common hope for a better tomorrow. Their warmth seemed almost filial before the moment died and each returned to the business of plotting the other's annihilation.

THE GOVERNMENT STRUCK THREE WEEKS LATER. Once again, I was caught near Salitre in the southern end of the zone when the air and artillery bombardments began. Behind it would come hundreds of enemy soldiers, spread out in a line running east to west and advancing north across several miles. We were about to be overrun.

In the midst of the early fighting, Raul Hercules summoned me to his secret command post for the sector. With my curiosity running high, I was introduced to their radioman, who was monitoring the enemy walkie-talkies with a U.S.-made Bearcat Scanner. As he manipulated the dials to pick up the various frequencies used by the government troops, I heard distinctly American voices issuing coded directives to the troops as well as asking questions of the Salvadoran commanders. Raul Hercules asked me if they were, indeed, *asesores norteamericanos* (North American advisors), and I said yes and left.

Contrary to the strictly limited role that U.S. advisors are supposed to play in El Salvador, these men obviously were, at the very minimum, acting in a command and control function. They could not have been any more than a mile or two from us. They and the Salvadoran soldiers were advancing steadily northward against delaying actions by the *compañeros*. The rest of us, maybe four hundred civilians in all, already were in flight up and around the volcano to the northeast and Palo Grande. That part of the volcano was heavily wooded, allowing us to make the first half of the journey under cover of trees—no one liked to *guindar* in daylight, but there was no choice.

The next part would be more perilous. We would have to move across exposed terrain. At that point, we received urgent instructions to stop and disperse ourselves as best we could. The order had come after an intercepted radio message pinpointed the location of an enemy tactical outpost. The site, an abandoned hacienda, was quickly surrounded and seized by the guerrillas, who found not only the radio but a dead captain with a copy of the entire tactical operations plan for the offensive.

I later saw the document. It was detailed down to radio codes and the hours they were to change. It laid out their logistical plans and even showed evacuation routes for their casualties. It also indicated that our own evacuation of civilians to the northeast was anticipated. About the time we would have made Palo Grande, soldiers from the volcano top garrison as well as a column cutting west from the Suchitoto highway would be there to trap us. The plan specifically mentioned the possibility of encountering as many as a thousand inhabitants from the Salitre area. There were no provisions for their capture, care, or evacuation. It did order that enemy dead were to be disposed of on the spot.

Capture of the government's battle plan posed a serious dilemma for Raul Hercules and the guerrilla command. Knowing that the hammer of the assault troops from the south meant to push us into the anvil of the soldiers to the north, the guerrillas could easily have surprised and killed hundreds of our would-be executioners. However, to deploy and then carry out the ambush would require leaving the civilians exposed and unprotected for several hours. If anything went awry, we were all dead. We, of course, knew nothing of this at the time. Scattered up and down the slopes of the volcano, the *campesinos* and their families sat in silent fear.

It was in this most unlikely of circumstances that Lupe, so long the bane of my existence, decided to make peace with me. She had been noticeably subdued in the several months following the capture and presumed execution of her companion, Camilo. She had put much less energy into her vitriol and sniped at me, I think, only out of habit.

I had changed, too. No longer appalled by the *sanitarios'* lapses and indiscretions, far less doctrinaire in the theory and practice of medicine, I wasn't so quick to judge or to intervene.

We worked together over a new mother who had delivered in the first hours of the *guinda*. Such precipitous labor was common during evacuation. This woman, over forty years old, had stopped by the trail for a half-hour, delivered her infant with the help of a neighbor, and then walked on. Lupe had hurriedly cut and tied the umbilicus.

She and I now worked together to complete the procedure. I acted as her assistant passing her clamps, razor blade, suture, and then Merthiolate as she more properly attended to the infant's umbilical stump. She admitted as I watched her that perhaps my "nail cocktails" weren't so foolish after all. Lupe then blushed and told me she was concerned that she was pregnant. She had not had her period since Camilo's departure four months ago. Her only other symptom was a little bloating. I told her without any secondary symptoms I doubted she could be pregnant and explained that about a third of the local women of childbearing age often skipped menstrual periods, sometimes several at a time. Stress, physical exertion, poor diet were all contributing factors to amenorrhea.

Our safety, in the end, outweighed the military value of going through with the ambush. As reluctant as they might have been to forgo such an opportunity, Raul Hercules and the rest of the comandantes had to give first priority to civilian security.

Several radio messages were sent out to Radio Venceremos and other stations. They, in turn, announced to the country that the insurgents of Guazapa had killed an enemy captain and obtained the full plan for the government invasion of their zone. Cockily, the announcements explained how the rebels now intended to trap and destroy two government units.

The tactic worked beautifully. The soldiers from the top of the volcano withdrew to their garrison and the column from the highway retreated. No doubt laughing at the guerrillas' premature announcement, the troops had no idea how close they were to finding us or being killed themselves.

IT HAD BEEN SIX MONTHS since our last major medicine shipment, which, if divided per capita, came to only a dollar's worth of medicine for each individual on the Front. We continued to lose supply columns such as the one on which Camilo "disappeared" in the fall. Despite promises and honest intentions, the IRC held only the one *consulta*. And our only other sources were those people brave enough to go singly into neighboring towns to purchase drugs directly from pharmacists—costly in lives and ineffective.

On the brighter side of the medical picture, two new physicians came to the Front in January of 1983. Both Latins, one was an experienced Salvadoran military surgeon and the other a Mexican who, like myself, was a general practitioner. I couldn't know it at the time, but it was their arrival as much as my own half-formed concerns about the scarcity of medical supplies that would lead to my departure from Guazapa just a few weeks later.

Oblivious to that eventuality, I looked only ahead to strengthening our *sanitario*-training programs and increasing the emphasis on preventive medicine. With another two physicians the burden of acute care medicine would be considerably lightened. Once again, I became the peripatetic gringo doctor, in town on schedule to deliver advice or hope, if not true medical care.

During that first circuit, Pedro came up to me with a request. A Latin journalist had come to the Front and was hoping he could interview me. Wary as I was about talking to anyone from the press, I consented on the ground that my observations of the situation, not my political views, would be the subject of the talk.

The journalist was very intense and clearly in sympathy with the guerrillas. Many months later, I found out that the interview had been published in several Central American and Caribbean papers. It was obvious that anything I had said had been put through his special filter. For instance, when I opined to him that several of Central America's economic problems could be attributed to the policies and actions of multi-national corporations, he wrote that I'd indicted "U.S. imperialism" for causing all of the sorry conditions there.

Even as I spoke to the man I promised myself never again. In that frame of mind, I met up with Pedro only a couple weeks later in still another part of the Front. Once again, he asked if I'd see a journalist and once again, contrary to my every intention, I found myself giving in to Pedro's supplications. This writer, he said, would be different. He only wanted a *norteamericano*'s perspective on what was going on in El Salvador. It was only for background—nothing on the record. Somehow, Pedro also conveyed the sense that I'd find my meeting an interesting one without, at the same time, indicating why that might be. Pedro was a very, very clever man.

My second interlocutor was thirtyish, a little paunchy,

dressed simply but in clean clothes, and sported yellow-tinted aviator glasses. He was a *chele* (light-skinned person), who introduced himself by the improbable name of Juan Alegría, or John Happiness.

If that wasn't enough to raise my suspicions, the tone and thrust of his questions definitely were. Coaxing me along as if I were a reticent child, he asked gentle, but pointed, questions about the organization of the Front. He obviously knew a great deal about it already. How did I evaluate the town councils? Were the cultural collectives functioning as well as they might? Did I know Selvin in Copapayo, the head of the agricultural production for the eastern zone?

I at first assumed only that Pedro had briefed John Happiness quite thoroughly. Then the conversation turned to broader matters. In a knowledgeable fashion he talked about napalm and white phosphorus as well as other violations of the Geneva Conventions. Did I know, he wondered, that the tiny Salvadoran Navy had begun mysterious night operations up the coastline and away from the curious eyes of the Acajutla stevedores? The sailors were unloading crates on the beach. Could I imagine what might be in them?

Here Pedro interjected with a few thoughts of his own. Without prompting from Mr. Happiness, whose ostensible aim had been to interview me, Pedro said he believed the shipments were more napalm and white phosphorus. He went on to say the secrecy might be due to the fact that the government had used up its entire military appropriation from the United States and was now obliged to smuggle in added "dirty" ordnance. Furthermore, he said, it was altogether possible that the secret shipments had another explanation. It could be the CIA setting up evidence of Soviet, Cuban, or Nicaraguan arms aid to the Salvadoran insurgents.

More guerrilla paranoia, I thought. I told Pedro his first two points seemed plausible, but that the third was a bit farfetched. This brought John Happiness back into the conversation.

He contended that both the CIA and the rightist armies it financed in Nicaragua had spent the previous two years trying to intercept the arms flow to El Salvador. The Reagan administration needed physical proof of a military aid link between the insurgents in El Salvador and the Soviet bloc. It had been an embarrassment, he felt, that only some radios and a few medical supplies could be demonstrated as having come to the rebels from outside.

He reminded me that the CIA engineered similar plots in Vietnam. There was evidence that North Vietnamese aid to the Viet Cong as well as the attack on U.S. warships in the Gulf of Tonkin had been staged to help justify escalation of the war. It would not be at all surprising, he told me, to one day hear over the government radio that many tons of Soviet-bloc arms had been uncovered in a guerrilla zone. What better proof could there be that Communists, not patriots, were directing and supplying the rebels?

The conversation continued for some time. Alegría explained that roughly 1,000 Salvadorans were dying each month; the great majority of them civilians killed by government forces in non-combat related circumstances. Maybe that didn't seem like much to me, but El Salvador's population is fifty times smaller than that of the United States. Their loss every month, he exclaimed, is equivalent to the total number of people the U.S. lost in fifteen years in Vietnam—slightly over 57,000 dead.

This was one reason why the insurgents were pursuing a negotiated settlement. The FMLN realized it could be several years until they achieved a military victory and the continued bloodshed was too costly. In addition, they worried about the economy. The Salvadoran Ministry of Finance estimated that 1.5 billion dollars had already left the country for Miami and Swiss accounts in the past twenty-four months. There would be no economy left if that were to continue.

Juan Alegría clearly was something besides a journalist. We discussed Africa, where he saw a model for resolution of the civil war. The British had stopped the bloody Rhodesian revolution through negotiations. The war, which had pitted white supremacists against black Marxist guerrillas, was finally ended by truly free and open elections in which the opposition could fully participate. Like El Salvador, they had first attempted to hold show-case elections in which the guerrillas couldn't safely campaign under white police and army providing "security." Rhodesia became Zimbabwe, in the end, by way of ballots, not bullets.

According to Juan Alegría, the United States would never control the death squads. It would mean delving into the farthest reaches of the Salvadoran military and ruling elite. If the United States truly believed in self-determination for the people of El Salvador, negotiations were the only rational means to that end. As it was, he believed, American intervention was paranoic. U.S. security wasn't threatened by the civil war; inevitable change, and the loss of face as well as hegemony were what frightened the Reagan administration.

With that, Juan Alegría concluded the meeting. Only after several days and much prodding from me did Pedro at last concede that this was no journalist I'd met. John Happiness was a pseudonym for Fermán Cienfuegos, head of the National Resistance, one of the five main "tendencies" under the FMLN umbrella. Put another way, he was one-fifth of the guerrilla high command, as senior an officer as there is among the insurgents.

Pedro smiled at my astonishment.

"You should be flattered," he said, "that such a comandante wished to hear your views."

"Pedro, I believe you have that turned around," I answered. "The comandante did most of the talking."

To his credit, Pedro did not tell me I wasn't as dumb as I looked.

IT IS POSSIBLE that Pedro knew even then, by the middle of January, that I was going to leave the Front. The meeting with Cienfuegos had been no accident, nor was the comandante indulging a whim when he asked to meet with me. The pleasure of my company notwithstanding, Fermán Cienfuegos had taken the opportunity to argue his case before a *norteamericano*.

The guerrillas were deeply resentful of their portrayal before the U.S. public and the world. They blamed both the West and the East for promulgating the notion that they weren't fighting the revolution on their own. When, as was common, press accounts referred to them as "left-wing terrorists" they were quick to point out that the "terrorists" in El Salvador were the death squads who killed and destroyed not in the name of the people but out of corrupt malice. By definition, a *compañero* could not be a terrorist.

This sensitivity was reflected in their strict rules of engagement. Civilian casualties were to be avoided at all costs. Looting was proscribed. All conduct unbecoming a *compañero* was punishable.

In a recent and tragic case, a guerrilla ambush squad had seen a bus carrying government soldiers on its roof and attacked. Inside the vehicle had been civilians, several of whom were killed. At a *balance*, the *compañero* squad leader was proscribed for his rashness, stripped of his weapons, and put to work in a farm collective for three months. That individual, whom I recalled from the San Antonio Abad column, was humiliated by being given a slingshot to protect a field of sorghum against flocks of screeching green parrots.

It was very important to them to demonstrate their ideals in action before their POWs, too. As far as was practicable, the government prisoners were integrated into the community and allowed to see its structures in action before being repatriated.

The structures themselves were built upon ideals. As stressful and uncertain as their lives were, the people of Guazapa hewed to strict codes of behavior.

In Zapote, for instance, a prisoner was taken in late January. He turned out to be well-known locally; the man had belonged to Fabián Ventura's death squad. Among his many crimes were the killing of two teen-aged boys and the rape of a pregnant woman. Since he was not a soldier, the guerrilla hierarchy decided it had no jurisdiction in the case. He was handed over to the Zapote Honor and Justice Commission.

These commissions existed in most of the villages. They amounted to a sort of rude judiciary that settled issues of social justice. A typical dispute might involve community land-use policies, the right of a *campesino* to take shelter in an abandoned house, or the ownership of a stray pig or cow. Conflicting claims to the distribution of possessions of families lost in air raids or massacres were also routinely handled by the Honor and Justice Commissions.

From my experience, their courts weren't bothered by incidents of domestic violence and child abuse, two very common police blotter entries in the U.S. In a typical American county hospital, for instance, many pediatric "injuries" are suspected cases of parental abuse or neglect. In Guazapa, I didn't treat a single battered wife or abused child in all the time I was there. These people didn't appear to be so innately violent as is widely argued by those who say the current level of murder and mayhem in El Salvador is merely part of their tradition of violence. I imagine, as well, the ban on alcohol in the Front encouraged family stability.

Nothing nearly so serious as rape and murder had ever confronted the Zapote commission. For two days, they grappled with the case, calling witnesses including the rape victim, who identified the defendant as her attacker. There was little doubt that he was guilty, but there was much concern about what to do about it.

At last, the Honor and Justice Commission decided that he must be executed. But not a single one of the five-member panel believed it was within their rights to do so. After a round of consultation with the Front's civilian *responsables*, it was decided to open up the issue to the entire village. A public trial, of sorts, would be held.

I was in Zapote for the trial, which was convened at 8:00 A.M. sharp on a day in early February. At least two hundred people gathered under the shelter of a eucalyptus grove to hear the evidence. The accused stood before them, guarded by a pair of militiamen. Behind them were seated the commission members. Its head, a woman, acted as judge.

There were no formal pleadings or points of law debated

The judge explained that the accused was known to have committed many murders as a death squad member, but that the only issues of concern at the moment were the killings of the two teen-aged boys and the rape of the pregnant woman.

The murder case rested on circumstantial evidence. No one had actually witnessed the killings. When asked for his version of the incident, the defendant acknowledged having been with a death squad that committed the actual homicide, but denied having taken part himself. As for the rape, he said, the woman had voluntarily had intercourse with him.

She was too distraught to answer his charge; her mother was the only family member to rise and speak for the prosecution. Her evidence was of her daughter's emotional trauma following the alleged attack, as well as the cuts and bruises she'd suffered. The mother also testified that her daughter had miscarried shortly afterward.

The judge summed up the evidence and then opened the trial to public debate: What were they going to do with the man? The first consensus was that he was indeed guilty as charged. One group of *campesinos* called for his instant execution, while others invoked the memory of Archbishop Romero. What would he have us do, they asked.

Next, the difficulty of keeping him under constant guard was discussed. Except for POWs, no one was ever detained in Guazapa. The only form of civil or criminal punishment was assignment to one of the agricultural collectives. Since this prisoner was such a menace, this was impossible. How long could they keep him locked up?

The question of rehabilitation came up. Would he, after three months, be safe enough to be let go in Zapote? After six months? Could a killer and rapist ever be trusted among them?

Slowly, hesitantly, the group was inching toward a distasteful conclusion: the defendant would have to be killed. Even those who adamantly resisted a death sentence conceded that he probably knew too much by now about their security system to ever be set free. Moreover, they could articulate no practical alternative to execution.

Still, he might somehow have survived had he not then spoken on his own behalf. A thin, sallow-faced man of perhaps thirty or thirty-five, he rose and spoke in a reedy voice. He obviously knew that his life hung on his words.

First, he confessed to the crimes and apologized for them. He said they'd been committed at a time when he didn't understand, when his attitudes had been molded by the brotherhood of the death squad. Now, he said, he realized how wrong he had been and how much he wished to work to atone for his sins.

That part of the speech won him some points. But then he sealed his own fate. The judge questioned him closely on the death squads, wanting to know which organization he belonged to and who, if any, of its members were still at large in the area.

He answered that he had belonged to ORDEN and had been paid by Fabián Ventura. The defendant quickly added, however, that the local ORDEN chapter outside Aguilares had been disbanded. He claimed not to have carried out any activities for many months. He had entered the Front with friends looking for a stray cow.

"Tell us why you joined," said the judge.

He explained that death squad members enjoyed special privileges. Among the several he mentioned was special preference for agricultural loan credits and promise of year-round employment on Ventura's hacienda. Then he added that if you were invited to join, you couldn't say no because that would prove your sympathy lay with the subversives.

"Who was the first person you killed?"

"A subversive," he answered mechanically.

Several people shouted that they wanted to know what he meant.

"Well," he answered, "it was a *campesino* who was active in a trade union. I can't recall his name."

The murder, he said, was conducted by a six-man squad, three veterans and three recruits. He described how the peasant was dragged from his house in the night and then slowly hacked to death with machetes. Each member of the squad had to participate. Each had to cover himself with the victim's blood. This practice, he explained, tied all the members together in guilt and responsibility for the deed. From the moment you first killed with a team, you were bound to them by this common responsibility. Anyone who tried to leave the brotherhood was marked for death himself, lest he give evidence against the others.

His admissions left the *campesinos* no choice but to execute the prisoner. The Honor and Justice Commission's original decision was ratified by a show of hands.

That afternoon one of the lay ministers from the local base Christian community offered him absolution and read the last rites. A grave was dug and the man was blindfolded. In front of a handful of official witnesses he was then shot and buried.

The trial and execution created a pall over Zapote. No one could argue the necessity of the villagers' action, but few of them thought it right and proper to take the man's life. No matter the gravity of his acknowledged crimes, an ideal had been compromised. At a moving service that night, they all prayed for the man's soul and asked forgiveness for what they had done.

A FEW DAYS LATER Jasmine and I, and our two new colleagues, met to discuss the state of our fledgling health care system. Jasmine gave them a brief history of our efforts, ending with the current situation. She turned it over to me. I spoke of our hopes for formalizing and expanding *sanitario* education, for increasing and diversifying the output of natural medicine production, and for more community education initiatives.

Jorge, the new surgeon, was blunt. How could he be expected to operate without suture, anesthesia, or antibiotics? He suggested that one of us leave the Front to raise money and then buy the medicines we needed. He seemed a bit pompous; it reminded me of myself many months before. But his suggestions were practical and obvious. Neither Jasmine nor I thought in those terms; we were usually trying to conserve or stretch what little we had. I suggested we discuss other alternatives first. There was a silence.

We then began to consider who among us was the best qualified for such a mission. When the three others stared at me, it dawned on me that the decision had been made.

I agreed to leave the Front for sixty days, but cautioned that if I sought humanitarian aid, it would be for civilians in both government- and guerrilla-controlled El Salvador.

Meanwhile we put together a wish list. Looking forward to the day when we could practice something besides crisis medicine, we put vaccines down as one shopping item. We wanted stethoscopes for all the *sanitarios* and baby scales for the clinics. Teaching aids were added to the list, as well as texts, eye charts, even—hope against hope—the luxury of a microscope for the main hospitals.

I was ambivalent about leaving the Front. While I did look forward to seeing my family and friends, I felt guilty leaving as invasion rumors began again.

Nothing of my leaving could be mentioned; I would disappear as suddenly and without explanation as Jasmine had done in the summer. The last I saw of her, she was debriding Fredi, a five-year-old victim of white fire who was covered with phosphorous burns. Her hospital was still as littered as I'd first found it. Impassive as ever, she squinted at me in the dark main ward, and then offered a strong handshake.

"Que le vaya bien," she said. (May you go well.)

Alirio was designated as my replacement as civilian doctor. Just as Pedro had accompanied me on my rounds in the late spring and summer, Alirio now came along to learn the patients, meet the *sanitarios*, and begin to assume my responsibilities. I could tell he'd practiced under similar circumstances, and I was pleased with the ease with which he fit in.

I had already seen some of my old friends for the last time. Magdaleno, for instance, was gone with his column the last two times I visited Salitre. At this writing, I understand he is still alive and remains the all-Guazapa champion weapons snatcher. Word has it that the old man's most recent prize was an M-60 machine gun.

I did see Chepe once more on my last trip to Tenango. His hiccups long since cured, I found him as usual out in his corn patch hoeing away and humming to himself. The loss of his dog, Tical, in the last invasion, seemed to have aged him even more. When he saw me, he instantly noticed my most recent hat had disappeared. The sun had burnt the bald spot at the back of my head.

"So Camilo, has your hat disappeared?" he asked.

"Sí, está desaparecido," I answered.

He pulled off his own weathered Stetson and handed it to me. It had been his son's hat and still showed the hole from the bullet that had killed his boy two years ago. The hat was Chepe's most prized possession.

I tried it on and to my relief found the hat several sizes too small for me. It perched on my head like a beanie.

"Chepe," I said, "I think my gringo head is too big for your lovely hat."

He laughed and embraced me.

"Then you will join me for coffee?" he asked.

I did and then marched off with the promise to find something big enough to cover my head.

My final visit with Rutilio, old David's nephew, and his wife, Ita, had come many weeks before on December 3. This was the anniversary of the 1980 abduction, rape, and murder of four American churchwomen by Salvadoran National Guardsmen. That crime is remembered each year with candlelight services at the many base Christian communities in Guazapa. I carried with me a quote from one of the nuns, Ita Ford. That night I shared it with Ita. "I don't see that we have control over the forces of madness," Sister Ford had written her mother. "And if you choose to enter into other people's suffering, you at least have to consent to the possible consequences."

Many times during my year in Guazapa, I'd turned to those lines for strength. After a sermon and prayers and a commemorative speech by Rutilio, Ita lit three candles for the dead women and carried the lights outside. Just a couple days before, Flor's oldest daughter had been out on the porch at night to work on the school's next-day lesson plans. Not twenty minutes after she'd sat down with the single candle to write by, a Huey came roaring high overhead in the darkness, machine guns spitting at the light of the candle. It was a miracle the girl wasn't killed—the next morning we saw the line of fire in the dust not a foot from her desk.

I reminded Ita of this as we stood watching her votive offering glow in the night. Her answer was that yes, it was a risk, but a small one compared to the sacrifice the four American women had made. One day, she told me, she would light little candles for them in the cathedral.

My farewell to Raul Hercules was somewhat more formal. I sat with Pedro at the hospital on New Year's Day as he recounted the Army major's speech of the afternoon before. Raul Hercules strode into the room and handed me an envelope.

"Camilo," he said, "I have something special for you." He was gone before I could open it.

My mind flew to my parents; I could conceive of nothing short of an emergency or tragedy to warrant a sealed communication. It was only the second envelope I'd opened in a year.

Instead, I found ten *colones* (about three dollars) inside, together with a handwritten message from Alma and Raul Hercules. "Thank you for your sacrifices on behalf of the civilian population of Guazapa," it read in Spanish. "Please use this for something you may personally need."

Except for Jasmine, the only person to whom I could offer an actual goodbye was Pedro. He was, after all, in charge of arranging for my departure. As I prepared to join my armed escort to leave Palo Grande for Copapayo and the boat that would take me north on the first leg of my journey, Pedro stopped by the hospital for the last time.

It was uncomfortable for me. In my experience, heartfelt farewells entail either tears or forced bonhomie. Neither suits my style. Pedro. however, saved the situation by giving me a quick embrace, an adiós, and then changing the subject.

He had an interesting problem. Recently, his wife had given birth to their fourth child, a boy. Pedro had gone to San Salvador and called her in Costa Rica.

"What name have you given him?" he'd asked.

"Como tú," she'd replied. (As you.)

That was well and fine, he told me, except that his wife knew him by several pseudonyms. *Como tú* could be anything from Alejandro to César to Roberto, possibly even Pedro.

I gave him my well-worn volume of Pablo Neruda's poetry, and we parted. To my successor, Alirio, I entrusted the distribution of the rest of my possessions. My radio was to be given to the Palo Grande hospital collective. The Swiss Army knife was promised to Rutilio. For Flor, there was the small crucifix a *campesino* had given me my second week on the Front.

Then I was off for Copapayo

I SPENT MY LAST FULL NIGHT on the Front in Copapayo with Frederico's family. Only Aurelio, the *compañero* son, was missing from the family table that night.

They knew both from the fact I was clean shaven and had an armed escort that I was leaving, but we couldn't talk about it. The evening would be another non-goodbye goodbye. It was my unofficial going-away party, a quiet fiesta to mark the unspoken truth that Camilo, the gringo doctor, was leaving Guazapa.

Frederico recalled his joy the night I delivered his only grandson, Selvin and Lia's infant. He spoke of the younger years when he and Miguel were the local gallants, days before the arthritis set in and their eyesight failed. He wished that this revolution, the one that would succeed, had begun while he was still strong enough to do more than tend his *milpa*.

I snapped a family photograph the next morning. I intended the picture as a remembrance of the family and a gift I would give them when I returned. It turned out to be many weeks before I could have it developed. By then, circumstances dictated that I could not return to Guazapa. Frederico's family subsequently was slaughtered by the soldiers, erased to its last member, save Aurelio, the *compañero*. The single photo is all that remains of them.

As I waited for nightfall that final day, I decided to visit the base Christian community where Uncle Gabriel was Delegate of the Word. A few old *campesinos* were there, most of them familiar to me as friends of Miguel and members of the Radio Club.

As we drank coffee and chatted, one of them asked me why it was I never carried a weapon. I explained that I was a Quaker; they laughed when I told them Quakers were so named because they literally shook in the presence of God at their meetings.

Radio Venceremos came on with an afternoon bulletin in the midst of our talk. Another government offensive was building. We began to hear the sounds of aircraft far across the Front almost as soon as the announcement was made, and the noise only intensified as the day wore on.

Our conversation turned to the possibility of another *guinda*, then turned back to the topic of my pacifism. It was slow going for me. I talked about the precepts of non-violence and how my experiences in Vietnam had changed my outlook so dramatically. I could tell from their intent stares that they were struggling to relate their concrete existence to my world of ideas. Archbishop Romero, I offered, was also committed to non-violence.

"Yes," Gabriel immediately said, "and look what they did to him!

"You, Camilo," he continued. "You gringos are always worried about violence done with machine guns and machetes. But there is another kind of violence that you must be aware of, too.

"I used to work on the hacienda," he went on, pointing southwest toward the abandoned estate near Platanares, the hacienda where I'd watched the dance on Ché Guevara's anniversary. "My job was to take care of the *dueño's* dogs. I gave them meat and bowls of milk, food that I couldn't give my own family. When the dogs were sick, I took them to the veterinarian in Suchitoto or San Salvador. When my children were sick, the *dueño* gave me his sympathy, but no medicine as they died.

"To watch your children die of sickness and hunger while you can do nothing is a violence to the spirit. We have suffered that silently for too many years. Why aren't you gringos concerned about that kind of violence?"

No one said another word. We sat still for several minutes, listening to the crescendo of fighting from the south and sipping our coffee. Gabriel had a stricken look on his face, as if he'd violated some taboo. I tried to smile at him, but the best my gesture could do was stir him to a final comment.

"Tell your people," he said, "they could start base Christian communities too."

Night came, and I climbed into the boat. Frederico and Isabel saw me off and handed me half a roast chicken for the long trek north. "Go with God," was the last I heard as we silently rowed out into the lake. Copapayo was dark. Behind it loomed the volcano, now swathed in moonlight and lit up, every few seconds, by the flash of incoming artillery rounds.

Guazapa X had begun.

EPILOGUE

MARCH 1983

THE BATTLE OF GUAZAPA—The Guazapa guerrillas thought they had won their battle.

They had no idea the Army was preparing the strongest attack ever mounted against Guazapa. . . .

. . . Rebel leaders passed down an order for *aguinda**—a mass exodus. *Las masas*—the local civilian supporters of the guerrillas—quickly began slaughtering pigs and chickens so they wouldn't fall to the Army. Around midnight, a guerrilla force led a silent column of some 2,000 civilians through Army lines and across the road past Suchitoto while the Army stayed in its barracks. Mothers cupped their hands over mouths of crying babies. . . .

. . . The next morning the parade of refugees stopped to rest by a clear stream. In the distance a cloud of black smoke rose above Guazapa—the sign that the Army had seized the

---

*Don North had heard the word *guinda* as *aguinda*. None of my El Salvadoran sources are able to explain how the word for sour cherry has come to be the word for flight in the night.—the author

261

area and was demolishing everything in sight. As the rebels pushed on toward the nearby town of Tenango, they began hearing reports that the Army had killed a hundred civilians at the front end of the *aguinda*. Outside Tenango, the signs of the slaughter were everywhere: charred and scattered bits of clothing, shoes and schoolbooks. When the survivors reached Tenango, a local resident, Roberto, pointed out shallow graves where he said government troops had buried dozens of men, women, and children after executing them with guns and machetes. When I saw the bodies of the victims, vultures had already picked their skeletons clean, and village dogs had begun to carry away the bones.

The Tenango villagers said the elite, U.S.-trained *Brigada Infanteria Reaccionaria Immediata Atlacatl* had committed the atrocities. As evidence, they showed us chalk graffiti marks left by the soldiers congratulating the Atlacatl Brigade on its second anniversary. . . .

. . . At Lake Suchitlan, about 2,000 civilians waiting to cross in six small rowboats looked like a miniature Dunkirk. At 6 P.M. the army quit for the day, its usual practice. Eventually the entire group crossed the lake and marched on for two days to San Antonio Los Ranchos, a rebel way station.

The rebels stayed for five days in San Antonio Los Ranchos, and then the order came to begin the return march to Guazapa. . . . Finally we arrived at the scorched remains of Guazapa. Rotting bodies of slaughtered cows and horses littered the area. . . . The scene brought back memories of the Vietnam War, which I covered. The El Salvador government also hoped to win the hearts and minds of the people with a rural "pacification" plan.

That night San Salvador radio quoted the government as saying that it had spent $5 million in U.S. military aid during the invasion of Guazapa. I asked a rebel commander for a final tally of guerrilla casualties. Since the Army went into Guazapa, he said, it had managed to kill 100 civilians and wound 20 guerrillas—and eliminate all of five rebels. If the commander's body count is accurate, each dead guerrilla cost $1 million.

Don North, *Newsweek*, April 25, 1983

Author's note: This story of Guazapa X was late being reported because it took Don North 42 days to leave the controlled zone.

WHITE HOUSE URGES SALVADOR TO CALL ELECTION THIS YEAR—The Reagan Administration has urged the Salvadoran Government to advance the date of presidential elections from next March to later this year, State Department officials said today. . . .

. . . The Reagan Administration had hoped to keep the planning secret so the announcement would be seen as a Salvadoran initiative. The purpose in moving up the election date, officials said, was to dramatize the Salvadoran leaders' commitment to democratic rule and national reconciliation. The plan was also supposed to help the Reagan Administration to persuade Congress to approve $60 million aid for the Salvadoran Army.

Bernard Gwertzman, *The New York Times*, March 3, 1983

SALVADOR ARMY'S TROUBLES—El Salvador needs better battle leadership, personal motivation, and field training as much as it needs ammunition, helicopters, and guns according to American and Salvadoran officials here.

. . . [The] army is now fighting a 9-to-5, five-day-a-week war against guerrillas that are active 24 hours a day, seven days a week.

An American officer recalled that on a recent visit to a combat unit he was briefed by its commander and executive officer. When he returned to his helicopter to leave, he found the commander and his executive officer in civilian clothes waiting for a lift back to the capital. It was Friday evening. . . .

Drew Middleton, *The New York Times*, March 5, 1983

* * *

CHARLES CLEMENTS, M.D.

U.S. REJECTS POPE'S VIEW ON SALVADOR—U.S. Ambassador [to El Salvador] Deane R. Hinton on Monday hailed Pope John Paul II's visit to embattled El Salvador but made clear that the pontiff's call for a dialogue between the Salvadoran government and leftist guerrillas has not changed U.S. opposition to a negotiated settlement of the war. . . .

Juan M. Vasquez, *Los Angeles Times*, March 8, 1983

WEINBERGER LINKS SALVADORAN WAR TO GLOBAL COMPETITION—Defense Secretary Caspar W. Weinberger yesterday referred to the stakes in El Salvador's civil war in terms of global competition between the United States and Soviet Union, saying a communist victory in El Salvador could pressure the United States to pull out of Europe and Asia to defend its southern borders. . . .

. . . The defense secretary's comments came on the heels of President Reagan's request to Congress last week for an additional $110 million in military aid for El Salvador on the grounds that the conflict threatens U.S. national security.

David Hoffman, *Washington Post*, March 11, 1983

U.S. SAYS $25 MILLION LOAN TO EL SALVADOR HAS VANISHED—The U.S. Embassy said in a report released Tuesday that $25 million lent to El Salvador's land reform program has disappeared, and it recommended that the U.S. funds be written off as a loss. . . .

UPI, *Los Angeles Times*, March 16, 1983

APRIL 1983

REPORT OF A CONGRESSIONAL FACT-FINDING MISSION TO EL SALVADOR SPONSORED BY THE UNITARIAN UNIVERSALIST SERVICE COMMITTEE—All of the military officials we talked to felt frustrated by criticism of civilian combat casualties. [Salvadoran] Air Force Commander Bustillo claimed that his forces identify their targets as carefully as possible, but "sometimes you don't know if you are dealing with a civilian situation or with the guerrillas. . . ."

. . . The Air Force considers Guazapa, the area of the heaviest bombing, a "free-fire zone," within which all targets are legitimate because of its importance to the fighting. . . .

> Entered into the *Congressional Record* jointly by Representatives James Oberstar, D-Minnesota; James Jeffords, R-Vermont; and Bill Richardson, D-New Mexico.

Author's note: A Western military official told the delegation that the Salvadoran military was continuing to use napalm from an unknown source and against the advice of U.S. military advisors.

PUBLIC OPPOSES U.S ROLE IN EL SALVADOR—By a wide margin, the American public opposes U.S. involvement in war-torn El Salvador, saying that this country's efforts to prevent an overthrow of the Salvadoran government by leftist rebels are not morally justified, are not vital to U.S. national defense, and will not end in victory according to the latest Los Angeles Times Poll.

The nationwide poll, taken as the Reagan Administration is seeking to formulate a winning strategy in El Salvador and battling with Congress for more military and economic aid for the Central American country, also reveals that a majority of Americans are against the use of U.S. troops there— even if the Salvadoran government were about to fall to the guerrillas. . . .

> David Treadwell. *Los Angeles Times*, April 12, 1983

SALVADOR ARMY'S ABILITY DOUBTED IN U.S. REPORT—Senior United States military commanders concluded two years ago that even with increased military assistance from the United States the Salvadoran military as then constituted could not defeat opposition guerrilla forces, according to Reagan Administration officials.

CHARLES CLEMENTS, M.D.

The comprehensive, highly classified analysis of the Salvadoran military was prepared in 1981 by Brig. Gen. Frederick F. Woerner Jr., who is now based in the United States Southern Command headquarters in Panama. . . .

. . . "If anybody at this table read that Woerner report with a God-given brain, I can't understand how that person could think you can attain a military victory, yet that is what we are pursuing in El Salvador," Senator Edward Zorinsky, Democrat of Nebraska, said. . . .

. . . The report is primarily an evaluation of the Salvadoran armed forces, and particularly the command structure. Defense Department officials familiar with the report said it generally portrayed the Salvadoran military as inadequately trained, armed, and directed, and was particularly critical of the officer corps.

The report, the officials said, blamed the officer corps for attempting to use conventional tactics against unconventional forces. It also criticized the officers and top commanders for misusing military funds and equipment and condoning attacks against civilians.

> Raymond Bonner & Philip Taubman, *The New York Times*, April 22, 1983

SPECIAL REPORT: *Medical Mission Report on El Salvador*—. . . Wherever we turned we found the chilling effects of the ever-widening devastation to health and health care that has been caused by the breakdown of education, the slashing of budgets for national health programs, and the repression of human beings by the systematic use of terror in ways that are hideous and frightful.

The persecution of health personnel is real. It began in 1979 and intensified through 1981, when a group of doctors, nurses and medical students protested the killing and kidnapping of patients and doctors in the hospitals—sometimes even during surgery. Retaliation against this group by death squads, suspected of being government forces, was swift and brutal.

The group's members "disappeared," or fled to avoid death, or were killed. . . .

. . . Aid to this war-torn country should emphasize life-giving sustenance rather than arms and military equipment.

Alfred Gellhorn, M.D., *New England Journal of Medicine*, April 28, 1983

MAY 1983

EL SALVADOR LOSING THE WAR, BRASS AT PENTAGON CONTEND— Top Pentagon military officers say bluntly that the U.S.-supported government in El Salvador is losing its war against guerrilla opposition. . . .

. . . In a series of interviews, the Pentagon officers said they did not believe the present aid program for El Salvador— aimed mainly at training more Salvadoran troops—has a reasonable chance of success. . . .

. . . The interviews with the ranking officers, who spoke on the conditions that they not be quoted by name, became a symposium for frustration. . . .

. . . "What this is going to come down to," one said "is whether the Salvadorans themselves can get their act together. If there is to be a win, it will be a Salvadoran win—and maybe that's the best we can hope for."

James McCartney, *Miami Herald*, May 20, 1983

U.S. 'EYES' ON SALVADOR CONFIRMED—U.S. night-seeing AC130 airplanes, flying without weapons or ammunition, have been operating secretly over El Salvador for the past several weeks to try to detect infiltration of arms to Marxist guerrillas, the Pentagon said Monday. . . .

. . . Earlier this month, the Pentagon acknowledged that the sophisticated Airborne Warning and Control System planes have been flying in the Central American area, watching for small planes carrying weapons from Nicaragua to El Salvador.

Combined Dispatches, *Miami Herald,* May 24, 1983

U.S. SETS ASIDE $6 MILLION TO ASSIST SALVADOR ELECTION—The Reagan Administration plans to spend $6 million to $8 million to underwrite El Salvador's cost of holding presidential elections later this year, an Administration official said today.

Expenses the United States expects to cover include the organization of a major voter registration drive, establishment of a national poll-monitoring system and modernization of El Salvador's vote-counting procedures. Consideration is also being given to creating a central registry that would use computers to maintain an accurate roll of all voters. . . .

Philip Taubman, *The New York Times,* May 26, 1983

JUNE 1983

IN EL SALVADOR, BEING A POLITICIAN MEANS RISKING YOUR LIFE— Members of the largest anticommunist political party in El Salvador still risk their lives engaging in politics.

The threat comes mostly from the right, not from the Marxist-led left. . . .

. . . The continuing assassinations of Christian Democrats and other civilians are one of the main concerns of the United States Congress as it debates Reagan administration aid requests for El Salvador. Aid has been tied to improvements in the human rights situation. In July, the administration is required to certify once again that the situation has improved, and it is expected to do just that.

But the constant assaults on the Christian Democrats appear to be aimed at weakening the political center—between El Salvador's militant extremes of left and right—which the administration professes to be trying to bolster. . . .

Daniel Southerland, *Christian Science Monitor,* June 7, 1983

*   *   *

U.S.-TRAINED SALVADORANS TEND TO QUIT—Only 15 percent of the Salvadoran soldiers trained by the United States two years ago are still in the army, and nearly half of those trained last year are already gone, the Pentagon said Tuesday.

The Pentagon figures also showed a heavy attrition rate among officers. Of 500 young officers trained at Ft. Benning, Ga., last year, only half remain on active duty, the Pentagon said. It costs the United States an average of $9,000 to train one Salvadoran soldier. . . .

Combined Dispatches, *Miami Herald*, June 15, 1983

U.S. PROMOTING LATIN POLICY—The White House has launched a coordinated government public relations campaign to persuade special-interest groups and other Americans that President Reagan's efforts to counter communism in Central America are vital to U.S. security.

"The judgement of history on this president will probably be based on what happens in Central America," said Faith Ryan Whittlesey, director of the White House office of public liaison. . . .

. . . "Every businessman who asks me about natural gas or consumer product safety, I ask to help us on Central America," Whittlesey said. . . .

. . . She said anti-communist appeals are being made to ethnic groups, and Jewish organizations are being told that forces most hostile to Israel—including the Palestine Liberation Organization, Libya, and Eastern European nations—are supporting leftists in Central America. . . .

. . . Administration officials are urged to sell Reagan's Central America policy in all speeches and public appearances, regardless of the audience or primary subject matter. . . .

Lou Cannon, *Washington Post*, June 17, 1983

SALVADOR'S LEADER REBUFFS CONGRESS—The Provisional President of El Salvador said today that he would not comply with United States Congressional stipulations that his Government begin unconditional discussions with the insurgents.

The rejection could upset the Reagan Administration's efforts to win approval of an increased aid package for El Salvador.

The Salvadoran, Alvaro Magana, who was here for consultations with Reagan Administration officials, said he would rather suffer a termination in American military and economic aid than conduct open-ended negotiations with guerrilla leaders. . . .

Phillip Taubman, *The New York Times*, June 19, 1983

U.S. ENVOYS AIR VIEWS ON EL SALVADOR—U.N. Ambassador Jeane J. Kirkpatrick said in a separate meeting with Washington Post editors and reporters that the U.S. stake in Central America is "a new fact" that the U.S. public has not assimilated fully. She called for public debate about what she said are new Soviet expansionist techniques in the area. . . .

. . . Kirkpatrick likened the Soviet Union to the Roman Empire, saying the Soviets have organized "a sort of international communist brigade" to help leftist rebels worldwide.

The brigade involves "tens of thousands of troops" from Soviet allies including Angola, Benin, Mozambique, Ethiopia, Algeria, and Nicaragua, all coordinated and deployed out of Moscow in a way not seen before, she said.

Soviet garrisons police the rebel efforts "to make sure they don't change their minds," Kirkpatrick continued. . . .

Joanne Omang, *Washington Post*, June 28, 1983

TROOP USE IN SALVADOR NOT BARRED—President Reagan, asked whether he would send combat troops to Central America, responded. . . . "It's an old saying that presidents should never say never. . . . They blew up the Maine."

Lou Cannon & Juan Williams, *Washington Post*, June 29, 1983

WITNESS TO WAR

JULY 1983

REAGAN NAMES 12 TO LATIN PANEL—President Reagan today appointed the 12 members of his National Bipartisan Commission on Central America and told it to report by Dec. 1 on how to build a national consensus behind a policy of dealing with "threats" to United States interest in the region.

The commission, headed by former Secretary of State Henry A. Kissinger, will be free to look into whatever elements of the region it chooses. . . .

Francis X. Clines, *The New York Times*, July 20, 1983

THE MISSION THAT FAILED—"He came, he saw no one, but he conquered Congress," one European diplomat in El Salvador remarked last week after U.S. special envoy Richard Stone's abortive peace mission to Central America. Stone's scheduled meeting in San Jose, Costa Rica, with four representatives of the major Salvadoran guerrilla groups never came off. But his trip did score points on Capitol Hill. Headlines trumpeting the "Salvadoran Rebuff" of Washington's peace initiative helped quiet congressional critics who were opposing an additional $50 million in military aid for El Salvador because they argued that the administration was not trying hard enough for a negotiated settlement.

How hard the administration really did try with the Stone mission was unclear. Members of the guerrilla delegation argued that Stone's trip was staged solely for domestic consumption. Aides to Costa Rican president Luis Monge—who arranged the meeting and tried to save it—complained that Washington had doomed the mission by violating an agreement that the talks be "informal, private, and frank" and alerting the press. . . .

Beth Nissen, *Newsweek*, July 25, 1983

SALVADORANS LOSE LAND WON IN AGRARIAN REFORM, U.S. FUNDED STUDY SHOWS—A U.S.-funded study of the land-to-the-tiller phase of El Salvador's agrarian reform program indicates that between 11 percent and 14.5 percent of the beneficiaries have been thrown off their land and that evictions are continuing at the same level as last year. . . .

. . . The figures appear to contradict the Reagan administration's certification report to Congress on El Salvador last week. That report said support for the program "from the armed forces has arrested the (eviction) problem."

Sam Dillon, *Knight-Ridder Newspapers*, July 28, 1983

REAGAN DENIES AIM IS BIGGER PRESENCE IN LATIN COUNTRIES—President Reagan, asserting that the United States was "not seeking a larger presence" in Central America, said tonight that his Administration's plans for military exercises were aimed at providing "a shield for democracy and development" in the region. . . .

Steven R. Weisman, *The New York Times*, July 27, 1983

SALVADORAN REBELS REPORTED TO GET LITTLE ARMS AID—The flow of military supplies to Salvadoran rebels from outside the country has been only a trickle for many months, according to officials here and in Washington.

A senior Reagan Administration official, interviewed in Washington several days ago, said "that's true," when asked about reports that Salvadoran guerrillas were receiving only small amounts of ammunition and weapons from Nicaragua, where a Marxist-dominated junta controls the government. The official also said the Salvadoran rebels had little need of such aid. . . .

. . . Salvadoran military officers do not assert that the supplies from external sources are a major factor in the civil war this year, or that they are arriving in high volume.

Charles Mohr, *The New York Times*, July 31, 1983

AUGUST 1983

ARMY'S TOLL DOUBLES IN EL SALVADOR—The number of Salvadoran soldiers killed during the past year in combat with anti-government guerrillas doubled the figure from the previous year, and the overall government casualty rate rose by more than three-fourths to 6,815 dead, wounded, or missing in action, the Salvadoran defense minister said today. . . .

. . . The casualty count amounted to one-fifth of El Salvador's total 33,000-man military establishment. U.S. military here said the proportion was high compared to other conflicts.

Edward Cody, *Washington Post*, August, 12, 1983

SALVADOR WAR 'GOING MUCH BETTER.' WEINBERGER SAYS—Saying the war in El Salvador is "going very much better," Defense Secretary Caspar W. Weinberger said Thursday that U.S. training of Salvadoran government troops is beginning to pay off in the fighting against leftist insurgents.

"There has been significant improvement in a number of the categories we use to measure these things," Weinberger told reporters, "(in) government casualties, engagements with guerrilla forces and things of that kind. It looks as if the training is beginning to take hold . . . morale and leadership are improving, so I think it is substantially better."

Rudy Abramson, *Los Angeles Times*, August 19, 1983

SALVADORAN ARMY SAID TO LOSE MOMENTUM—The Salvadoran Army, frustrated by low levels of action in recent weeks, has lost some of the fighting edge that is gained when it seized the initiative against leftist guerrillas earlier this summer, according to Salvadoran and other military sources. . . .

. . . Western sources acknowledge that the current slack period is showing the army still has trouble maintaining its initiative—a primary concern of U.S. trainers here.

Moreover, divisions within the Salvadoran officer corps are deep enough so that one commander, Lt. Col. Jorge Adalberto Cruz, accused some of his colleagues of spending too much time at the beach or at home instead of fighting. . . .

. . . In his outspoken comments to U.S. reporters Sunday,

Cruz accused some of his colleagues of laziness and preoccupation with politics and money. . . .

. . . "When I make requests (to the high command), nothing happens. It goes in one ear and out the other," he said.

Robert McCatney, *Washington Post*, August 31, 1983

SEPTEMBER 1983

THE 'NOWHERE' DIALOGUES—After months of preparations and more than a little stalling, Salvadoran government officials and their leftist guerrilla opponents finally sat down for a talk last week. . . .

. . . On his fourth trip to the region as Reagan's representative, [Richard B.] Stone could cut no deals. Salvadoran officials see him as an unproven diplomat whose job may have more to do with wooing American public opinion than stopping the war in El Salvador. After Reagan appointed Kissinger to head a special commission on Central America, Stone's mission appeared to be a sideshow. Stone has accomplished "virtually nothing," said one senior Salvadoran official. A guerrilla official was hardly more complimentary. . . .

James LeMoyne & Robert Rivard, *Newsweek*, September 12, 1983

SALVADORAN-LABOR FRICTION REACHES FLASH POINT AS UNION LEADERS ABDUCTED—The relationship between this embattled country's workers and their government has reached a crisis point, according to union leaders, workers, and the United States labor advisors here.

Three directors of major unions have been abducted and disappeared this week. Over 100 people involved in union activity have disappeared this past month, labor officials here say.

"The situation is very grave," a U.S. labor advisor remarks.

"But rather than confront that problem the military is attempting to crush the union movements, as it did in 1979.". . .

. . . "This is the last chance for El Salvador," he adds. "If they do not stop these death squads, I cannot see the purpose of giving them aid. And without U.S. aid, the guerrillas would take this country in two months."

Chris Hedges, *Christian Science Monitor*,
September 30, 1983

OCTOBER 1983

BOMBINGS DRAG INNOCENT INTO WAR—. . . I've seen the awful fear of innocent people caught under bombs in the middle of wars that they had no part in starting, from Vietnam, Laos and Cambodia, through Cyprus, Afghanistan, and Beirut. . . . And all the preparation I'd had in all those other wars was no shield against the shock of coming upon Salvadoran victims sprawled in the streets where bombs had littered them.

The children seemed to have been killed by the blasts alone. Four that I saw were frozen in the act of fleeing, arms and legs clutching at the air, mouths wide open in fear. Their mothers were mutilated by the bombs, torsos and limbs torn apart, their lives ebbed way in the blood-soaked pavement. We counted 17 civilians dead in the streets. . . .

. . . Tenancingo was the third Salvadoran town bombed this year by the newly acquired A-37 aircraft provided the Salvadoran government by the United States.

Like San Jose Guayabal in June and Berline in February, Tenancingo had the misfortune to be occupied by left-wing guerrillas who overpowered the local army garrison. The government response was to send in its new bombers as the first reaction. But in the cozy little towns in rural El Salvador, homes are made of adobe and clustered close together. The people usually don't have a chance to flee. . . .

. . . I had presumed that the bombing and the helicopters were in support of a counterattack by Salvadoran infantry against the guerrillas. But I was wrong. The Salvadoran army was 20 miles away and did not come in until two days later. . . .

. . . Newsmen looking into the bombing found several American officers stationed in El Salvador willing to excuse the attack on the grounds that the margin of error was, according to one colonel, "acceptable in terms of what we did in Vietnam.". . .

. . . Vietnam is being invoked more and more by the American military people in El Salvador as though it was the role model for this conflict . . . when word got out that a . . . news team . . . could document the civilian deaths by bombing, a senior American grumbled that the press was losing the war effort here "just like it did in Vietnam." . . .

Peter Arnett, *Atlanta Constitution*, October 2, 1983

BIG SHARE OF COSTS OF SALVADORAN WAR BORNE BY U.S.—The U.S. government and working-class Salvadorans are bearing an increasing share of the cost of fighting the war here, according to official statistics and senior Salvadoran officials.

At the same time the small upper class has retained its dominant role in the economic life of the country despite widely publicized reforms instituted in 1980 to redistribute the nation's resources, according to these officials.

This pattern has caused moderate Salvadorans both inside and outside the government to question for whom the war against Marxist-led guerrillas is being fought.

Before ending his tour as head of the U.S. Military Group here last summer, Col. John D. Waghelstein publicly criticized wealthy Salvadorans for sending their money and their sons out of the country and thus weakening the war effort.

One western diplomat remarked acidly that while America's founding fathers pledged their lives, their fortunes, and their sacred honor to their country, El Salvador's upper class pledge the Army's lives, Washington's fortune, and only their sacred honor.

WITNESS TO WAR

When Planning Minister Manuel Antonio Robles was asked recently about criticism that the war is essentially being fought to protect the interests of the 6 percent of the population who earn more than $240 a month, he replied, "Really, it is true." . . .

Christopher Dickey, *Washington Post*, October 3, 1983

EL SALVADOR 'DEATH SQUADS' MORE ACTIVE AS RIGHTISTS WORRY ABOUT LOSING POWER—A spate of brazen kidnappings, killings, and bombings in recent weeks by anti-communist "death squads" has alarmed even Salvadorans jaded by years of turbulence. . . .

. . . In the past month the death squads . . . associated with national security forces and right wing parties have kidnapped five university professors, killed 15 union members and officials, bombed a radio station and the home of several Jesuit priests and spirited away the third-ranking official of the country's Foreign Ministry. . . .

. . . On Saturday, for example, Roberto d'Abuisson, president of the Constitutional Assembly and head of El Salvador's most extreme right-wing party, labeled yet another union leader as a Communist, and claimed he has proof that the official had been secretly supporting leftist guerrillas. That accusation was particularly disturbing because on five other occasions public denunciations by Mr. d'Abuisson, a cashiered army major, have been followed by the murder of the person accused. . . .

Brenton R. Schlender, *Wall Street Journal*, October 7, 1983

SALVADOR: DIALOGUE WITH REBELS OFF—Provisional President Alvaro Magana says that his government's intermittent dialogue with the leftist opposition has been called off and he now hopes for a military solution to El Salvador's civil war. . . .

Sam Dillon, *Miami Herald*, October 8, 1983

WHY DISTRUST OF U.S. RUNS SO DEEP—If former Secretary of State Henry Kissinger and his study commission look below the surface on their swing through Central America, they are bound to discover that the U.S. has another foe there besides Marxist-inspired rebels. The second enemy: America's own history in the region.

The Reagan administration insists that its current military maneuvers in the area—involving naval flotillas on both sides of the isthmus and thousands of U.S. troops in Honduras— are designed to help the region defend itself against Cuban and Soviet-supported revolutions. But the big problem is convincing skeptical Latins that the armed presence this time differs from that of the past.

Over a period of nearly 150 years, U.S. armed forces swept into Central America and the Caribbean more than 60 times to topple governments, install friendly regimes, aid or suppress revolutions, and support American business interests. . . .

. . . It is against this background that Latins are debating America's motives now that the U.S. is again flexing its military muscle . . . says Latin American scholar Robert Leiken. . . . "It smells a lot like the old gunboat diplomacy."

Susanna McBee, *U.S. News & World Report*, October 17, 1983

SALVADORAN SAYS HE KILLED U.S. WOMAN—A national guardsman charged in the murder of four United States churchwomen has said in a written confession that he raped and killed one of them under orders from a superior.

Carlos Joaquín Contreras, one of five guardsmen accused in the Dec. 2, 1980, slayings, said in the statement that he was acting on orders from Sgt. Luis Antonio Colindrés, who is also charged in the killings.

Mr. Contreras's statement quoted Sergeant Colindrés as saying he was also acting on orders from superiors. But Mr. Contreras said he did not know who Sergeant Colindrés was referring to.

AP, *The New York Times*, October 27, 1983

NOVEMBER 1983

EL SALVADOR'S ROMAN CATHOLIC LEADERS TARGETED BY DEATH SQUADS—Clandestine death squads have mounted a major campaign of intimidation against the Roman Catholic Church here.

The Salvadoran church's two top leaders, Archbishop Arturo Rivera y Damas and Auxiliary Archbishop Gregorio Rosa Chavez, have received public death threats. And communiqués attached to bodies of recent death squad victims have denounced Catholic church and lay workers who call for dialogue between the government and insurgent forces. . . .

. . . When Archbishop Rivera y Damas was in hiding in 1977 because of similar threats, death squads issued a series of pamphlets that read: "Be a patriot! Kill a priest."

Commenting on the threats, Rosa Chavez says, "We are used to repression and we have learned the high price one pays for speaking out against injustice." . . .

Chris Hedges, *Christian Science Moniter*,
November 14, 1983

SALVADOR VILLAGERS CLAIM TROOPS SHOT UNARMED LEFTIST SUPPORTERS—Residents of three small towns in northern El Salvador told foreign journalists who visited the area that army troops rounded up and shot to death more than 100 leftist sympathizers earlier this month.

The journalists said Thursday they saw 20 bodies and what appeared to be seven fresh mass graves and were given a list of names of 118 victims.

The armed forces high command confirmed Thursday that there were "about 100 casualties" in the area around Lake Suchitlan but said the bodies were apparently those of guerrillas killed in battle. . . .

. . . The journalists went to the [town] of Copapayo . . . to check on reports . . . troops from the army's U.S.-trained Atlacatl infantry battalion "massacred more than 100 people" Nov. 4. . . .

The broadcast [of Radio Venceremos] said the victims were noncombatant supporters of the guerrillas. . . .

The journalists who visited [area] towns Wednesday said residents told them the victims surrendered to army troops and were herded into houses and killed with submachine-gun fire and grenades.

. . . "We talked to a lot of people in the three towns and they all had the same version," said one of the journalists, who asked not to be identified.

Combined Dispatches, *Miami Herald*, November 18, 1983

Author's note: On December 25, 1983, I was notified that Janet and her entire family, with the exception of Aurelio, were victims of this massacre.

DECEMBER 1983

SALVADORANS SAY U.S. IS GIVING MIXED SIGNALS—. . . Ambassador Pickering said last Friday that future military aid to El Salvador would be at risk if the Government did not prosecute suspected death-squad members. Less than three days later Mr. Reagan used the pocket veto to kill the bill requiring the Salvadoran Government to show progress in human rights.

Such unclear signals from Washington—strong oratory coupled with a refusal to tie aid to progress—has left many Salvadorans with the impression that military aid will continue despite the country's human rights record. . . .

Lydia Chavez, *The New York Times*, December 3, 1983

SALVADOR LAND PLAN: NEW OBSTACLES—During the last three years, El Salvador's limited progress in land redistribution has been cited by the Reagan Administration as a bright spot in the country's move toward democracy.

But this view appears to be dimming as a result of the vote in the Constituent Assembly Tuesday night . . . that would slash the amount of land available for future distribution by more than half. . . .

. . . As a result only about 72,000 acres instead of the original 173,000 acres would be available for redistribution to farm workers under this phase. . . .

Lydia Chavez, *The New York Times*, December 15, 1983

U.S. IS RETHINKING PLAN TO REBUILD EL SALVADOR—Here in [San Vicente], the province that was to be a showcase for a U.S.-backed pacification plan, guerrilla propagandists lecture children in schools funded with U.S. economic aid, and guerrilla patrols move down roads that are being repaired with U.S. funds, U.S. and Salvadoran officials confirmed last week.

These officials also confirmed that six months after the much bally-hooed pacification program began here, guerrillas are still active through San Vicente province. In fact, according to local officials, they are so strong that in some cases they have dictated work conditions on projects funded by the U.S. Agency for International Development (USAID).

Other projects simply have been abandoned for lack of security, putting the Salvadoran government in the embarrassing position of so far having been able to spend only half the $4 million in U.S. aid earmarked for infrastructure reguilding projects in the first six months of pacification. . . .

. . . In San Felipe, road-gang foreman, Jose Gomercindo Vallencia, recalled what happened when he was hired to build a road leading from the nearby Pan American Highway to isolated hamlets in the northern parts of the province. Early in December the guerrillas visited him and said they wanted to see the road built with manual labor, rather than with heavy equipment, to provide more and longer employment for the road crew.

They threatened to destroy road-grading equipment and tractors if they were used. The equipment is now parked on the Pan American Highway, which is patrolled by soldiers who can protect it. But less than a mile away, the road crew is working with pick and shovel. . . .

Rod Nordlund, *Philadelphia Inquirer*, December 19, 1983

*   *   *

SALVADOR CLERIC SAYS 6,096 DIED—The Roman Catholic Auxiliary Bishop of San Salvador said today that 6,096 people had died in El Salvador's political conflict this year, most of them killed by the armed forces and right-wing death squads.

"It is almost a rare thing to die a natural death in this country," Msgr. Gregorio Rosa Chavez said in his Christmas message at Metropolitan Cathedral. "It is almost a miracle."

Bishop Rosa Chavez attributed 4,736 of the killings to the armed forces and right-wing death squads. . . .

AP, *The New York Times,* December 26, 1983

JANUARY 1984

BATTLING ON TWO FRONTS—In two year-end raids leftist insurgents not only captured and held El Salvador's fourth-largest military base for some eight hours but blew up the Cuscatlán suspension bridge, a span that had come to symbolize 20th-century progress for Salvadorans. . . .

. . . In the last days of 1983, rebels raided the hilltop headquarters . . . near El Paraiso . . . the attack proved a serious blow both to the army and army morale. After learning that 700 of the 1300 troops based in the garrison were away on illegally-authorized holiday leaves and 200 other soldiers were absent on patrol, the guerrillas struck. . . .

The twin attacks underscored the continuing problems that American military advisors have faced in turning the Salvadoran army from a Praetorian guard of the rich into a modern fighting force. . . . Some junior officers have even told their soldiers to wear street clothes under their uniforms so if need be, they can be dressed for surrender. . . .

. . . Rightists in the country have begun to complain about U.S. meddling. After last week's military setback, editorials appeared in the right-wing press demanding the resignation of the army's high command and an end to American intervention. . . . (O)ne of the most notorious death squads warned in a communiqué last week, "We will not allow the gringos to come here and make decisions about military command changes. . . ."

> John Kohan, Timothy Laughran, and
> Johanna McGeary, *Time*, January 16,
> 1984

REAGAN PLANNING ARMS AID INCREASE FOR EL SALVADOR—The Reagan Administration is preparing to ask Congress for $250 million in military aid for El Salvador, nearly four times the current figure for this year, a White House official said today. . . .

. . . The Presidential commission on Central America, headed by former Secretary of State Henry A. Kissinger, submitted a report to Mr. Reagan on Wednesday for substantial immediate increases to military and economic aid to the region including a five year economic aid commitment of $8 billion.

The report said increased aid was necessary to counter Soviet and Cuban involvement in the region, which was portrayed as a fundamental danger to the United States. . . .

> Hedrick Smith, *The New York Times*, January 13, 1984

U.S. CLAIMS LAND REFORM MAKES GAINS—The State Department in a report fulfilling a congressional requirement told Congress Wednesday that 1983 was a year of "important consolidation and forward movement" in El Salvador's land reform program.

The report was issued in compliance with legislation calling on the State Department to "certify" progress of land redistribution. . . .

. . . El Salvador's reform progress has been "halting and painful" at times, the department said . . . but the over-all record is one of "significant progress." . . .

> AP, *Washington Post*, January 26, 1984

*   *   *

CHARLES CLEMENTS, M.D.

SLAVADOR PRESSES HUNDREDS INTO MILITARY—Hundreds of young people have been pressed into the Salvadoran Army this month after being stopped by military patrols. . . . "They are recruiting people all around here," said Manuel Guzman, the mayor. . . . Mr. Guzman, 63 years old, estimated that about 600 youths had been picked up since the campaign began early in January.

. . . According to residents and relief workers who travel in the countryside, the conscription campaign appears unusual because of its scale and because special efforts are apparently being made to draft young men who are educated.

Education Ministry officials said that in at least two outlying towns, Yamabal and Sembera, primary schools will not open as scheduled next month because teachers are afraid they will be taken for military service if they are seen about. . . . The official said the number of male students who have enrolled for the coming year at the (local) high school . . . is down by 90%.

. . . Besides schoolteachers and high school students, recruiters have pressed engineers, agronomists, and seminarians into service, according to residents and local officials.

. . . Salvadoran law subjects all young men to the draft, though diplomats said that in practice the sons of the small elite are rarely inducted against their will.

Stephen Kinzer, *The New York Times,* January 30, 1984

FEBRUARY 1984

U.S. AIDES FEAR SALVADORAN SETBACK, EVEN A COUP, IN ELECTION'S WAKE—United States officials say the Reagan Administration is seriously concerned that the outcome of next month's presidential election in El Salvador could jeopardize rather than strengthen democratic rule. . . .

. . . The officials said the focus of the . . . concern was the presidential candidacy of Roberto d'Abuisson, the leader of the far-right National Republican Alliance. The Administration was said to feel that a victory by him could polarize El Salvador's civilian leadership and produce an upswing in human rights abuses by security forces and right-wing death squads. . . . The officials added that the Administration was also concerned over the candidacy of José Napolean Duarte, who represents the Christian Democratic Party [who they said] the Salvadoran military viewed with suspicion and might move to overthrow. . . .

Phillip Taubman, *The New York Times*, February 2, 1984

EX-ENVOY ACCUSES 6 SALVADOR EXILES—A former United States Ambassador to El Salvador accused the Reagan Administration today of deliberately ignoring specific and detailed information about six Salvadoran exiles living in Miami who, he said, have been directing the actions of death squads in their home country. . . .

. . . Mr. [Robert E.] White also asserted that the Reagan Administration had known "for three years that Roberto d'Abuisson planned and ordered the assassination of Archbishop Arnulfo Romero, which occurred in March 1980. The Archbishop was an outspoken opponent of violence.

The information about the six exiles, the Archbishop's assassination and other details about the death squads "was reported to Washington" by cable in 1981, he said, but "over the last three years, the Reagan Administration has suppressed the facts."

He added, "it is now clear that the Administration covered up vital documents from the Kissinger commission and the Congress and I can no longer remain silent." . . .

Joel Brinkley, *The New York Times*, February 3, 1984

SALVADORAN LAND PROGRAM IS CRITICIZED—An internal United States Government report last month warned the Reagan Administration that the future of El Salvador's land redistribution program, a cornerstone of United States policy there, is bleak.

The internal Government audit, dated Jan. 18, said that

despite some successes, most farm cooperatives created under the first phase of the land program "are not financially viable." . . .

. . . A separate, confidential report prepared for the United States Agency for International Development by a private consulting company, said that the Salvadoran Government lacks an effective mechanism for preventing diversion of American aid money to private use. . . .

AP, *The New York Times*, February 15, 1984

ABUSES DISCLOSED IN AID PROGRAMS IN LATIN NATIONS—United States economic assistance programs in Central America suffer from extensive mismanagement and corruption, according to State Department audits and a Congressional study.

At a time when the Reagan Administration has proposed major increases in economic aid to the region, these reports show, many of the institutions responsible for distributing American assistance have had difficulty handling the present level of financing.

Abuses cited in the reports included the illegal diversion of funds for private gain, fraudulent accounting procedures, and spending that never reached the people it was intended to help. . . .

Phillip Taubman, *The New York Times*, February 20, 1984

U.S. IS CONSIDERING EMERGENCY ARMS FOR EL SALVADOR—Secretary of State George P. Shultz said today that the Reagan Administration is considering giving El Salvador emergency military aid, without waiting for Congress to act, so its army can maintain pressure on the insurgents in the coming election period. . . .

Mr. Shultz acknowledged that the Administration was considering sending military equipment to El Salvador under parts of the law that allow military goods to be paid for as much as 120 days after they are received. . . .

. . . One of Mr. Shultz's sharpest exchanges was with Senator J. Bennett Johnston, Democrat of Louisiana.

"It seems to me the situation is deteriorating and we are losing the war," Mr. Johnston said, "and I would suggest that the best explanation I can come up with for why we're losing the war is because we're losing the war for the hearts and minds of the people, which is very regrettable. And why that is, is perhaps because of the death squads and the lack of human rights in El Salvador." . . .

[Mr. Shultz said,] "If I may make a comment, I would have to just flatly disagree with most everything you've just said." . . .

"On the military side, there are ups and downs," Mr. Shultz said. "Right now, from all I can read, the El Salvadoran military are on some sort of 'up.' "

Bernard Gwertzman, *The New York Times*, February 22, 1984

ACKNOWLEDGMENTS

MUCH MORE THAN PERSONAL INITIATIVE took me to El Salvador and then saw me through to the completion of this book.

I offer to my family the gratitude of an errant son and brother for the trust which sustained me through many difficult times.

To Bill Monning and Dana Kent of Salinas, Calif., as well as the several other friends and colleagues who helped found the Salvadoran Medical Relief Fund, I'm indebted for both material and emotional support.

Terry Savery, friend and confidant, gave me steady encouragement.

Kathy Robbins, my literary agent, provided me direction, understanding and confidence.

Tobi Sanders, my editor, was attentive and forbearing.

Stephen G. Michaud played a crucial role in the preparation of the text. While I am solely responsible for its content, I relied upon his skill, patience, and dedication to produce the manuscript.

Claudia Prose was a selfless, tireless assistant, invaluable in every phase of the project.

The North American Congress on Latin America graciously supplied staff and research assistance. Many individuals within the American Friends Service Committees, the Vietnam Veterans of America, and the Judson Memorial Church were generous with their personal support.

My final and most important acknowledgment is of the warmth, faith and courage of so many Salvadorans.

CHARLES CLEMENTS, 39, is a Distinguished Graduate of the U.S. Air Force Academy, and, as a C-130 pilot in Vietnam, flew more than fifty combat missions before he became disillusioned with U.S. involvement. He later enrolled in the University of Washington School of Medicine, from which he graduated in 1980. He also holds graduate degrees in business administration as well as public health.

He has returned to the United States to help found the Salvadoran Medical Relief Fund in Salinas, California. His testimonies before Congress and the American people are an ongoing effort to promote peace with justice in Central America.

Copies of the PBS documentary "Witness to War" (30 minutes, color) are available from: First Run Features
153 Waverly Place
New York, N.Y. 10014

Special Offer
Buy a Bantam Book
for only 50¢.

Now you can have Bantam's catalog filled with hundreds of titles plus take advantage of our unique and exciting bonus book offer. A special offer which gives you the opportunity to purchase a Bantam book for only 50¢. Here's how!

By ordering any five books at the regular price per order, you can also choose any other single book listed (up to a $4.95 value) for just 50¢. Some restrictions do apply, but for further details why not send for Bantam's catalog of titles today!

Just send us your name and address and we will send you a catalog!